Memories of Dress

Memories of Dress

Recollections of Material Identities

Edited by
Alison Slater, Susan Atkin, and
Elizabeth Kealy-Morris

BLOOMSBURY VISUAL ARTS
LONDON • NEW YORK • OXFORD • NEW DELHI • SYDNEY

BLOOMSBURY VISUAL ARTS
Bloomsbury Publishing Plc
50 Bedford Square, London, WC1B 3DP, UK
1385 Broadway, New York, NY 10018, USA
29 Earlsfort Terrace, Dublin 2, Ireland

BLOOMSBURY, BLOOMSBURY VISUAL ARTS and the Diana logo are trademarks of
Bloomsbury Publishing Plc

First published in Great Britain 2023
Paperback edition published by Bloomsbury Visual Arts 2024

Cover design by Holly Capper
Cover image: Soul Dress, Lesley Beale, 2020 © Lesley Beale, 2020. Photograph by
Freddy Griffiths. Reproduced with permission.

A catalogue record for this book is available from the British Library.

A catalog record for this book is available from the Library of Congress.

ISBN: HB: 978-1-3501-5379-0
PB: 978-1-3503-7046-3
ePDF: 978-1-3501-5380-6
eBook: 978-1-3501-5381-3

Typeset by Deanta Global Publishing Services, Chennai, India

To find out more about our authors and books visit www.bloomsbury.com and
sign up for our newsletters.

To our children Elsie, Alice, and Colin

Contents

Illustrations

Contributors

Dr. Susan Atkin is Deputy Division Head for Fashion Design at Manchester Metropolitan University, UK. She has been at Manchester Met. since 2012 and currently teaches at both undergraduate and postgraduate research levels. Before her academic career, Susan was designer-owner of the independent womenswear label Electricity. Susan's PhD considered Manchester's cultural identity through exploration of the links between the city's music and local fashion culture. Subculture, identity, bricolage, and the concept of local fashion continue to be key areas of the research. Her research has led to lecture requests and talks beyond academia, including at the Whitworth Art Gallery, Manchester, UK.

Lesley Beale is the craft curator at Lakeside Arts, Nottingham, UK, running their contemporary craft fair and championing young makers through a visiting lecture program in professional development. She is also an artist interested in the process of making. Through the predominate medium of textiles, Lesley places ritual at the heart of her practice, which is process-led rather than artifact-led and often performative. She is currently undertaking a practice-led PhD at Nottingham Trent University, using autoethnography and autotopography to explore ritual and death in a secular society.

Professor Elizabeth Chin is an anthropologist with a multidisciplinary practice that includes performative scholarship, experimental ethnography, and arts-based technology interventions. She is the author of *Purchasing Power: Black Kids and American Consumer Culture* (2001) and *My Life with Things: The Consumer Diaries* (2016). Currently editor-in-chief of *American Anthropologist*, she is invested in care, generosity, and transparency in scholarship and publishing. She is the core faculty in the MFA program Media Design Practices at ArtCenter College of Design, Pasadena, United States.

Dr. Soljana Çili is Senior Lecturer in Psychology at University of the Arts London and Lecturer (Teaching) at University College London, UK. She holds a Bachelor of Psychology (Hons) and a PhD in Psychology. Her research focuses on the relationship among autobiographical memory, mental imagery, and the self in psychological disorders and in cognitive-behavioral therapy. It also explores the impact of fashion and fashion industry practices on individuals' sense of self and well-being, as well as the relevance of dress for memory and the self.

Jo Jenkinson is Reader in Fashion and Deputy Head at the Manchester Fashion Institute, Manchester Metropolitan University, UK. Her research interests focus on dress, music, and youth, exploring how experiences of youth live with us in our continuing life trajectory. This temporal aspect of experience has been further explored in her project "Portrait Youth," which uses the language of dress and styling to enable diverse groups of young people to articulate their narratives of youth. Her recent publications include "Wear Your Identity: Styling Identities of Youth through Dress—A Conceptual Model" (2020) in *Fashion, Style & Popular Culture*.

Zsofi Juhasz completed her BA (Hons) Fashion at Manchester School of Art, UK, in 2017. Her chapter develops work which was awarded the Dean's Prize for outstanding undergraduate research. Her chapter is one of the first written in English to consider memories of home sewing in Socialist Hungary and draws from primary research interviews with the author's grandmother, who was a dressmaker in Hungary during this period. Since graduation, Zsofi has worked on private commissions and as a costume maker in stop motion animation. She completed an MA in fashion knitwear design at Nottingham Trent University, UK, in 2022.

Dr. Elizabeth Kealy-Morris, originally from the United States, is Senior Lecturer at Manchester Metropolitan University, UK, lecturing in critical theory and graphic design practice within fashion communication subjects. Through her research, Elizabeth seeks connections between cultural memory, dress, identity, disability, and wellness. Responding to how society has adapted to and resisted the wearing of Covid face masks during the pandemic, she co-organized and co-led the January 2021 international symposium *Face Off: The Provocation and Possibilities of Mask and Head Coverings*, hosted by the Manchester Fashion Institute. Elizabeth's research into "body dressing work" has featured in the *Guardian* newspaper as well as publications, including *Culture Costume and Dress* (2018).

Dr. Alison Slater is Senior Lecturer in Design History specializing in dress. She coordinates the contextual studies framework across Manchester School of

Art, Manchester Metropolitan University, UK. Alison's research investigates how memories, emotions, and feelings influence encounters with material objects. Her PhD research, funded by the AHRC, into working-class women's memories of dress in the Second World War has featured in *Fashion on the Ration* (Imperial War Museum North, 2015–16) and the BBC Radio 4 documentary *From Rags to Riches* (2017). Her research into materiality in oral histories of dress is published in *Critical Studies in Fashion & Beauty* (2014).

Dr. Jane Webb gained her PhD in 2004 in social history and material culture, having initially trained in art history and anthropology. The process of visual and material practice forms an important part of Jane's research methodologies. She works with archives, historical geographies, and collections of dress and other objects to explore individual histories of personal experience and emotion. Jane's teaching experience is rooted in delivering contextual studies for design programs, working with students through creative practice, curation, and writing. Jane is currently Director of Education in the School for Cross-Faculty Studies, University of Warwick, UK.

Dr. Ben Whyman is the manager of the Research Centre for Fashion Curation, University of the Arts London, UK, where he project manages and researches for exhibitions, publications, and events. Ben's PhD explored menswear collections housed in the V&A Museum and the Fashion Museum, Bath, to expand conversations around the biography of objects, material culture, and acts of remembering. He has presented his research at conferences and is featured in publications, including a chapter on couturier Hardy Amies for *London Couture: British Luxury 1923-1975* (2015), *Archivist* magazine (2015), *Critical Studies in Men's Fashion* (2017), and *Dandy Style: 250 Years of British Fashion* (2021).

Acknowledgments

This book began its life in a different world. Our lives, both personally and collectively, have changed in so many ways since work commenced. Our discussions began in summer 2017, when Susan was pregnant with Alice; our contract with Bloomsbury was signed in October 2019, while Alison was on maternity leave with Elsie and shortly after Elizabeth's son, Colin, had left home for university. We agreed on a deadline for the following summer with no imagination of what would unfold in the months in between as the Covid-19 pandemic and its fallout transformed our lives.

A huge thank you goes to our contributors Lesley Beale, Elizabeth Chin, Soljana Çili, Jo Jenkinson, Zsofia Juhasz, Jane Webb, and Ben Whyman for their commitment from early ideas through to completion against the backdrop of change and uncertainty. Our gratitude extends to our colleagues Andrew Warstat, Philip Sykas, Fiona Hackney, and the anonymous reviewers, whose comments have informed the development of our co-authored and solo chapters. Our appreciation also goes to our former tutors and others who have inspired and informed our academic research journeys to date. We are immensely grateful to Frances Arnold, Rebecca Hamilton, and Yvonne Thouroude at Bloomsbury Academic, whose recognition of circumstances, encouragement, support— and more than one extended deadline—through the challenges of lockdowns, forced separation from loved ones, working from home, juggling childcare during nursery closures, and health issues have enabled this volume to make it to fruition.

Special thanks, and apologies for the late nights close to deadlines, go to our partners: Terry, Ben, and Chris, our children, and our extended families for their support.

As our lives have been transformed, this book has offered a distraction and focus through difficult times. *Memories of Dress* has evolved through a period where life, loss, and grief have been ever present; it has been a privilege to be able to remember and write about memory at a time that will inevitably come to define this period of our lives. In addition to being dedicated to our children, this volume is dedicated to those we have loved and lost from 2020 to 2022.

The editors, authors, and publisher gratefully acknowledge the permission granted to reproduce the copyright material in this book. Every effort has been made to trace copyright holders and to obtain their permission for the use of copyright material. The publisher apologizes for any errors or omissions in the above list and would be grateful to be notified of any corrections that should be incorporated in future reprints or editions of this book.

Introduction

Memories of Dress: Recollections of Material Identities is a story about dress but is also about more than dress. The ideas presented span the academic contexts of dress history, fashion studies, material culture, cultural studies, and memory studies and attempt to present a balance of personal recollected experiences alongside a critical understanding of select theories of memory. Dress is defined as the complete style of clothing and adornment worn (*Oxford English Dictionary* 2022), with fashion meaning the prevailing styles of dress which are "adopted by groups of people" (Hoskins 2014: 4) and are always "context-dependent" (Davis 1992: 8). The focus on everyday experiences seeks to contextualize and assimilate how memories of past identities are reported through the recollection of clothing worn at a particular time. As Joanne Entwistle (2000: 112) asserts, there is "a complex relationship" between fashion, dress, and identity. "The clothes we choose to wear can be expressive of identity . . . [but] our clothes cannot always be 'read,' since they do not straightforwardly 'speak' and can therefore be open to misinterpretation" (Entwistle 2000: 112). We use *Memories of Dress* as a tool to explore the ways that our clothes "speak" of our past selves and our belonging to wider social and cultural groups at specific times. The auto/biographical memories are analyzed using self-interpretative methods that unpick the meanings behind and reasons why particular clothing is worn.[1] This approach recognizes the challenges of presenting both a "(unique) individuality and conformity to (shared) group identity" (Craik 2009: 3; see also Woodward 2008) and that the same garment can mean different things in different social, cultural, and political contexts (Barnard 2014; Tulloch 2002).

Told from the perspective of the wearer in the present,[2] the chapters in this volume explore the individual negotiations of where "internal and external worlds" of personal and public identities meet (Breward and Evans 2005: 3). Sometimes the wearer speaks or writes, at other times a biographical interpretation is applied in retrospect through garment analysis and/or contextual research. What is consistent is that garments discussed are framed in the present moment in time through a social or material encounter with the past. The subjectivities of memory are central to the narratives presented. Personal feelings about motivations, attitudes, and values of wearing or not wearing are held in—and shared through—memory. The analysis of recollections in this volume seeks to get at the heart of the "connotative personal meanings" of the clothes we wear through critical memory work (Weber and Mitchell 2004: 255). The lens of memory enables experiences of dress and its role in everyday life to be explored according to different contexts, locations, and life stages (Taylor 2002; Weber and Mitchell 2004; Woodward 2007; Buse and Twigg 2016). The focus on everyday dress means that, where fashion is explored, discussion is focused on the wearer's experience in the context of prevailing sartorial modes of the time rather than on catwalk styles or high-end designer looks. The contextualization of where memories of dress map onto contemporary fashions, alongside traditional dress practices, highlights the relevance of auto/biographical memories as a method to explore the motivations and meanings in everyday clothing choices. Narratives of personal practices and self-identity are presented to assist an understanding of the way that we negotiate the rituals of dress in everyday life as well as the public and private tensions of fitting into wider social and cultural groups. The complexities of past clothing choices are reflected in intersectional perspectives and distinctions, including, but not limited to, social class, ethnicity, age, and disability, according to the wearer's circumstances and identity—both at the time when memories were formed and at the time when memories were recorded.

The authors in *Memories of Dress: Recollections of Material Identities* critically investigate auto/biographical memories of past sartorial practices from multiple standpoints to present a comprehensive overview of theoretical, material culture, and practice-led approaches to histories of dress. We explore the ways in which dress is remembered and how dress features in the patterns of everyday life and memories of lived experiences. Memories of dress feature prominently in auto/biographical memories, including oral histories, yet traditionally they have not been subjected to the same degree of academic scholarship as other sources of evidence (Biddle-Perry 2005).

Mapping the Field

Memories of Dress sits within a community of work which broadly covers the subject of dress history, fashion studies, and memory. At the couture and ready-to-wear levels of the fashion and dress spectrum, we are accustomed to viewing clothes by high-end designers, and a number of catwalk shows and collections have been analyzed using theories of memory (Lau 2014; Zborowska 2014;

Toussaint and Smelik 2017). In contrast, memories of fashionable styles and everyday dress from the perspective of the wearer have helped us understand the relationship between identity and clothing, including discarded garments (Guy and Banim 2000; Banim and Guy 2001; Bye and McKinney 2007; Woodward 2007), dress memorabilia (Masuch and Hefferon 2018), footwear (Sherlock 2014, 2016), and treasured garments (Wood 2020). Secondhand dress and fashion in "vintage" style have also been explored as a cultural memory object (Jenss 2015).

The embodied and material nature of "worn clothes and textiles" makes them suited to memory work because of their intimate proximity to the body (Hunt 2014: 207). Our use of textiles and dress in everyday life captures our bodily activity through use, wear, and tear; the malleable surfaces of fabrics are impressed with imprints of our routines, and cloth itself becomes a form of memory archive (Wilson [1985] 2010; Stallybrass [1993] 2012; Stallybrass and Jones 2000; Hunt 2014). As Peter Stallybrass has argued, writing about a jacket belonging to his deceased friend, Allon: "cloth *is* a kind of memory" ([1993] 2012: 69). Clothing holds the "traces" of those who wore it (Gibson 2015: xv; see also Miller 2008). As such, garments are a form of archival information that can transport knowledge from past to present (Woodward 2007; Hunt 2014). The material memory of dress enables an emotional connection with others that also extends beyond the human life span (Stallybrass ([1993] 2012; Ash 1996; Stallybrass and Jones 2000; Hallam and Hockey 2001; Miller 2008, 2010; Hunt 2014; Slater 2014; Gibson 2015). Garments, such as Allon's jacket, shape and share memories after bereavement (Stallybrass [1993] 2012; Ash 1996; Simpson 2014, 2019). However, as Daniel Miller's (2008: 36) work on materiality reminds us, "clothing is not forever, it changes and fades." Discarded or lost garments can reside in memory long after the life of the material object (Stallybrass and Jones 2000; Woodward 2007; Slater 2014; Spivak 2014; Buse and Twigg 2016).

Memory work can support our investigation and understanding of dress as material objects (Bide 2017). It can also reveal more about the way that clothing links us with other people. In research into Renaissance clothing, Peter Stallybrass and Ann Jones (2000: 275) identified that late sixteenth-century garments reflected "social relations" in materialized forms. In research into clothing kept but no longer worn, Maura Banim and Ali Guy (2001: 207) found that memories of dress stored "a connectedness with others." Cheryl Buckley (1998) identified similar connections through recollections of home dressmaking in her own family. Sophie Wood's research also found that men and women valued treasured garments because of remembered "emotions of love, feelings of comfort, and connections to others or to other selves" (2020: 223).

Through a series of autobiographical and literary pieces focusing on the female dress garment, Sandra Weber and Claudia Mitchell (2004), and their contributors, explored embodied identity from the perspective of the wearer, including "emotional" aspects of clothing and appearance (4). They recognized the communicative challenges of dressing, both in the act of wearing and in articulating nonverbal experiences, as well as the complexities involved in contextualizing the social and private aspects of embodied memories (Weber and Mitchell 2004). As Sophie Woodward (2007: 58) identified, "multiple histories [can be] woven into cloth," but the meanings of these connections cannot fully be understood without the narrative of a wearer or owner.

Clothing is, therefore, an auto/biographical "tool for storytelling, remembering and identity construction" (Buse and Twigg 2015: 16), with narratives of auto/ biographical memories of dress simultaneously being personal, social, and political (Woodward 2007; Chong Kwan, Laing and Roman 2014, Gibson 2015). Dress can be a material and embodied transmitter of memory, particularly at times of changing identity, through aging, and for those with dementia whose personal narratives may be more fragile, but for whom dress continues to play an enduring role in their memories and sense of identity (Twigg 2009, 2010; Buse and Twigg 2013, 2014, 2015, 2016; Slater 2014). Julia Twigg (2009: 1) reminds us that dress can provide a "fruitful field to explore the narrative of peoples' lives" as the tensions between social expectations and identity play out in our wardrobes. Memories of dress can also assist the framing of personal recollections within historical time. Marita Sturken explains that "memory establishes life's continuity; it gives meaning to the present, as each moment is constituted by the past" (1997: 1). This holds significance within dress history and fashion studies, as Twigg explains: "clothes also make the passage of time visible, as styles pass into history, moving from being cutting edge to out of date and dowdy, to quaint and odd and—possibly—to intriguing and beautiful" (2013: 76). Heike Jenss echoes this in what she defines as "fashioning memory," where the "temporal dynamics of fashion" enable us to see what is new and what is old, though perhaps still desirable, through "the desire to recall—though usually with a temporal twist—through a certain distance of time" (Jenss 2015: 140; Wilson [1985] 2010; Stallybrass and Jones 2000).

Building upon these approaches, our volume considers how recollections of everyday dress practices are situated alongside findings from dress history, fashion studies, and material culture. We pick up Carole Hunt's (2014) proposal that cloth could be seen as a special case in the field of memory studies. The chapters within our volume investigate concepts of material and cultural memory, as well as framing individual experiences within (and outside of) the collective identities of a broad range of social and cultural groups. Our examination of the emotional aspects of clothing and appearance gathered through memories of dress gives insight into men's and women's public and private lives. Auto/ biographical narratives are contextualized by considering motivations and experiences at the time clothing is worn, the changing sense of self over time, and how memories of dress serve individuals and groups of people at the time of recollection. Alongside material culture approaches, we place the immaterial meanings contained within and around clothing at the time it was worn and the time of recollection at the forefront of our stance.

Concepts, Histories, Objects, Practices

As the aforementioned literature shows, existing accounts tend to use memories in support of other methodological approaches: this volume places memory at the heart of its methodological and theoretical framework. The chapters are explained at this point in order for our discussion of memory theory in the remainder of this introduction to weave connections between the different chapters and ideas in the volume. A shared list of references for the volume is also provided as a resource for future researchers, with only primary sources (including interviews, newspapers, magazines, and archive material) referenced in notes within each individual chapter.

The chapters in this book are organized into four parts. The first of these (Part I), "Concepts," presents a stand-alone chapter by psychologist Soljana Çili, which frames memories of dress, and other material possessions, in relation to autobiographical memories and concepts of self. Through the examination of how autobiographical memories link to self-esteem and psychological well-being, Çili considers the way in which clothing memories can provide anchors of continuity despite the sense of self changing over time. The definitions of autobiographical memories established in Çili's chapter carry forward to the rest of the volume.

Part II of the volume, loosely framed as "Histories," presents three chapters focused on personal experiences of dress in the recent past. Ordered chronologically, these chapters contextualize personal recollections in the social and cultural circumstances in which the clothing was worn at that time.

Alison Slater's chapter uses oral evidence to explore working-class female dress in industrial towns in Lancashire, northern England, during the Second World

War. Personal recollections from nine women, gathered through interviews for oral history, are used to explain how, despite limited clothing stock, working-class women managed their family's dress to ensure social and cultural notions of respectability were achieved through their visual public appearance. Framed through the lens of "collective memory" of a small group of women, Slater examines age and generational differences in her interviewees' memories of wartime dress and "making do." She also reflects upon her own role in shaping and sharing the collective memories presented in the chapter.

Zsofia Juhasz's chapter explores memories of dress in socialist Hungary through an interview with her grandmother, Julianna, who had Alzheimer's disease at the time of interview. Juhasz investigates the tensions between socialist ideals of women's dress and limited resources during the Hungarian socialist era versus individual desire for self-expression and solutions found through home sewing and accessing the skills of a local seamstress. Juhasz focuses on how narrative identities are shaped through remembering and retelling past experiences, considering Juliana's sense of self as she recalled this time in her life. Juhasz also examines how, despite fading in other aspects, her grandmother's memories were enhanced through remembering the tactility of making and wearing clothes.

Susan Atkin's chapter uses oral testimony to examine men's memories of dress from the Madchester movement (1986–96), a key period in the popular history and cultural memory of Manchester, England. Through the accounts of her interviewees, who were active members of the movement, Atkin considers how styles of dress, music, and leisure practices are cultural signifiers that impact the reasons that period is remembered and represented as it is within the mythology of the city. Atkin also frames male experiences of subcultural dress within traditional contexts of British working-class life and within a global fashion market where American clothing and media were used to reflect belonging to Madchester both in the period and in memory.

Part III of the volume, "Objects," presents three chapters exploring memory through the lens of material culture, surviving garments, and associated ephemera that are engaged with to investigate the wearer's motivations and biography at the time clothing was worn and how it survives to this day.

Jo Jenkinson's chapter considers how "memory toolkits," including dress, music, and photographs, gathered by seven female participants as representations of their youth, were used together in a multisensory interview environment. She examines the interviewees' personally selected images, objects, and soundtracks as mnemonic devices that reveal changes and continuations in concepts of self-identity from the time an autobiographical memory was formed to the time it was related in interview. Jenkinson conceptualizes the term "memory wardrobe" to describe the way we remember and imagine ideas about dress, the body, and emotional connections between the two—both material and immaterial, real and potential. Framed within the age of her participants, this study of youth shows how memories of clothing and concepts of youth are carried from the past to the future through retained music soundtracks, dress, and snapshot photographs.

Ben Whyman's chapter analyzes theater writer and literary editor Ken Tynan's Tommy Nutter jacket, held in the collection of the Victoria and Albert Museum, London, to investigate how garments are evidence of materialized memory. Whyman uses the term "post-wardrobe" to describe the selection of museum-held garments that were once part of an active wardrobe that have at some point been rationalized, edited, and a small proportion stored. Through material culture analysis and an analysis of the relationship between bodies, memory, and clothes, Whyman explores how such a garment can become a transmitter of experience, personal biography, and history. The materiality of Tynan's jacket is presented as a recollection—a narrative of memories recorded in cloth—encountered after the life of the wearer.

Jane Webb's chapter examines the intersection of personal memorial and academic study in the clothing collection at Platt Hall in Manchester, England. The chapter explores museums as places of stored memory for families to commemorate their loved ones and where clothing that once had another life ends up. Webb considers how, after periods of dormancy, curators and researchers bring their own informed interpretations to objects within museum collections. Using three garments to trace material memories back from donor to wearer, Webb suggests ways in which the personal and professional motivations for collecting dress might intersect, providing opportunities to understand clothing in museums in even richer ways. Her imagined memory, grounded in historical evidence, offers a different perspective on how we listen to and tell biographical stories of dress over time and across generations.

The final section (Part IV) of the book, "Practices," considers practice-led approaches to memories of dress including autoethnography, autobiography, and making.

Elizabeth Kealy-Morris' chapter presents an autoethnographic investigation of memories of "not fitting into" the everyday dress of the suburban American female body in the late 1970s and 1980s due to a spinal deformity requiring she wear an orthotic from eleven to fourteen years of age. Kealy-Morris uses the term "body dressing work" to describe how her experience of not fitting into certain dress styles due to disability sat against an idealized notion of body image and health within her cultural group. Kealy-Morris articulates personal memory via family photographs and autoethnographic prose, and cultural memory is explored through a study of the casual fashion style of sportswear known as "the American Look" and, in particular, the shift dress, a key garment to emerge from this style. Kealy-Morris demonstrates that the cultural myths of America are embedded into expectations of the dressed female body and the work of the presentation of the self to enable fitting in.

Elizabeth Chin's chapter traces the cultural heritage of Chin and her daughter through the making of a quilt that shares the chapter's title "Black/White/ Yellow." Begun in response to a request to write for this book, Chin's quilt is an assemblage of garments and fabrics that are personally symbolic, some of which were owned by her multicultural family. As this clothing is joined with other representative fabrics, it is reassembled into an object for a different purpose that reflects upon traditional quilt-making practices. Chin's narrative of making is presented as a series of cuts and joins that reflect upon race versus ethnicity and the ways in which dress, making, and memory practices can be used to perform self-acceptance, diversity, and protection. Imaginative histories accompany personal recollections to fill some silences of her family's past and reveal the remaining tensions that—along with the completion of the quilt—are still to be negotiated by future generations.

Lesley Beale's chapter uses both autoethnography and practice-based research to consider how clothes—and memories of them—bear witness to our lives and deaths. Framed in the context of a secular society, reflecting on parental loss and changes to bereavement practices during the Covid-19 pandemic, the chapter discusses ritual and ceremony associated with death. Beale uses her primarily textile practice to forge new rituals grounded in bodily materiality and repetition, exploring the journey through grief when a loved one is lost. At the end of a human life span, memories of dress become more about the presence of absence and move into the realm of biography for both the wearer and those left behind to continue the process of memory.

Through these chapters, the reader is invited into the mind of the wearer and researcher to try to understand the centrality of clothing memories in our recollected experiences of everyday life. When introducing their co-edited book on dress narratives of memory, body, and identity, Weber and Mitchell (2004) propose: "ask women to talk or write about dresses, and without much prompting, they will regale you with detailed snippets from their lives, anecdotes that start out ostensibly about clothes, but end up being about so much more"

(3–4). We have also found this in our editing of this volume where, while memories of dress—from both women and men—are the focus, many pertinent and interesting asides have arisen within the contributing chapters. Because of this, we have taken the editorial decision to enable a generous use of notes within our chapters to offer the reader a wider context that contributes to an understanding of the book's primary focus and the different voices represented.

Memory: Some Theories and Definitions

As our title suggests, memory runs as the central thread in this volume. While memory is deeply personal, our academic research is underpinned by select theories of memory which enable chapters on a diverse range of topics to come together in one publication. The field of memory studies has exploded since the late 1970s largely in line with feminist, and more recently wider intersectional, developments; postmodern thought has questioned structures of power and discourse and challenged traditions in history and historiography. In the early 1980s, the focus was largely on recovering experiences deemed to be missing from accepted accounts resulting in a flurry of local history projects, including oral histories. Academic work saw another resurgence in publications from the mid-1990s as we reached the end of a millennium. Milestones and anniversaries tend to bring renewed interest in memory work, particularly for public forms of memorialization. This book situates itself within some of the theory produced in the last fifty years: it cannot and does not claim to cover all relevant literature that could assist an understanding of memories of dress. We have selected some key terms—"popular memory," "collective memory," "cultural memory," "nostalgia," and "myth"—that are explored further here and picked up at various points throughout the volume.

According to the Popular Memory Group (1982: 207), popular memory is "dominant memory" that sits outside of academic history. The group explored the term by considering how "a sense of the past is produced: through public representations and through private memory (which, however, may also be collective and shared)" (207). Access to public representations of memory is contested and political ideology can sway what becomes central and what is "marginalized or excluded or reworked" (Popular Memory Group 1982: 207). Ultimately, popular memory is what people "believe rather than what historians tell them" (Smith 2000: 1). Popular memory of dress is often the kind of representation of the past that we see in fictional, sanitized, and/or glamorized portrayals of dress in film and television or more general concepts that are commonly associated with a particular period; for examples, see Slater, Atkin, and Kealy-Morris in this volume.

Collective memory is based on the principle that a group of people has a shared memory of the past (Halbwachs 1992; Connerton 1989; Nora 1989; Misztal 2003; Olick, Vinitzky-Seroussi, and Levy 2011). Theories of collective memory are attributed to French philosopher and sociologist Maurice Halbwachs, who in 1924 wrote: "there exists a collective memory and social frameworks for memory; it is to the degree that our individual thought places itself in these frameworks and participates in this memory that it is capable of the act of recollection" (1992: 38). Halbwachs argued that it was only within the society and culture to which they belong that an individual can articulate personal recollection. This led him to propose that the frameworks of collective memory inform all aspects of autobiographical memory. This stance has caused "unease" among some historians, who have instead adopted alternative terms adapting Halbwachs' concept (Green 2004: 36). However, the importance of social relationships in memory work today is underpinned by Halbwachs' ideas and add a "unique and valuable perspective to our understanding" of the past (Olick, Vinitzky-Seroussi, and Levy 2011: 36; Assman 1995; Green 2004). It is widely accepted that there are as "many memories as there are groups . . . memory is by nature multiple and yet specific; collective, plural, and yet individual" (Nora 1989: 9; Misztal 2003). It is the role of current members of a group to keep their collective memory alive. The chapters by Slater, Atkin, Jenkinson, and Beale in this volume demonstrate that Halbwachs' (1992: 53) theory that the "framework of collective memory confines and binds our most intimate remembrances to each other" is particularly relevant to the study of dress among a group of people with a shared experience.

Cultural memory signifies the ways in which characterizations of societies and cultures originate and are questioned, challenged, and altered while also woven together with history and popular culture. It is therefore highly contested (Sturken 1997; Bal, Crewe, and Spitzer 1999). At its core, cultural memory is the practice of a society determining which contemporary stories will be remembered to be told in the future; contributions to cultural memories are able to happen at any point and can occur both at the time of the event or afterward. This made memory a political force for Michel Foucault (1975: 25), who noted that "if one controls people's memory, one controls their dynamism." Cultural memory is produced in many ways, for example, via monuments, murals, photographs, films, books, performances, exhibitions, and local or national events, which then become interwoven with wider culture and circulated further (Bal, Crewe, and Spitzer 1999). The appeal of cultural memories, and thus their circulation, varies in accordance with popular culture and the zeitgeists of the time. We propose through this volume that the situated, embodied, everyday practice of dressing (Entwistle 2000) places clothing at the center of cultural production and therefore a primary site of memory work. We argue that cultural memory of dress can influence the way a cultural group perceives itself, as shown in Atkin's chapter in this volume, and the bodies that wear, or are unable to wear, particular sartorial styles—as demonstrated by Kealy-Morris' autoethnographic study on disability in Chapter 8. We also suggest that drawing upon cultural memory, which often occurs through a mix of imagery, sound, narrative, and imagination, can enable individuals to make sense of both their past and current lives and identities (Jenss 2015; see also the chapters that follow by Slater, Atkin, Jenkinson, Webb, Kealy-Morris, and Chin).

Nostalgia can play a role in how we make sense of our past from the present. Originally a seventeenth-century diagnosis for homesick soldiers (Boym 2001), the term has evolved to be directly linked with experiences of modernity and consumer consumption, including fashion (Jenss 2013). Nostalgic remembering is often emotionally complex, reflecting a blend of both positive and negative recollected emotions, of happiness and a bittersweet sense of loss, as well as an awareness of finitude (Sedikides, Wildschut, and Baden 2004). In relation to identity, nostalgia offers opportunities for analytical and reflective analysis both in isolation and in social and cultural contexts of the time and comes to the fore when change is present. In their study on the role of nostalgic memorabilia in psychological well-being, Christoph-Simon Masuch and Kate Hefferon (2018: 357) coin the term "dress nostalgia" to conceptualize how many of their participants were attached to clothes they perceived as meaningful and had kept for a long period of time. We note how many of our contributors have presented memories of dress when reminiscing about past selves that involve "sentimental recall of the past and direct references to social connectedness or significant others" (Masuch and Hefferon 2018: 357; see Slater, Juhasz, Atkin, Jenkinson, Whyman, Kealy-Morris, Chin, and Beale in this volume). Stirring both positive and negative emotions, the garments remembered–while not always physically kept–have acted symbolically as reminders of change and personal development and can have an impact on well-being, a concept developed by Çili in Chapter 1. We also adopt Keightley and Pickering's (2012: 11) view that nostalgia is not just a desire for a sense of self and belonging but also "a response to the desire for creative engagement with difference, or a sign of social critique and aspiration" that can accommodate desire or longing for progressive and utopian ideals, often deriving from an imagined past.

Following Woodward (2009), we do not use "myth" in its popular definition as an untruth nor do we use Roland Barthes' ([1957] 2009) definition.[3] As Woodward (2009: 99) explains, dress like "classical mythology cannot be understood in isolation from storytelling (such as, Homer) or dramatic re-enactments (such as, Sophocles) nor can the myth of street style be seen as somehow separate to what people wear, how they talk about fashion, or what is in the high street." Woodward (2009: 99) notes that fashion myths are often a-temporal and uses "Italian timeless elegance" as an example. Heike Jenss (2015: 37) also alludes to this when defining "zeitgeist narratives" to describe how when we use decade labels when referring to past times, such as the 1960s, we are not just using numerical shorthand to define a period of ten years but referencing a time that represents a wider imaginary and often mythic construction of time. This is also the case in Atkin's and Jenkinson's chapters in this volume where interviewees who grew up in the second half of the twentieth century recall their memories of dress and music in their youth.

Mythology is formed when multiple accounts come together, including individual and collective memories, and academic and popular discourse. Raphael Samuel and Paul Thompson (1990) explain that mythology has a power in everyday life and memory is continually reshaped to make sense of the past from the perspective of the present. They suggest that even while what is being recollected may be true, what is both said and unsaid is what makes it a myth. Because of this, even recent history can be mythologized as it is recalled both individually and collectively (Samuel and Thompson 1990). History and myth are inseparable: accounts of the past—and we argue this is whether written or oral— are told by a teller who, in order to be heard, needs their tales to be authoritative and appropriate (Tonkin 1990; see also Slater and Atkin in this volume). What is authoritative and appropriate is interpreted in line with traditional and contemporary ideals and philosophies (Lévi-Strauss [1978] 2000; Lummis 1987; Campbell 2008). More recent work by Emily Keightley and Michael Pickering (2012) recognizes the value of "remembering as a creative process" (42). They argue that since memory is always "*re*-presented in the present," it is never passive, and any discussion of memory needs to acknowledge that recollected experiences are both product and process (Keightley and Pickering 2012: 42 [original emphasis]; see also Jenkinson and Webb in this volume). The notion of truth in memory is therefore less important than understanding why that story matters to an individual or group of people.

Recollections of Material Identities

Memories of Dress: Recollections of Material Identities presents new perspectives that combine approaches from dress history, fashion studies, and cultural studies to explore the ways in which dress is remembered while recognizing the value of material culture approaches and studies based on surviving garments. Our understandings and interpretations are foregrounded in the immaterial meanings contained within and around clothing at the time it was worn and at the time of recollection. Termed "material identities," this approach encourages discussions of personal sartorial motivations and tensions with collective understandings of public appearance to be articulated and explored. This volume brings together multiple voices to tell stories that encompass and contextualize different circumstances and experiences, including those whose narratives are missing from existing literature or museum collections.

History has traditionally favored survivors and has privileged narratives of wealth and power. Dress history is no exception. Many of our internationally regarded museum collections are founded on bequeaths from wealthy families whose personal archives support the documentation of their heritage. As the chapters by Whyman and Webb demonstrate, the dress we encounter in museum collections tells us something about the status of the original owner, perhaps the designer, and the conditions of use and storage over a garment's life, which are the traces of life that remain in our clothes when the self is no more—what Whyman terms here as "materialized memory" (following Krasner 2010; Abel 2013). The garments in personal and institutional archives, including those examined by Jenkinson, Whyman, and Webb, evidence the former lives of their wearers and say something about the person that kept or donated them. As Arjun Appadurai (1986: 41–2) identified, objects have "life histories" and "biographies" and therefore distribute knowledge during their life span. Marius Kwint (1999: 3) states that there is "an open dialogue between the object, the maker and the consumer in constructing meaning." The physical properties of objects, and our sensory engagement with them, mean that the histories of our possessions become part of our own biographies (Stewart 1993; Woodward 2007). The stories we tell about ourselves and others through dress are shaped by material encounters.

Saulo B. Cwerner's (2001: 79) study of the wardrobe as both the set of clothes owned and the traditional site of storage within the home where most of our encounters with clothing begin and end reminds us that most of our clothing spends its time between uses "at rest." Webb's chapter in this volume applies

Cwerner's ideas of the domestic to museum storage. Also of relevance is the collection policy at the time of donation or curatorial purchase, and any revisions to this over time that have been used to rationalize what is kept and reflect how the institution sees itself in the wider local, national, or international social and cultural world. Whyman's definition of "post-wardrobe" reflects this afterlife status of stored and no-longer worn items in a museum collection.

The clothing we keep in our personal wardrobes reflects similar retention policies along the lines of the person I want to be, the person I am most of the time, the person I wish I could be, and the person I fear I might be (following Guy and Banim 2000; Bye and McKinney 2007; Woodward 2007). Stored clothing is about "both object and imagination (a memory, an aspiration, a fantasy)" (Tseëlon 2012: 24). In her chapter, Jenkinson's "memory wardrobe" describes a more personal experience linked to imagined memories. What is stored in our wardrobes or in our museum collections, whether real or remembered, is always curated and always selective. Each of the chapters by Jenkinson, Whyman, and Webb considers how retained clothing (and in the case of Jenkinson other artifacts, photographs, and soundtracks) are linked to an imaginary potential of memories of dress and their role in the liminal spaces between past, present, and future.

Personal memories of dress reflect similar concerns as the reasons why clothing is kept and are also curated: there is a choice in what we relate from what we remember, even if the processes of storage and retention are sometimes beyond our control and are affected by memory issues (Buse and Twigg 2013, 2014, 2015, 2016; Slater 2014). Where the firsthand testimony of others is presented in this volume, it draws upon oral history methods outlined by Lou Taylor (2002) who proposed that "since clothing is such a fundamental factor within everyday life and human experience, memories of dress should be able to make significant contributions to the field of oral history" (Taylor 2002: 242; Biddle-Perry 2005). Oral testimony enables the recovery of lost areas of experience from respondents with a variety of backgrounds and treats their recollections as valid evidence for research into aspects of living memory (Lummis 1987; Bornat 1989; Tosh 1991; Lomas 2000; Taylor 2002). The spoken memories of dress—collected through interviews, then recorded, transcribed, and reproduced by Slater, Juhasz, Atkin, and Jenkinson here—highlight and reflect important social and cultural experiences, ranging from individual to community.

Alongside oral accounts, autoethnographic practice opens new ways of writing, visualizing, and performing private and social identities through the analysis of the ethnography of one's own culture (Reed-Danahay 1997). The distinction with the autobiographical account is an important one. While both methods recall and represent memories from a personal, first-person perspective, autoethnography is a form of self-narrative that places the self within the social context in which it occurs. In this way autoethnographic practice enables the authoring of personal accounts that emphasize alternative meanings to dominant representation in a bid to challenge marginalization as well as gain agency and legitimacy in one's lived experience (Neumann 1996). Mihaly Csikszentmihalyi and Eugene Rochberg (1981: 16) propose that objects contribute to the development of identity when they "help create order in consciousness at the levels of the person, community and patterns of natural order." The three final chapters of this book, by Kealy-Morris, Chin, and Beale, each use autoethnographic practice to explore memories of dress: Kealy-Morris explores memories of daily dressing practice through wearing, choosing, rejecting, and constructing the self in the context of wider fashionable styles; Chin uses her family history to narrate the complexities of racial heritage in the United States; and Beale considers personal and collective rituals around death and bereavement.

Elizabeth Hallam and Jenny Hockey (2001: 1) state that we "explore memory through material objects that acquire meanings and resonances through embodied practice." Their examples around death rituals, including the tradition of mourning wear, show how we use objects to evoke memories. The performativity of memory through objects can be extended to the process of making. Leora Auslander (2005) states that human beings need objects to effectively remember and forget. She positions her argument under the title of "beyond words" to reflect the tacit nature of how this happens. Taylor (2013: 311) adopted Auslander's term for an embroidery created as a memorial to her grandmother. Taylor describes her embroidery, created by the emotional and instinctive ritual of stitching, as a "memory carrier" (2013: 309). There is a great tradition of textiles as memory carriers. As Lesley Millar (2012: unpag.) has written, cloth is "the membrane through which we establish our sense of 'becoming,' and formalize our relationship with the external world . . . clothing holds the memory of our time and connects us with memories of other times and other places." In this volume, Beale and Chin demonstrate that memories lie not just in the material object itself but in the embodied practice of its creation; Juhasz's analysis of her grandmother's dressmaking narratives shows that memories of making can remain when other aspects of recall become less certain. Rituals and traditions involving textiles and dress are complex and culturally specific. Decisions we make around the clothes we wear matter greatly to our identities within our social groups. In this way, our regular engagement with dress as an intimate object, kept in the safety of hearth and home—and sometimes in museums—informs who we are as people (Csikszentmihalyi and Rochberg 1981).

Clothes as material objects are recognized for their value as "memory prompts" (Weber and Mitchell 2004: 256; Gibson 2015: xv). The retained clothing (whether in a personal or museum collection) and personal photographs depicting clothing discussed in this book play a similar role to the notion of *lieux de mémoire* by Pierre Nora (1989), as a site of memory that represents and visually articulates traces of the past in the present (Slater 2011). Where photographs are presented here, they are acknowledged both in their popular definition as *holding* memory and as visual examples that *produce* memory, as "mechanisms by which the past can be constructed and situated within the present" (Sturken 1999: 178). Marita Sturken notes that "the personal photograph is an object of complex emotional and cultural meaning, an artifact used to conjure memory, nostalgia, and contemplation" (1999: 178). As such, snapshot photographs can conjure both memory and mourning, a view of a moment captured and lost in its small frame (Sturken 1999). Marianne Hirsch (1999: xiii) posits that the people and events captured in a family snapshot result in a "familial looking." We see familiar faces in a particular, often positive, light, which can act "as a screen" and an "instrument of cultural dialogue and cultural memory" (Hirsch 1999: xiii). Therefore, familial collective memory can surround a personal photograph in half-truths, myth, and amnesia.

Taylor (2002) also reminds us of the importance of the role of the photographer and the context and culture in which an image is framed. The photographs used in this volume, which take the form of personal snapshots, professional media images, and evidence of creative practice outputs, serve memory as "records" of the past that take the reader (or viewer) on a journey beyond their personal experience (Kwint 1999: 2). The time a photograph was taken is also important; most of the personal photographs in this volume date from the pre-digital age and were taken on film, printed (using a dark room), and retained for a future reference. In this book, it is the storytelling of memory that helps us begin to interpret the "relationship between the image and what it shows" (Kuhn 2002: 13). The related auto/biographical recollections presented alongside photographs contextualize these visual documents for a more personal, complex understanding of the motivations and decisions relating to the garment/s portrayed in the wider context of its consumption.

Photographs can also serve as "archives of public memory" (Wilson 2013: 94), triggering recollections and interest in the past and the styles of the time where clothes of the past are shown as "embodied or 'animated'" (Jenss 2015: 124–5). Jenss explains that media photographs (and film) offer an understanding of how clothes were worn and moved on the body which offers the opportunity for reinterpretation, in the spirit of the time (for the case of Jenss, and also Atkin in this volume, this was the 1960s). Jenss (2004) argues that dressing in original garments produces a feeling of individuality and sophistication. In her 2015 volume, investigating German 1960s enthusiasts, Jenss notes that original clothes of the period, made and worn during that time are seen as "witnesses of their time. . . . They convey a visual as well as physical experience of and link to the past, forming a kind of material, mobile meeting place with the sixties" (Jenss 2015: 105). Atkin (2016: 232) has noted the different fabrics and fit of original garments "*feel* different" for the wearer. The chapters by Atkin and Whyman in this volume further explore how garments can evoke auto/biographical memories of their original time period through their materiality and how personal narratives can provide a more nuanced understanding of the garments shown in media photographs.

Several chapters in this volume include personal snapshot photographs shared via interviews. Where Slater, Juhasz, and Jenkinson's interviewees discuss photographs, these were used as a means of "social performance" (Langford 2006: 223; Kuhn 2010; Slater 2011). Photographs were used to "furnish" recollections, to "constitute a picture of the past," and to "stimulate" remembering and prompt narratives that may "have remained dormant, repressed, or forgotten" (Kwint 1999: 2). One of Slater's interviewees showed two photographs to demonstrate limited quantity of dress despite the passage of time alongside her recollected experiences. The scenes depicted in the professional images in Atkin's chapter were remembered by her interviewees and assisted the analysis of related memories of the garments shown. Used alongside soundtracks in Jenkinson's research, photographs enabled imaginative remembering of dress of the past, adding context—and also color—to black-and-white imagery. Kealy-Morris and Beale use representations of close kin and themselves captured in particular moments to support reflexive practices and autobiographical memory. Beale's photographs of her parents allow space for mourning through discussion of their lived experience in times and clothing from before her own lifetime. The distinct embodied quality of these photographs as representations of clothing once worn reminds us of the central importance of the body to any aspect of clothing (Woodward 2007). A photograph of dress usually records the body that is wearing, has worn, or offers the potential to wear the garment in the future. As Elizabeth Wilson wrote, "snapshots, photo-journalism and news pictures capture people wearing clothing in the situations in which they actually wear them, in the street, at home, at parties . . . [as] clothes *in use* . . . they show us [what] *really was*" (Wilson 2009: 68–9 [original emphasis]). Calling them "ghostly traces," Susan Sontag (1977: 8) suggests that photographs play a talismanic role as a mnemonic device, summoning our bodily past into present reality. The photographs of dress of past selves and deceased loved ones elicit memory and mourning for what Entwistle (2000) termed "embodied practices," for the body wearing the clothing in the photograph or the absent body that once wore the garment is now photographed on a hanger or draped on a mannequin (Wilson [1985] 2010, 2009). Yet the auto/biographical memories that accompany these visual representations fill the space where the body was and in doing so places the wearer back at the heart of the story.

The memories of dress presented here represent a range of material identities through garments that are both real and imagined, owned and discarded, visual and written, embodied and disembodied. The exploration of material identities through the lens of memory offers a unique perspective by articulating, examining, and contextualizing the meanings and motivations, both collective and public, personal and private, behind the clothes we wear at different times and in different circumstances, places, and life stages. In *Memories of Dress*, we encounter traces of material garments and immaterial clothing practices that extend beyond the life span of object and sometimes beyond the life span of the owner/wearer. We pick up the challenge written by Taylor in 2002, also acknowledged by Weber and Mitchell (2004), that "one of the voids of dress history has been its failure to examine emotional responses to dress and appearance" (Taylor 2002: 102). As Sophie Wood (2020) concluded in her research into treasured garments, "clothes are too often studied removed from the people that fill them up, both physically and emotionally" (246). The memories of dress presented in this volume, whether through concepts of self, histories, objects, or practices, situate the wearer's recollected experience—auto/biographical, collective, cultural, and imagined—at the heart of each chapter. The complexities of human memory are acknowledged and embraced from the first chapter, which establishes autobiographical memory as the grounding concept of "self," to the last, which imagines memories of dress in an intergenerational journey from past, to present, and future. This is a story of identity, belonging, and difference told in and through memories of dress.

As with all works of memory, the narratives presented in this volume make no claims toward truth or representation. There are silences—both personal and collective—which we acknowledge as having as much importance as what is included in this volume (following Passerini 2005). In the first instance, the memories presented here exist because of successful memory storage and retrieval processes. In the second instance, they exist because at some time, and in some form, these recollections were recorded and preserved. For everything that is remembered, something else is forgotten or goes unreported. Once memory enters the realm of the social, cultural, or collective, it is in part "metaphor" (Erll 2011: 304) and thus any attempt to understand from beyond personal experience is inevitably and always subject to interpretation. As Carolyn Steedman (2001) has written, the search of history—and memory as is the case in this volume—is a search for self-identity in the present, "for all the ideas, and times, and images that will give us, right now, solidity and meaning in time" (77). As the chapters in *Memories of Dress: Recollections of Material Identities* show, these searches come in various forms, and each demonstrates what Judith Simpson (2019) has termed the "mnemomic and affective power" of clothes (159). The memories of dress presented in our volume show what can be gained when we seek an understanding of our embodied auto/biographical relationship with clothes and how these are carried with us, from snippets of our earliest autobiographical memories, to the performance of identities past and present shaped by the society and culture in which we live, to whatever remains in memory in our later years, and even to the material garments that survive to tell a story beyond a human life span.

Notes

1 "Auto/biography" is used as an overarching term that covers autobiography and biography and interrelations between these types of writing, applied here to writing about memory. Our definition aligns with that of the British Sociological Association's (2022 [online]) "Auto/Biography Study Group," encompassing "the interrelations between biography, autobiography, text and lives, and the relationship between the differing genres of representing lives. The forward slash in auto/ biography denotes the critical interrelationship between the self and the other, the private and public," and extends this to cover memories of lives, told through clothes, from both perspectives.

2 Present in this context means the time when the story was recorded or told. This may be at the time of writing for this volume or at the time of data collection in an earlier empirical study. Dates are provided when accounts from earlier research are included.

3 Barthes defines myth as socially constructed notions that are drained of their original meaning (removed from context and without history) that are accepted without question and with different meanings. In *Mythologies* ([1957] 2009), Barthes takes a negative stance on myth, presenting popular cultural objects, defined as myths, that have been re-presented with different meanings that often benefit the bourgeoisie and capitalist culture.

Part I

Concepts

1

Personal Objects and Dress as Instruments for Anchoring the Self, Remembering the Past, and Enhancing Well-Being

Soljana Çili

In William Faulkner's ([1951] 1996) *Requiem for a Nun*, the attorney Gavin Stevens states that "[t]he past is never dead. It isn't even past." This statement captures very well the nature of the past as something that is no more and yet stays with us, often kept alive by the emotions and mental images associated with it; the meanings we have attached to it; or people, places, and objects that remind us of it. The aim of this chapter is to present existing literature on the relevance of autobiographical memory for our sense of self and the role of personal objects in the memory-self relationship. The chapter begins with an introduction to autobiographical memory. Next, I focus on the way in which personal objects, including dress, are linked to the self and trigger memory retrieval. I argue that possessions can serve as both anchors of the self and threads which link our past, present, and future, thus influencing our perceptions of self-continuity and psychological well-being. I conclude by highlighting the need for further research which can help us to better understand the role of dress in our lives.

Understanding Autobiographical Memory and Its Functions

Broadly speaking, memory involves encoding and storing information that we can subsequently retrieve and use. We have different types of memory (see Baddeley, Eysenck, and Anderson 2015). We can, for example, remember facts or semantic information, such as the name of Albania's capital city. We can remember skills we may have acquired over time, such as knitting or riding a bicycle. We can also remember scenes from our lives. In fact, autobiographical memory involves memory for self-relevant information and episodes from our personal past which happened in a specific time and place (Baddeley, Eysenck, and Anderson 2015; Nelson and Fivush 2004).

Autobiographical memories serve three main functions: social, directive, and self (Bluck et al. 2005). The social function involves sharing personal experiences to develop, strengthen, or maintain interpersonal relationships. The directive function involves using our memories and the lessons learned from them to direct or manage our behavior as we go about our daily lives, for example as we make plans or decisions, solve problems, and adapt our behavior to the situations we find ourselves in. It helps make our behavior more efficient and potentially ensures our survival (Pillemer 2003). Finally, the self function involves using past experiences to construct a coherent and continuous sense of self which is conducive to psychological well-being (Bluck et al. 2005; Conway, Singer, and Tagini 2004; McAdams 2015). According to Dan P. McAdams (2015), we use our experiences to weave a narrative or life story which helps us understand who we used to be, who we are, and who we may become; how we came to be; and how we are one person despite all the different selves we have developed over time. This life story or narrative identity is an essential component of the self. Definitions of the self in psychology are often based on the conceptualization proposed by William James, one of the founders of the discipline. According to James (1890), the self involves the *I* and the *Me*. The *Me* encompasses what the *I* observes and attributes to itself, for example our individual personality traits, roles played in life, goals, values, and narrative identity. On the whole, the self enables us to reflect about ourselves and regulate our emotions and behaviors as we adapt to our environment (Leary and Tangney 2012).

The Memory-Self Relationship and Its Relevance for Psychological Well-Being

According to McAdams' (2015) model of personality, narrative identity starts developing in late adolescence and early adulthood, when our cognitive abilities become more complex and we face societal pressures to develop an identity. At this stage, we engage in autobiographical reasoning, a process in which we attempt to make sense of our experiences and link them to each other and to aspects of the self which are illustrated by or have changed as a result of these experiences (Habermas and Bluck 2000). Among other things, during this process we try to make our personal history coherent and formulate self-event connections, which are statements indicating links between our experiences and our sense of self (Pasupathi, Mansour, and Brubaker 2007). For example, I can understand what I value as I make the self-event connection: "My negative reaction to seeing others treated unfairly shows how much I value justice and fairness." In this case, memories of episodes in which I have experienced anger and intervened in situations I considered unfair illustrate an aspect of myself. In the same way, I can think about how specific experiences have changed me and formulate self-event connections reflecting this change, for example: "The challenges I faced at university as a first-generation student made me more resilient." Even in this example, I am drawing a conclusion that helps me understand myself and my life.

The life story is a constant work in progress as we add, remove, or edit/reinterpret episodes or chapters from our past or anticipated future (McAdams 2015). As the story changes, so does our view of ourselves and our life, which may become more positive or more negative. The outcome depends on factors such as the way in which we interpret or narrate our experiences, which in turn is influenced by things like gender and culture (see, for example, McAdams 2015; Nelson and Fivush 2004; McLean and Syed 2015; Wang 2021). It also depends on the kind of experiences we have and remember. We forget most of the events we experience in any given day. The experiences that we remember in the long run and eventually include in our life story are usually relevant to our long-term goals (Conway and Pleydell-Pearce 2000; Singer and Salovey 1993; Conway, Singer, and Tagini 2004). This association between long-term autobiographical memories and goals is evident in the reminiscence bump, a phenomenon which involves adults' tendency to remember a disproportionate number of experiences from their adolescence and young adulthood—normally between the ages of ten and thirty (see, for example, Koppel and Berntsen 2019; Munawar, Kuhn, and Haque 2018). There are multiple explanations for its existence. For example, some accounts emphasize the fact that adolescence and young adulthood feature many memorable first-time experiences (Pillemer 2001), as well as experiences which are crucial to the development of our identity and long-term goals (Conway and Pleydell-Pearce 2000).

Because of their relevance for the self and factors such as enhanced recall, many of the memories from the reminiscence bump and the rest of the life span are what Singer and Salovey (1993) call self-defining memories. These memories are vivid and associated with intense affect, come to mind frequently, maintain close links with similar memories, and revolve around our enduring concerns. Ultimately, these memories become part of what the self-memory system (SMS) model refers to as the long-term self: a structure comprising conceptual information about one's self and autobiography (see, for example, Conway, Justice, and D'Argembeau 2019; Conway, Singer, and Tagini 2004). The content of this long-term self is thought to be organized in the form of goals and self-images which represent our past, present, future, desired, or feared selves (Conway, Justice, and D'Argembeau 2019). The SMS model proposes that we are able to adapt to and deal with our environment because, when we face shifts in our circumstances, a relevant self-defining memory and working self are activated. The working self consists of a subset of the goals and self-images of the long-term self. It is the aspect of the self that is "on air" or active at any point in time and guides our thinking, emotions, and behaviors. For example, when I enter a classroom, one of my "lecturer" working selves is activated and guides my teaching and interactions with students.

The SMS model is supported by evidence suggesting that, when we recall specific memories, the activation of a working self related to these memories may contribute to transient changes in emotions, self-perceptions or self-evaluations, and behavior (for a review, see Çili and Stopa 2019). For example, recalling positive memories is associated with experiencing positive emotions (Josephson, Singer, and Salovey 1996). Compared to recalling negative self-defining memories, recalling positive self-defining memories is also associated with experiencing higher self-esteem after recall (Çili and Stopa 2015). These effects are partly due to the fact that autobiographical memories are typically characterized by autonoesis, a sense of the self mentally traveling in time and reliving the events they depict (Tulving 2002). They are not necessarily confined to the moments following retrieval. In fact, autobiographical memories can have long-term effects on psychological well-being and mental health. Among other things, memories can be associated with low well-being and symptoms of psychological disorders. This can occur when they depict adverse or traumatic experiences, have an overall negative emotional tone, are described with a low sense of agency (e.g., autonomy) and connection with others, and are associated with negative meanings or self-event connections (Adler et al. 2016; Çili and Stopa 2019; McLean et al. 2020).

Autobiographical memories may affect the self both when we voluntarily recall them and when they come to mind spontaneously. Their retrieval can be triggered by internal factors such as emotions. For example, intense anxiety may elicit the recall of one or more experiences in which this emotion was felt. Often, however, the retrieval of memories or associated mental images is triggered by stimuli in our environment, such as music (Belfi, Karlan, and

Tranel 2016; Sakka and Saarikallio 2020) or smell (Hackländer, Janssen, and Bermeitinger 2019). Among the most important external cues to trigger memory retrieval are material possessions or personal objects. Following is an account of the role that these objects, including dress, play in the memory-self relationship.

Personal Objects, Autobiographical Memory, and the Self

There is an intimate relationship between material possessions and the self. In his seminal work *The Principles of Psychology*, James (1890) stated:

> *In its widest possible sense*, however, *a man's Self is the sum total of all that he* CAN *call his*, not only his body and his psychic powers, but his clothes and his house, his wife and children, his ancestors and friends, his reputation and works, his lands and horses, and yacht and bank-account. All these things give him the same emotions. If they wax and prosper, he feels triumphant; if they dwindle and die away, he feels cast down,—not necessarily in the same degree for each thing, but in much the same way for all. (James 1890: 291–2 [original emphasis])

According to James, the self consists of what individuals identify with and experience emotions toward. He argued that the "Me" (James 1890: 291) involves three related aspects: the social self (how we are recognized and regarded by others); the spiritual self (the subjective self comprising of our psychological attributes); and the material self (concrete people, places, or objects that we identify as belonging to us). In the last century, the material self has attracted significant attention in psychology and areas such as sociology, philosophy, fashion, and marketing. Research has focused primarily on personal objects, which are usually defined as objects individuals have become attached to and emotionally invested in, potentially because they have acquired some special significance (see, for example, Csikszentmihalyi and Rochberg-Halton 1981). While they can be used for the purpose for which they were designed, objects can also be used symbolically (Belk 1988; Csikszentmihalyi and Rochberg-Halton 1981; Dittmar 1992; Habermas 2001; Habermas and Paha 2002). First, they can symbolize the self and help us communicate different aspects of it, such as our social position, ethnic background, or personality (Dittmar 1992). In fact, evidence suggests that we can draw relatively accurate conclusions about people's personality based on their possessions (Gosling et al. 2002). Second, objects can remind us of our experiences and selves (Belk 1988; Csikszentmihalyi and

Rochberg-Halton 1981; Dittmar 1992; Miller 2008, 2010; Van den Hoven, Orth, and Zijlema 2021). They can thus serve as extensions of the self.

Russell W. Belk (1988) argues that the extended self includes what individuals consider to be theirs. This comprises, but is not limited to, the persons, places, and objects they feel attached to. According to Belk (1988: 159), possessions serve as manifestations of the self and as a "personal archive or museum" which enables us to reflect on our past, how we have changed over time, and where we are headed. Indeed, research suggests that objects can elicit the retrieval of autobiographical memories, transporting us to our past or to an imagined desired future (Breen, Scott, and McLean 2021; Habermas and Paha 2002; Kroger and Adair 2008; Zijlema, Van den Hoven, and Eggen 2019). Research on university students, for example, has found that they use different spaces in their dorm rooms to construct and reflect different past, present, or future selves or to reflect the same self in different ways through their belongings (Breen, Scott, and McLean 2021). They use personal objects not only to remind themselves of their past, but also to regulate their emotions (Habermas and Paha 2002). They may do this more frequently during times of role transition, such as starting university or relocating, which may involve separation from significant others and a discontinuity in the sense of self (Habermas and Paha 2002). Overall, research suggests that "mnemoactive objects" which elicit memories are often valued more than other objects, regardless of their financial importance (Jones and Martin 2006: 1587).

Given the close relationship between memory and the self, Tilmann Habermas argues that using objects for mnemonic purposes can strengthen our sense of self-continuity and the idea that the different selves these objects remind us of are actually part of the same person (Habermas 2001; Habermas and Paha 2002). Objects associated with specific moments or periods in our lives can act as anchors for the person we were, feared, or aspired to become at the time. They have fixed those selves in time and can thus remind us of them through their physical presence or their presence in photo albums. By traveling back in time and remembering these past selves, we are able to establish links between them or between them and our current or future selves. Through objects, we can also reconcile different or conflicting selves and thus create a narrative about ourselves that is both continuous and coherent. Aaron C. Ahuvia (2005), for example, reports a case study on a young woman who grew up in a ranch in Nebraska, United States, but worked as a marketing executive in Chicago. Her loved objects, such as antique family heirlooms and cooking/entertaining gadgets, seemed to represent both her rancher and her urban selves. They helped her reconcile these different selves in a coherent life narrative which took into account her rancher past self and her urban "present and aspirational future self" (Ahuvia 2005: 179). Her antiques, however, seemed to represent both her rancher self and the sophisticated taste of her urban self. They thus enabled her to reduce any perceived tension between these two selves.

Further research supports the idea of material possessions as extensions which expand the self beyond our physical body or as anchors which fix specific past selves in our minds. For example, Rosellina Ferraro, Jennifer Edson Escalas, and James R. Bettman (2011) suggest that possessions become linked to the self if they reflect domains on which individuals base their self-worth, such as academic achievement, appearance, or relationships. Kimberly Rios Morrison and Camille S. Johnson (2011) found that possessions may be particularly important as self-extensions for individualists—people who base their self-definitions on their unique characteristics—when their self-views are threatened. Christina Buse and Julia Twigg (2014) suggest that for patients with dementia, who experience memory loss and changes in their sense of self, objects can be particularly important in providing a sense of security and connection to past selves. Anna Pechurina (2020) demonstrates the relevance of objects from the homeland for migrants' identities. Other research highlights the fact that individuals tend to report distress and a sense of loss when they lose personal objects, for example as a result of damage, natural disasters, or moving into institutions such as care homes (Belk 1988; Kroger and Adair 2008; Lollar 2010). In fact, Belk (1988) argues that such objects are usually retained until they are no longer needed to maintain a sense of self, no longer correspond to our current or ideal self, or no longer fit with our narrative for our life. This pattern of retaining and discarding is reminiscent of the lifecycle of clothes which, as personal objects, can be highly relevant to the self.

Dress as Personal Object and Its Relationship with Memory, the Self, and Well-Being

As mentioned earlier, James (1890) believed that the material self also comprised one's clothes. He wrote:

> We so appropriate our clothes and identify ourselves with them that there are few of us who, if asked to choose between having a beautiful body clad in raiment perpetually shabby and unclean, and having an ugly and blemished form always

spotlessly attired, would not hesitate a moment before making a decisive reply. . . .
We all have a blind impulse to watch over our body, to deck it with clothing of
an ornamental sort. (James 1890: 292–3)

This emphasis on clothes was expressed throughout his writings and, according to
Cecelia A. Watson (2004), was also visible in his dressing style. James is described
as wearing casual clothes unless formal dress was "absolutely necessary" (Watson
2004: 217). Even the formal dress he sports in his portraits included polka-dot ties
which, according to Watson, were deemed unfashionable and made him stand
out—something that was to be avoided by the "well-dressed man of the latter half
of the 1800s" (2004: 218). For Watson, James' unique style reflected his personality,
particularly his energy and approachability. In fact, although dress may be part of
the material self, it is closely related to the spiritual and social selves.

Like other material possessions, clothes are used for utilitarian purposes, such
as protecting us from the elements, and for symbolic ones. In fact, we use dress
to draw inferences about others regarding characteristics such as demographics,
competence, personality, and mood (Lennon et al. 2014). We use it to express
our individuality and distinctiveness, as well as our group membership (Cox
and Dittmar 1995). We also use it to strategically manage the impressions we
create on others, for example in the workplace (Peluchette, Karl, and Rust
2006); to camouflage perceived physical flaws or accentuate body parts that we
are comfortable with or proud of (Clarke, Griffin, and Maliha 2009; Frith and
Gleeson 2008; Tiggemann and Lacey 2009; Masuch and Hefferon 2014); to boost
our morale (Tiggemann and Lacey 2009); and to manage emotions/mood (Kang,
Johnson, and Kim 2013; Masuch and Hefferon 2014). Qualitative research by
Alison Guy and Maura Banim (2000: 316) suggests that, at least among women,
clothes may be associated with different aspects of the self: the actual self ("the
woman I am most of the time"); the ideal or aspirational self ("the woman I want
to be"); and the feared self ("the woman I fear I could be"). This is in line with
Sophie Woodward's (2007) conclusion, also based on qualitative research, that
women consider their knowledge of who they are and who they can be when
choosing what to wear. Taken together, these findings support James' (1890) idea
about an intimate connection between dress and the self. This connection seems
to extend to multiple or possible selves, which are conceptualized as part of
individuals' long-term self in psychological literature (see, for example, Conway,
Justice, and D'Argembeau 2019; Markus and Nurius 1986).

Given its connection with the self, its constant presence in our lives, and the
fact that we experience it through multiple sensory modalities (Slater 2014;
Woodward 2007), it is not surprising that dress has mnemonic value and can

be cherished like other personal objects. Clothes help maintain a record of our history and memories (Cox and Dittmar 1995; Woodward 2007). We may become particularly attached to and retain over time clothes which are associated with special occasions or emotional memories linked to our childhood and youth, significant people in our lives, love, or home (Bye and McKinney 2007; Niinimäki and Armstrong 2013). These clothes may help establish a sense of self-coherence and self-continuity by anchoring the selves that were dominant or active at the time we wore them and by reminding us of these selves. A blouse my mother wore for over twenty years and recently gave to me reminds me of the early years in which she wore it—difficult and yet overall happy years in which I was moving from childhood to adolescence. The outfit I wore at my PhD graduation reminds me of the girl who was finally confident in her abilities and yet fearful of what came next in her life. As I reflect on who I have been through the clothes I see in my wardrobe and photo albums, I can see how I have changed over the years and how I am still, in many ways, the same person I was then. The fact that my clothing style has not changed much over the years strengthens my perceptions of consistency. When changes in one's life are accompanied by wardrobe changes, clothes may arguably remind individuals of more distinctive selves and turning points in their life. Woodward (2007: 52), in fact, suggests that women may use the clothing in their wardrobe "as a means to work through their biography." She describes a participant whose wardrobe reflected her transition from a working woman to a full-time mother and homemaker. For this participant, the work clothes that she no longer wore were powerful reminders of who she used to be and could be. In a similar vein, Buse and Twigg (2016) suggest that both kept and absent but remembered clothes help patients with dementia maintain a sense of self-continuity. Among other things, clothes can remind them of their occupational history and times when they were different from their current self, for example independent and energetic.

Because autobiographical memory is relevant for the self and psychological well-being, it is reasonable to assume that dress may affect well-being through its connection to both memory and the self. Research in this area is limited, but the existing literature suggests that dress may affect well-being through its short- and long-term impact on the self. In terms of short-term impact, evidence suggests that wearing specific clothes can influence our psychological processes. For example, Barbara L. Fredrickson et al. (1998) found that wearing a swimsuit rather than a sweater increased state self-objectification—the preoccupation with appearance and physical competence experienced during the research—in males and females. In females, this was associated with higher body shame and poorer performance in a mathematics test. According to the authors, the shame might have been due to the fact that females face stronger cultural demands to meet specific appearance ideals. The poorer test performance, on the other hand, might have resulted from self-objectification exerting a negative impact on females' cognitive resources. In more recent research, Bettina Hannover and Ulrich Kühnen (2002) found that the way participants described themselves varied depending on what they were wearing. Participants wearing formal clothes to the experiment endorsed more formal adjectives such as "strategic" and fewer casual adjectives such as "easygoing" to describe themselves compared to participants wearing casual clothes (Hannover and Kühnen 2002: 2517). Hajo Adam and Adam D. Galinsky (2012) found that wearing clothes imbued with symbolic meaning can affect cognitive processes such as sustained attention, which is the ability to remain focused on an activity or stimulus for an extended period of time. In one of their experiments, participants wearing a white lab coat presented to them as a medical doctor's lab coat performed better in a task requiring sustained attention compared to participants wearing an identical lab coat presented as an artistic painter's coat and to participants who saw the lab coat presented as a doctor's lab coat but did not wear it (Adam and Galinsky 2012). Taken together, these quantitative psychological studies support the qualitative research coming from disciplines such as anthropology and material culture studies. Both Daniel Miller (2010) and Woodward (2007), for example, argue that dress does not just express the self; it also changes it. Adam and Galinsky (2012: 918) introduced the term "enclothed cognition" to describe this change, that is, the systematic influence that clothes have on wearers' psychological processes and behavioral tendencies.

Repeated contact with clothes related to autobiographical memories and the self may also have a long-term impact on psychological well-being. Qualitative research by Christoph-Simon Masuch and Kate Hefferon (2014, 2018) found that participants viewed clothing practices as a source of positive emotions and feeling good about the self. These authors argue that, in this way, clothes contributed to their hedonic or subjective well-being. They suggest that clothes also contributed to participants' eudaimonic well-being, which involves a sense of meaning, authenticity, self-expressiveness, and self-actualization or realizing one's potential. This is because their participants reported a nostalgic attachment to clothes which were associated with specific meanings and reminded them of past selves, personal growth, and important relationships. Even when they were no longer worn or were worn occasionally, clothes seemed to act as "meaning-making resources" which helped participants to reflect about the past and integrate their past selves, potentially contributing to a sense of self-continuity (Masuch and Hefferon 2018: 355). It may be argued that they facilitated autobiographical reasoning and the development of participants' narrative identity. Amy R. Loder and I also suggest that clothes may contribute to well-being. In our study (Loder and Çili, forthcoming), participants indicated a favorite garment; described a memory associated with it; rated memory characteristics such as positive and negative valence, intensity of the associated emotions, vividness, and the influence of the memory on their self-perceptions on a scale from 0 (not at all) to 10 (extremely); and completed a measure of psychological well-being. Participants' memory characteristics suggested that many of them were self-defining memories. Participants' level of psychological well-being was positively correlated with the extent to which their memory was positive. It was negatively correlated with the extent to which the memory was negative and with the intensity of the negative emotions associated with this memory.

The findings of Masuch and Hefferon (2014, 2018) and those of Loder and Çili (forthcoming) need to be treated with caution. The methodological limitations of our studies, including the small sample sizes, mean that none of us can make causal claims regarding the impact of clothes on participants' psychological well-being. Furthermore, it is important to keep in mind that individuals differ in the extent to which they cherish clothes for their symbolic or mnemonic value. For some, the utilitarian value of clothes is what matters and clothes may thus have a limited impact on their well-being or no impact at all. Nevertheless, these two studies suggest that clothes may contribute to psychological well-being not only by helping maintain a sense of self-continuity and self-coherence, but also through the transient changes they trigger when related autobiographical memories are retrieved. These changes may be related to enclothed cognition (Adam and Galinsky 2012). At their root may lie the activation of specific working selves. Based on the memory-self relationship literature presented earlier in this chapter, I propose that wearing, seeing, or remembering specific garments may be accompanied by the activation of working selves which are related to the symbolic meanings associated with these garments and/or with particular autobiographical memories. For example, in Hannover and Kühnen's (2002) study, wearing formal clothes may have triggered the activation of working selves that for participants were related to formal settings or memories, such as educational or professional ones. When asked to endorse adjectives describing them, participants may have been describing these working selves. Since the activation of a working self may be associated with shifts in emotions, self-perceptions, and behavior (Çili and Stopa 2019; Conway, Singer, and Tagini 2004), I believe it may be the reason why individuals are able to use clothes to boost their morale (Tiggemann and Lacey 2009) or manage their emotions (Kang, Johnson, and Kim 2013).

The kind of working selves activated when individuals wear, see, or remember specific garments may depend on the memories or meanings they are associated with. For example, wearing clothes associated with positive memories and meanings may elicit the activation of working selves which contain positive self-images and trigger positive emotions. Expanding on Masuch and Hefferon's (2014, 2018) account, I propose that repeatedly wearing, seeing, or remembering these clothes may influence psychological well-being by potentially making positive working selves more accessible and positive emotions chronic. Increased accessibility of positive working selves may enhance individuals' self-esteem. Frequently experienced positive emotions may then contribute to well-being by promoting resilience and enhancing information processing and problem-solving (Fredrickson 2001). Nostalgia, which can be elicited by specific garments (Masuch and Hefferon 2014, 2018), may also play a role. Defined as a bittersweet longing for one's past (Sedikides and Wildschut 2018), nostalgia can have both positive and negative effects on well-being (Newman et al. 2020). Among other things, it can enhance individuals' sense of connectedness with others and their sense of self-continuity, which can contribute to a sense that one's life is significant, purposeful, and coherent (Sedikides and Wildschut 2018). Through its association with specific autobiographical memories and a potential connection with related working selves, dress may thus promote a positive, continuous, and coherent sense of self. Ultimately, it may influence individuals' hedonic and eudaimonic well-being.

Conclusion

As the literature reviewed in this chapter suggests, autobiographical memory is crucial to our sense of self and psychological well-being. Personal objects and dress are strongly associated with both autobiographical memories and the self, in some ways helping autobiographical memory perform its directive and self functions. Despite what advertising slogans would have us believe, we are not merely the sum of our possessions or what we wear. Nevertheless, possessions— including dress—may be an important *part* of the self. It is for this reason that they have such important implications for the way we see ourselves and our life.

Of course, more experimental and longitudinal research is needed in order to understand their role as cues for memory retrieval and their contribution to the self and well-being. Only then can we be confident about the causal mechanisms involved, the magnitude of their impact on well-being, and how this impact unfolds over time. A better understanding of these mechanisms may help us develop better interventions for patients with dementia or individuals such as forced migrants who struggle to establish a sense of self-coherence and self-continuity following a traumatic experience or loss of personal belongings. It may also help us develop strategies for encouraging attachment to clothes and promoting long ownership rather than quick disposal. In turn, this may help to reduce the negative environmental impact of the fashion industry. We can only hope that the growing research in this area, together with works such as the current volume, can push the field forward.

Part II

Histories

2

Remembering Respectability

Collective Memories of Working-Class Dress in Wartime Lancashire

Alison Slater

Figure 2.1 Working-class women in their local community, Hollinwood, Oldham, 1939. Unknown photographer. Author's own photograph.

This chapter explores memories of working-class female dress during the Second World War. It draws from oral evidence gathered through interviews with nine women, aged between seven and twenty-two years old in 1939, who lived in the area to the north of Manchester, England, during the war.[1] The parameters of the study recognized that experiences of war and wartime dress varied according to social status and geographical location (Walford 2008). The interviewees were categorized as "working class" if they (or their father or husband) worked in a lower-class occupation and they lived in a working-class neighborhood.[2] Interviewees also self-defined their class status by opting to take part in a study of working-class wartime dress (Roberts 1995: 6–7; Bourke 1994; Slater 2011).[3] Focusing on this geographical area, around the towns of Bolton and Oldham, situates the interviewees' recollections in a strong nonconformist religious tradition and in small, local communities where clothes played a significant role in the presentation of public identity.[4]

The chapter draws heavily upon oral evidence, which is informed by two types of memory. The first is autobiographical, which begins with firsthand experience and ends with "subjective remembering" (Tulving 1983: 11). William Brewer (1986) suggested that autobiographical memories take three forms: personal memory (including mental images of recollected experience), factual information about the self, and generic personal memory (including a general image of the past but not of a specific event).[5] Autobiographical memories provide the "basis for an individual's life story" (Paller, Voss, and Westerberg 2009: 187) that reflects both an "autonomous sense of self" and more generic recollections of "social conventions and relations" (Ross and Wang 2010: 403). Individual circumstances and the wider culture at the time of remembering affect how we access memories of the past and how important we deem them to be (Ross and Wang 2010). Personal recollections are "mediated" by cultural codes (Sangster 1994: 23). Therefore, in research that relies upon autobiographical memory, the role of culture and "collective memory" must also be considered.

The social frameworks of collective memory, a concept developed in the 1920s by Maurice Halbwachs (1992), provide a scaffolding against which personal memories are framed.[6] When we think about the events of our past, including preparation for and answering questions during an interview, we reflect upon it. Memories of childhood and adolescence, like those of my interviewees, are based on autobiographical recollections but are also informed and sometimes changed by subsequent experience.[7] This can include wider social and cultural references that are used to "orientate" our own recollections (Olick, Vinitzky-Seroussi, and Levy 2011: 19; Lummis 1987; Ross and Wang 2010). Memory practices do not happen in a vacuum: belonging to different social groups influences what and how we remember. As Sue Campbell (2008: 42) explains: "we remember with and in response to other people" and sharing "shapes" memories. Memory is framed from the perspective of the present self but is influenced by the many experiences and voices that have spoken into an episode, from the time a memory was formed to the time it is reported. The sharing of memory enables the survival of cultures and social practices from one generation to the next (Halbwachs 1992). Thus, shared memories reach "into the most minute and everyday details of our lives" (Connerton 1989: 2), including memories of dress.

Recollections of personal possessions are reported according to an individual's sense of self that "extends forwards and backwards in time" (Belk 1990: 674). This is particularly the case with clothing memories. As Julia Twigg (2013) explains, "clothes anchor people's understandings of the past and measure the passage of time" (76) and recollections of dress connect "personal and historical time" (77). Collective memories of dress are found in this connection: where individual experiences of dress map onto shared experiences of belonging to different social groups, for example, a family, a group of friends, a school, a workplace, a local community. This chapter considers how this sense of social belonging impacted what was worn and what was reported as oral evidence. The study of women of a similar age, social circumstance, and geographical location assists this exploration of collective memory, particularly as it is framed within a specific period of history.

Memories of Working-Class Wartime Dress

The Second World War was a unique period in modern British history,[8] when government restrictions dictated how many clothes were permitted and what the styles of these clothes should look like (Sladen 1995; Reynolds 1999; Walford 2008; Howell 2013; Summers 2015). Clothing rationing was introduced on June 1, 1941, and required everyone above the age of four to provide coupons for new items.[9] At first, sixty-six coupons a year were issued, this soon dropped to forty-eight, and by 1945, adults received thirty-six coupons a year (Wilson and Taylor 1989; Zweiniger-Bargielowska 2000). While the scheme placed all citizens in a similar position, it was never intended to level social boundaries and dress continued to signify status.[10] Colin McDowell (1997) recognized the efforts of working-class women to keep "decently, let alone smartly, dressed" when their average 1940s wardrobe included "one of each item, except underwear, and lots of gaps . . . a little sentimental jewellery and, for decency, a hat" (39). When my interviewees were asked "did you have a lot of clothes during the war or not?," their responses emphasized the limited quantity of clothing owned:

AW2: No, no, no we didn't.[11]

DS: Oh not a lot, no, no, cos you couldn't get them.[12]

AL: No [Laughs], no love: just enough to put on my back and wash![13]

HB: Not a lot no . . . I mean money was tight, you know?[14]

Clothes were generally considered "basic" (HB), "adequate," and "nothing outstanding" (AW2). The interviewees' wartime wardrobes tended to consist of one or two dresses, a skirt and a blouse, a small number of homemade jumpers and cardigans, one coat, two or three changes of underwear and one, maybe two, pair(s) of shoes (Slater 2011).[15] One interviewee emphasized the minimal storage needed for her whole family's clothing:

> JS: It sounds ridiculous but do you know that we didn't possess a wardrobe in our house! . . . My mother in her bedroom had a very big old-fashioned chest of drawers . . . and our clothes had to be folded carefully and placed in these drawers, so you can tell we didn't have many.[16]

The limited quantity of clothing owned meant that frequent clothing changes, including practices considered necessary for hygiene today, were not always possible.

> MF: Well you didn't used to change your knickers every day like we do now. . . . You used to put one pair on and it used to have t'last all week. . . . When you come to think how long you wore your knickers and things like that![17]
>
> MH: Underclothes . . . we changed every day but top clothes, no . . . you just wore them . . . unless you spilt something on them—probably for two or three days and then you would put clean on.[18]

Cleanliness was important as clean clothes signified care in appearance. Garments were looked after to ensure they lasted as long as possible by folding or hanging them up after wearing, brushing to remove visible dirt, and laundering (by hand) when needed. But it took considerable effort to maintain cleanliness with such a limited stock, as JS recalled:

> JS: With my school shirt—I only ever had one on the go at one time. My mother would wash them when I took them off a night and sit up until they dried and get up very early the next morning and iron them and she'd do that with knickers . . . she would have to keep on top of it like that.

Different levels of cleanliness were accepted depending on the type of garment and whether it could be washed; looking and feeling clean was what mattered most.

DS: I never remember going down feeling—going out—feeling dirty, yet they weren't always spotless! [Laughs].

JS: It sounds awful because my mother was immaculate and spotless clean and scrupulous about washing things but I think in some ways we put up with more dirt. I'm sure that's true, like in your coats and stuff.

Working-class wartime dress reflected economic circumstances, wartime restrictions, and a wider conservative attitude toward dress, particularly among those with less interest in fashion.

MH: Clothes . . . [were] just something you had to have to keep warm I think in the winter and err as I say, partly because of my upbringing, I was just never very fashion conscious, as long as it was comfortable, serviceable . . . I think that was partly erm of the war but also partly because of the attitude of mind and the fact that we couldn't afford a lot, but it would also have been considered rather frivolous.

AW2: I suppose I wasn't you know erm how should I say it? Very aware of appearance, I always wanted to look right. I can't say fashionable, I wasn't a fashionable person, so I can only say that I wanted to look fairly smart enough without [being] over the top.

While unnecessary frivolity was criticized for failing to fit the spirit of wartime (Rouse 1989; Ewing 1992; Breward 1995; Kirkham 1996), this was not a new concept among working-class families in Lancashire. A consideration toward appropriateness was evident in the interviewees' prewar, wartime, and early postwar clothing.[19] Everyday clothing acquisitions were prioritized according to what was needed, how long it would last, and what was available; personal preferences often came last, much to the dismay of those who wanted more fashionable styles. Working-class women had "good clothes sense" (Kirkham 1996: 170) but dressing up tended to be reserved for best or special occasions.

Memories of Dressing Up

In the context of limited clothing and finances, it was initially surprising that the interviewees discussed prioritizing the acquisition of best clothes.[20] The geographical focus of my research enables the oral evidence to be considered alongside reports from the Mass-Observation (MO) study of Bolton as *Worktown* from 1938 to 1942. This comparison assists an understanding of why dressing up was so important. A 1941 MO study found that "poorer people . . . 'dress *up*' to go *out*" (Change 1941: 45 [original emphasis]), a "special Bolton smartness" was also noted (46).[21] This was also echoed in memory:

> AW2: In public you would try a little harder to look smarter, at home you
> would wear old things really because again you didn't want to spoil the
> other things you were saving for going out.

> AC: It was important that you looked nice and went out on a Saturday night!
> [Laughs] . . . we made the best of what we could I suppose.[22]

Commentary from MO suggests that what some working-class people considered to be "smart" did not reach middle-class standards of dress. Investigators were "impressed . . . with the tendency for people in the very raggiest and shabbiest of clothes" to say they valued smartness over comfort (Change 1941: 45). However, in earlier research, JS had explained that the public display of a respectable class identity also presented an important visual distinction from a lower social group:

> JS: [A dress of floral print or gingham] would be what "respectable" children
> wore. I won't say what some wore, but that was respectable . . . mine were
> always beautifully washed and ironed, where other children went in dirty
> or smelly clothes . . . we were very class conscious. . . . You belonged to one
> class or another. We belonged to the class that wore caps, but there was this
> other "lower" class . . . I didn't mix with them.[23]

The visual difference between best and ordinary clothing was observed by Tom Harrisson, the lead researcher for MO: "Broadly, we found the whole of Worktown went up the social scale at the weekend . . . and the visible class distinctions of Tuesday become inextricably confused on Saturday afternoon. Weekend Worktown was a place superficially populated by well-to-do middle-classes—on an ordinary weekday, a city of wooden clogs, grimy faces and manual workers" (Harrisson 1942 cited in Highmore 2002: 104). Contemporary evidence supports that dressing up in their best attire was a regular means for working-class people to change their appearance, signify their respectability, and even visually defy their class status.

The oral evidence explains how such appearances were achieved. Many families would save up for an annual "best" outfit, usually purchased in spring, with a seasonal winter addition if finances allowed. HB would get a new outfit for Whitsuntide (Whitsun).[24]

> HB: You kept them for Sunday best then, until the year after and then you got
> some more you see. [Laughs] . . . Up to leaving school that carried on and

then you started work and you know, you think you've grown up then!
[Laughs].

DS also got a new "Sunday" outfit once a year:

> DS: We wore a hat when we went to church, you didn't go about without a hat
> in those days. Don't take much notice of me, this is just what I remember!
> [Laughs] . . . For work . . . you wore erm well old clothes, you know. Err, and
> then your other clothes went down for work clothes.

MH clarified that her newest clothes tended to be reserved for church on Sundays
for a period of time, but she didn't think of these as a "Sunday best."

> MH: Sunday—well not necessarily—certainly clean you see because in a way
> we didn't have Sunday best. Except when they were new then they were kept
> for Sunday certainly for a while or going out but mostly for Sunday because
> we didn't go out a lot otherwise.

In a discussion of what her mother wore, JS explained the recycling process
where clothing that was once reserved for best was eventually relegated to
ordinary daywear and at the end of its use, retained to wear for housework to
prevent damage to newer items.

> JS: My mother, in the morning, she would put on a very simple cotton dress, now it
> might have been a best dress at one time, I don't know . . . and she would wear
> an apron and this cotton dress . . . or erm if it was winter she'd perhaps wear a
> kind of a tweed skirt and a blouse or something like that, but those were quite
> old and err poor looking, best way I can describe them. And she'd wear those
> until she'd finished her housework and then we would have our "dinner" as
> we . . . called it in the middle of the day . . . then when . . . she'd washed up and
> cleared everything away she would go and have a good wash and change and
> these things that she wore in the morning . . . she'd wear them to go to the shops
> but she wouldn't, not that she went to many other places . . . I didn't realize
> 'til after the war that my mother would probably have loved to go to things at
> church but she wouldn't go because she didn't have smart enough clothes.[25]
> Erm so she didn't have much that she could change into, but she would change
> into a slightly better outfit for the afternoon . . . if we sent for the doctor, she'd
> change before the doctor came, she . . . wouldn't be seen in these things.

This cycle of consumption, of having one best (or better) outfit, assisted in the
public presentation of a smart, respectable appearance and achieved a visibly
better standard of dress than their circumstances might otherwise afford. The
timing by many of a new outfit for Whitsun meant that this could be worn to

parade the streets in Whit Walks: a moment where public appearances were particularly on show in the local community.

Occasions when working-class families knew a photograph would be taken were another time to dress up in best clothing. JS gave the example of wearing her best dress for an elementary school photograph, which ensured that the highest possible standard of appearance that could be achieved was presented on that day and preserved in the photograph in perpetuity.

> JS: I remember having a dress, I think it's on that photograph at school cos as I said it's funny, I think I've got my "best" frock on because we always had a "best frock," you know? That was important and the "best frock" I can remember . . . it was like err a silky type of material. . . . It was quite frilly and I thought I was the "bee's knees" in that. I loved that!

JS's positive memory of this garment emphasized that she felt better about herself wearing that dress; the fabric and style stood out and were more memorable than her ordinary clothes. She was one of several interviewees who used the slang term "the bee's knees" to describe the positive feeling of wearing a particular outfit.[26] Despite being uncommon today, the term was part of the interviewees' language at the time the memories discussed here were formed. Michael Adams (2009: 88) notes that the use of slang terms in everyday speech by young people is part of the "interlude" of youth, where they learn to fit into social structures and develop social identity toward adulthood. It is perhaps then significant that slang words used in the period being remembered also found their way back into an interviewee's vocabulary as they articulated their memories of adolescent dress.

Memories of Making Do

Starting work was memorable because of the challenge of sourcing appropriate clothing for the adult workplace after years of school uniform or children's wear.[27] AL left school on a Friday around her fourteenth birthday in December 1941 and started work in a tailor's shop making bespoke ladies and men's suits the following Monday:

> AL: And what am I going to wear for my first day at work? Well, I've only got my gymslip and my school—and I'm not wearing those! My dad said "Well you'll have to wear that lilac frock then." So . . . I had to wear a lilac taffeta bridesmaid dress, shortened, and a pair of silver shoes.[28]

In time, she utilized her developing sewing skills to make her old school uniform into a new skirt. The feeling of achievement was as memorable as her recalled anxiety of not having appropriate clothes to begin with.

> AL: My dad found me some white paint and I painted the shoes white. And then . . . being in the tailoring trade I'd learned a little bit about sewing . . . I took my gymslip, I cut it off at the yoke and attached the belt to the top and it made a very nice pleated skirt . . . and I suppose I got a blouse from somewhere or knitted a jumper.

Although the remake was undated, AL's account shows that working-class women were using techniques associated with the government's "Make Do and Mend" campaign in the early war years.[29] Most girls had been taught basic sewing and knitting at home and at school, which gave them the skills needed to make or alter garments to ensure their suitability for different occasions or to appear more fashionable (Slater 2010, 2011; Milcoy 2017). Recollections of regular and less creative mending and darning were more general, but these practices ensured that garments were serviceable for as long as possible.

The interviewees all reported activities that were later promoted as part of Make Do and Mend, and are now culturally associated with the campaign but did not discuss when the phrase entered their lives. It was the oldest interviewees who implied that official propaganda had a limited (if any) impact.

> DS: Oh I don't know anything about that . . . I do now but I didn't then . . . Well I think we probably did do some mending but I can't think of it as "Make Do and Mend."
> MC: I couldn't tell you . . . my mother would do it for us you see.[30]

Instead, a mentality of making do, including repairing clothes, was presented as a continued feature in the interviewees' memories of everyday life: from watching their mothers' mending in their early years; to helping with basic techniques in wartime; to taking over these responsibilities as they got older. The younger interviewees suggested that these practices continued long after the war:

> MH: I still think I have a bit of that attitude! [Laughs] It's ingrained!
> JS: My children say that's my motto "Make Do and Mend" because I've still kept up with that in a way.
> AL: Oh I still "Make Do and Mend" love, to be honest! Although now I can afford to buy clothes, but for many years after the war: if something got too tight, I let it out; if it got too short, lengthened it; the fashion made things shorter, I shortened them; for many years I made do, yeah.

The interviewees had at some point in their lives adopted the phrase "Make Do and Mend," and its popular memory meaning, as a catchall term for generic memories of prewar, wartime, and postwar mending and making do.

What making do meant in reality was most evident when the younger interviewees discussed their mother's clothing. Marriage changed working-class women's experiences. The majority gave up work, had children, and entered what Carl Chinn ([1988] 2006) termed "the hidden matriarchy," where they took on responsibility for household budgeting and gained a significant role in their local communities.[31] Working-class mothers were judged by their children's dress and public appearance. Their everyday decisions and actions were self-policed by a fear of becoming the subject of criticism and local gossip and, in the worst-case scenario, ostracization from their neighbors.[32] As JS explained:

> JS: Me mother wouldn't want me to wear anything that made me look what
> she would've called "cheap" . . . anything that made me look common! . . .
> she was a bit of a snob in some ways, she would want my clothes to look as
> though they'd come from a quality place even if they hadn't! [Laughs] . . . As
> I say, I learnt two things very early on in life when I look back: one was that
> we were very poor and the second was that we didn't let anybody know and
> I think those two things dominated most of this that you've asked me.

The interviewees with older female relatives in their lives—mothers, grandmothers, aunts, and even sisters—reported that these women had a significant impact on, and sometimes dictated, their experiences of dress. The impact of the lack of older female guidance was emphasized by AL:

> AL: My father and I . . . we just sort of . . . I don't know: I had no mother to
> guide me. I have no brothers or sisters, so I had no guidelines . . . I didn't
> mix . . . very much with other girls . . . and mothers and things like that.
> I had to use my own common sense and initiative to be able to wear
> something that was reasonably suitable.

The two interviewees who married and became mothers during the war, DS and MC, had little recollection about their own clothing once they had children, probably because there were few new or memorable items. As MC explained when asked about clothing purchased after clothing rationing ended:

> MC: I had my family [by then], so I couldn't, so who come first? Children
> didn't they?

The absence of distinctive clothing memories once the older interviewees had children was explained by the younger interviewees who recalled their own mothers' clothing in their formative years. JS remembered her mother having new black clothes to attend her maternal grandmother's funeral.

> JS: I don't know how on earth she got it because she wouldn't have much money . . . I can remember her wearing the black dress for years and years after . . . it was unusual for me: unusual that my mother had new clothes—that was very unusual—but that she had black.
>
> AS: So you don't remember your mum having new clothes during the war?
>
> JS: I don't remember my mum—I've thought and thought and thought—"did my mum ever go and buy herself anything during the war?" and really can't ever remember her buying new clothes. Again, she had a lot of "pass-ons" and my grandma . . . was wonderful at jumble sales. [Laughs] . . . she didn't buy clothes for us from jumble sales, because I don't think there were many children's clothes in the jumble sales, but she used to buy clothes for my mother. My mother had to have an operation on her feet when she was older and I'm sure it was through wearing shoes that crippled her because . . . it didn't matter what size they were—if there were a pair of shoes, she'd have to wear them.

It is likely that her mother prioritized black clothes because of the fear of what other people might think if she did not achieve the appropriate image of a respectable daughter mourning for her mother.

During her interview, MH presented two snapshot photographs taken on holiday, the first dated toward the end of the war and the other a few years later (Figures 2.2 and 2.3). She had chosen these in preparation for her interview as visual evidence that her mother's clothing did not change for several years.

Figures 2.2–2.3 MH (left) with her mother, *c.* 1944 and MH (right) with her parents, *c.* 1945/6. Unknown photographers © MH. Reproduced with permission.

MH: Now I've put those two together because they're different ages—I've grown—but my mother is still wearing the same hat.

AS: And the same skirt, and the same jacket as well?

MH: I think it is. Now that might have been an effect of the war; you didn't discard things just because you fancied a new one.

While having one outfit for many years may have been an impact of war, the oral evidence suggests it was more likely that MH's mother prioritized the clothing needs of her growing children and sacrificed new items for herself, instead making do with her existing clothing for a longer period of time.[33] Under the eyes of their local community, working-class mothers stage-managed their own and their family's public appearance to perform a respectable identity that both denied and disguised their true circumstances, and demonstrated their abilities to cope in times of hardship. As a result, memories of dress suggest that working-class mothers played a more significant role in their daughters' public identity than the occupation of their father, which was traditionally used for social classification.

Collective Remembering

The complex notion of respectability was demonstrated through appearance and behavior at the time of wearing and was also reflected in the oral evidence, where dress, class, gender, identity, family, and community "interweave and bind together a narrative" (Sandino 2007: 6). This narrative of self was told through a sense of belonging to a particular social group: to a community of women with something in common including, but not limited to, social class, economic circumstance, and geographical location. Autobiographical recollections were framed within the interview subject of wartime dress but presented to acknowledge the passage of time between then and now. Each interviewee recognized that she was both the same person in the past and the present, but like the world in around her, she was also different and changed. An acceptance of the potential fallibility of her own memory was also evident (Lummis 1987). Although there were variations depending on individual circumstances, a consistent desire toward respectability was shared by all interviewees. This shared sense of past implies a shared collective memory (Halbwachs 1992; Belk 1990; Misztal 2003; Wertsch 2009; Olick, Vinitzky-Seroussi, and Levy 2011), a collective remembering of dress among this group, that overlaps and interweaves personal experience and social connections.

The firsthand and secondhand perspectives of mother and daughter expressed generational differences between individual and collective recollections. The age of the interviewees during the war means their memories of this time are within the "critical period" for early memory (between the ages of five and thirty years) where reminiscence bumps, points of heightened recollection, occur in both autobiographical and collective memories (Schuman and Corning 2014: 157).[34] Living through a significant historical event, such as the Second World War, means personal experiences can be presented through a "collectively conceptualized" narrative of the period (Schuman and Scott 1989: 377). The generational differences between the youngest interviewees (born in c. 1930), who remembered their youth and their mothers' clothing, and the older interviewees (born in c. 1920), who experienced the changes brought about by marriage and children, highlight an older group of women with the personal experience to reject the collective memories of their children's generation (Lummis 1987; Mills 2016) and a younger group, whose personal experience was to some extent protected and influenced by their parents' generation. The memories of dress from the older interviewees may be particularly salient because they come from within "late adolescence and early adulthood when adult identity is crystallizing" (Belk 1990: 673). This is considered a key time for the formation of generational collective memories (Schuman and Scott 1989; Belk 1990). Significantly, it was the older interviewees who were able to reject collective narratives of the period, and the passage of time and changes in life stage—from daughter, to mother, to grandmother—enabled the younger interviewees particularly to look back on the role their mothers played in their formative years in new light.

Conclusion

While wartime dress was a point where autobiographical memories and collective memories of a significant world event coincided (Schuman and Corning 2014), the oral evidence suggests that personal circumstance is as important as age in framing personal memories and defining generational collective memories of dress. For example, the fact that leaving school to begin work meant a sudden change in clothes, reflecting a shift in both self-identity and visible appearance, provided a memorable marker at the start of the transitional journey from childhood to young adulthood. But mothers offered guidance and support for their daughters through this period of adult identity formation; it was the absence of AL's mother that made her memories of this change so stark. While the adult workplace was the beginning of a new social identity for working-class girls, it was getting married and having their own children that most impacted the experiences and memories of dress among the older interviewees. Interestingly, the older interviewees with firsthand experience were silent about this role, and narratives of maternal roles were narrated secondhand in the younger interviewees' memories of their mothers.

For working-class people, and other marginal groups, telling their own stories and sharing their memories is particularly important (Kuhn 2002). Research by Christina Buse and Julia Twigg (2016: 16) has shown that talking about clothes enables "storytelling at an embodied, material level" that is less impacted by impairments associated with aging. The sense of self-identity embodied in working-class memories of dress empowers those whose garments and experiences are underrepresented in traditional methods of storage, histories, archives, and collections. Peter Stallybrass ([1993] 2012: 75) wrote that "in the transfer of [physical] clothes, identities are transferred," and a similar process happens when we share memories of dress. But memory also transfers "responsibilities" from past to present (Poole 2008: 149). My interviewees had responsibilities, as the last in their generation able to preserve oral accounts of working-class dress and social life of this period, to ensure the survival of their familial and communal memories for the future (Samuel and Thompson 1990). Since the time of my interviews in 2009, all but one of the interviewees that I remained in touch with have died. It is now my responsibility to honor their memories of working-class wartime dress which ended up, as Weber and Mitchell (2004: 4) predicted, "being about so much more." A story about working-class wartime dress in Lancashire becomes a story about social relationships within a family and local community—where (primarily) working-class mothers drew upon traditional coping strategies to manage their family's dress and public appearance, and ensure their reputational survival, despite socioeconomic circumstance and wartime austerity. It is no surprise that against this backdrop the feelings of dressing up or successfully achieving a desired look, often shared in the colloquialisms of their youth, were particularly memorable.

Epilogue

Just as the autobiographical and collective memories shape oral evidence, my own memories shape this interpretation. As Cheryl Buckley (1998: 167) acknowledged, writing about dressmaking in her own family, it is sometimes hard to separate ourselves from our research as we "partly share" the memories that we report. I was born in Oldham, Lancashire, in a lower-middle-class family in the early 1980s, but my knowledge of this geographical area was shaped by the stories of my paternal grandmother, who died in 2009. Lillian was born in 1922 in Gatley, Cheshire, the eldest girl of seven children and moved to Oldham as a child. Her father was a cobbler and she worked in a munitions factory during the war. She married my grandfather in the early 1950s, and five years later they adopted my father. My research into working-class memories of northern dress is shaped around a general sense of working-class life in Lancashire in this period—an understanding that she imbued in me. An essence of the memories she shared with me has inevitably shaped what is presented here (Buckley 1998; Misztal 2003; Campbell 2008).

Three years after my grandmother Lillian's death, my father applied for his adoption records. In 2013, I discovered that my northern heritage comes solely from my adopted grandparents. My paternal birth grandmother Elsie, who died in 2021, was also working class and grew up with her mother and siblings in Bristol. Her parents' lives had been transformed by events of the First World War. They had four children together but never married and separated soon after Elsie and her twin brother were born. Until Elsie was reunited with her son in 2014, she told very few people about the baby she had and was made to give up for adoption in the late 1950s. Her silence about her past, part chosen, part enforced by others, offers stark evidence of the extent to which social attitudes toward public respectability underpinned all aspects of everyday life in the period of this research. Becoming pregnant before she was married set her on a hushed journey north to a mother and baby home in Cumbria and set in motion the events that would form my personal connection with this story. This collective memory of working-class dress is dedicated to both my paternal grandmothers and the role they each played in its creation.

Notes

1 "Oral evidence" refers to the interviewees' words, which were audio recorded and transcribed verbatim; my analysis contextualizes their oral evidence into oral history (following Lummis 1987). The ages of the interviewees were determined by the methodology which required women who were old enough to remember their wartime dress and physically and mentally capable of being interviewed. The 1939 ages correlate with the start of the war; by 1945 the age range was thirteen

to twenty-eight years. The grouping of "women" recognizes that we meet these women as mature individuals recalling their younger selves. For other sources on oral histories of dress, see Lomas (2000), Taylor (2002), Biddle-Perry (2005), Slater (2014, 2020), and Atkin (2016 and in this volume).

2 Occupations were categorized using the Registrar General's Social Classification, the principal system for socioeconomic analysis for most of the twentieth century (Rose 1995). The term "social group" is used for subsections of the working classes. For more about fashion and class, see Worth (2020).

3 Interviewees were recruited by newspaper advertisement, leaflet distribution, and word of mouth. They are identified by initials to adhere to consent agreements, and contextual information relevant to 1939–45 is provided in footnotes. My initials (AS) reference any questions cited from the interviews.

4 Nonconformists are protestant groups that have dissented from the Church of England. Many of the interviewees were Methodists, a movement founded by John and Charles Wesley in the eighteenth century. Nonconformist traditions informed an association between visible cleanliness and respectability that continued to impact the lives of my interviewees in the 1940s.

5 See Çili in this volume for a more comprehensive discussion of autobiographical memory.

6 See Coser (1992), Wertsch (2002, 2009), Olick (2008), and Olick, Vinitzky-Seroussi, and Levy (2011). As discussed in the Introduction to this volume, collective memory is one of several terms used to describe the social and cultural aspects of memory. While the term is attributed to Halbwachs, a French philosopher and sociologist, his work was informed by and sits alongside work by others from history, philosophy, psychology, psychiatry, and sociology in the early twentieth century (Olick, Vinitzky-Seroussi, and Levy 2011).

7 What is reported as oral evidence is grounded in personal experience but can be influenced by multiple factors. Some memories remain largely the same from origin to reportage, others change over time (Bernstein and Loftus 2009; Paller, Voss, and Westerberg 2009). There is no pure access to the past through either memory or history (Kuhn 2002). Contextual research plays a key role in the interpretation and verification of memory and, as the chapters by Atkin and Webb in this volume discuss, the process of reflection that informs and accompanies the narration of memory is part of the creative act of human memorial practice.

8 Great Britain declared war on Germany on September 3, 1939. Victory in Europe was declared on May 8, 1945, and over Japan on August 15, 1945. The official start and end dates are September 1, 1939, when Germany invaded Poland, to September 2, 1945, when Japan signed the formal declaration of surrender (Bartrop 2022).

9 Oliver Lyttelton, president of the Board of Trade, signed the order to introduce clothes rationing on May 29, 1941, with an embargo for publication until June 1

to limit advance purchasing (Hansard, HC Debate, June 10, 1941, 373: 9–10). The order to end clothes rationing, signed by Harold Wilson, president of the Board of Trade, on March 14, 1949, took effect the next day (Hansard, HC Debate, March 14, 1949, 462: 1738–44). Examples from a 1941 list of the number of coupons required include dress (non-wool): seven, wool skirt: six, blouse: four, sweater/cardigan: eight (two ounces of knitting wool was one coupon), underwear: one or two per item, pair of shoes/sandals: five (*Daily Sketch*, 1941, "New Official List of Coupons Needed for Clothing and Footwear," July 1: 4). Childrenswear required fewer coupons, but growing children needed more frequent clothing changes.

10 See Calder (1969), Wilson and Taylor (1989), McNeil (1993), Kirkham (1996), Zweiniger-Bargielowska (2000), Howell (2013), and Worth (2020).

11 AW2 (2009), interviewed by author, February 17. Aged fifteen in 1939, AW2 worked in a factory office, then in a shop. She lived with her father (Royal Air Force driver), mother, and two siblings in Rochdale. The identifier AW2 was used to differentiate her from another research participant and is retained here for consistency.

12 DS (2009), interviewed by author, October 29. Aged eighteen in 1939, DS lived with her father (postman), mother, and up to five siblings in Pendleton, Salford. She married in *c.* 1942/3 and had three sons. At some point she was a florist.

13 AL (2009), interviewed by author, January 16. Aged eleven in 1939, AL was a scholar then a shop seamstress, living with her father (bus driver) in Bolton. Her mother had died in April 1939.

14 HB (2009), interviewed by author, October 27. Aged nine in 1939, HB was a scholar living with her father (cotton mill worker, then factory worker), mother, and older brother in Oldham. During her childhood the family income was impacted when her father was out of work and then later injured in a workplace accident.

15 The quantity of clothing reported accords with a 1941 survey, by Mass-Observation for the Advertising Service Guild, into early experiences of clothes rationing of 188 working-class women in Gloucester who had on average 2.88 dresses, 0.35 costumes (matching jacket and skirt), 1.00 skirts, 1.35 coats, 0.31 mackintoshes, and 1.92 pairs of shoes. Researchers noted that "wardrobes were not checked on, and people had to remember them as they stood on the doorstep which must lead to incredible inaccuracy" (Change 1941: 13), although accuracy probably increased when fewer items were owned.

16 JS (2009), interviewed by author, February 19. Aged seven in 1939, JS was a scholar, attending grammar school on a scholarship from 1942. She lived in Chadderton, Oldham, with her father (laborer, then in the army), mother, and younger sister.

17 MF (2009), interviewed by author, October 29. Aged sixteen in 1939, MF worked in an aircraft factory. She lived with her aunt (cotton mill worker, then munitions worker) and uncle (coal miner) in Westhoughton, Bolton, and later lived with

friends. She would visit her father who lived in Colne, Lancashire; her mother had died in 1934.

18 MH (2009), interviewed by author, February 17. Aged seven in 1939, MH was a scholar, attending grammar school on a scholarship from 1942. She lived in Chadderton, Oldham, with her parents (green/grocers—her father was also a special constable) and older brother.

19 MH evaluated that behaviors continued from earlier periods of economic depression as "a mixture of both" necessity and habit: her parents "would have never overspent because they'd seen what could happen."

20 The best clothing discussed here was worn regularly rather than being special occasion wear for a particular event, with two exceptions: one examines the reuse of bridesmaid dress, the other how funeral clothes stood out in memory as rare example of new clothing.

21 The survey noted the impact of religious tradition and geographical location on this practice: "the difference is a valid and significant one, and representative of a considerable area of Northern England, especially the area of strong Nonconformist influence" (Change 1941: 46).

22 AC (2009), interviewed by author, August 10. Aged seventeen in 1939, AC was an office worker and lived with her parents (cotton mill workers) in Middleton Junction, Oldham. She married in 1945.

23 JS (2007), interviewed by author, May 31, as part of my MA Textiles (2005–7). The lower social group referenced has been labeled "roughs" by some historians (Roberts 1984: 5, 1995; Ross 1985; Thompson 1975); they probably could not afford aspirational attitudes to public identity.

24 Whitsuntide marks the Christian festival of Pentecost. In Lancashire, Catholic, Anglican, and Non-Conformist churches would parade in different Whit Walks on different days in their local communities. Dressing in white, new, or best clothes for Whitsun dates back to the nineteenth century (for further discussion, see Slater 2011).

25 Church activities were central in my interviewees' wartime social lives and "mapped key moments in community and family life" (Parker 2005: 217). For some this was about being part of local festivities (Chinn [1988] 2006), but for those with a Christian faith, including MH, a best outfit held fewer religious connotations. However, dressing up on Sundays was not linked to church attendance (Change 1941), and it was the local community rather than the church that demanded new clothing at particular times (Bourke 1994; Tebbutt 1995; Parker 2005). JS's account of her mother wearing older clothes to go to local shops, probably covered with a coat, using better clothing for occasional trips to the cinema or beyond her local community but having insufficient clothing for church events shows the complex social role of dress among this group.

26 Of US origin, dating from 1923, the *Oxford English Dictionary* defines it as "the acme of excellence." See also Jenkinson in this volume whose interviewees used this term.

27 The Education Act 1944 introduced the eleven-plus examination for all children in England. Working-class children who passed gained a scholarship to grammar school and those who did not pass went to secondary modern schools (Gillard [1998] 2018). Staying in school beyond the compulsory age of attendance (fourteen years old from 1939 to 1946) usually required a girl's parent/s to value her extended education and be able to manage their finances sufficiently so that her potential wage was not essential toward the family income. For those at grammar school, including MH and JS, wearing their uniform outside of school hours and school days (even on holiday) was another way to address limited clothing and present a respectable status in public.

28 Transcribed verbatim from recording. A gymslip is a sleeveless overgarment consisting of a "pleated skirt on a yoke," worn for school uniform in this period (Craik 2005: 152). AL explained that the lilac dress and shoes were acquired (probably gifted) when she was "previously . . . a bridesmaid at an old lady's wedding." Earlier discussions in this chapter around appropriate dress and the avoidance of unnecessary frivolity emphasize why this outfit was deemed inappropriate for work.

29 What is now remembered as "Make Do and Mend" was launched by the British government in June 1942, but by December 1942 it was still known as "Mend and Make Do" with the advertising slogan "to save buying new" (Zweiniger-Bargielowska 2000: 120). The official "Make Do and Mend" booklet, still available in reprint, was published in September 1943 to offer advice and technical guidance for clothing repair, maintenance, and methods of making new clothes from old items. The campaign has seen a resurgence in popular memory in line with ethical trends toward vintage fashion, recycling, and home craft. It features in almost all literature related to wartime dress, including Norman (2007), Howell (2013), and Summers (2015). For more about working-class experiences, see Slater (2010).

30 MC (2009), interviewed by author, April 30. Aged twenty-two in 1939, MC lived in Chadderton, Oldham, and worked in a cotton mill, with her father (warehouse man), mother, and five siblings. Her only brother died on a Royal Navy submarine in October 1940. MC married in 1942 and had two children.

31 The oral evidence supports Chinn's research from Birmingham, England, that despite the presumed patriarchal structures of society, the working-class family was dependent on the hard work and dedication of the working-class mother and her household management of limited financial and social resources.

32 See Roberts (1984, 1995), Ross (1985), Alexander (1990), Davin (1996), Tebbutt (1995), and Chinn ([1988] 2006).

33 AW2 emphasized that while parents "did without" for their children, her mother would not have considered this a sacrifice but an act of love and care for her family.

34 See also Çili in this volume. In empirical research, Schuman and Corning (2014: 152) found the "reminiscent bump for personal memories" was between five to sixteen years old; the bump for "national or world events" was between seventeen to twenty-four years old; and the "critical period" for early memory covered both age ranges from approximately five to thirty years of age (Schuman and Corning 2014: 157). The age ranges of my interviewees, from seven (the youngest in 1939) to twenty-eight (the eldest in 1945), map onto these findings. More recent research suggests that collective memory assists in the organization of autobiographical memories on a neurological level (Gagnepain et al. 2020).

3

Memories of Making

Home Sewing in Socialist Hungary

Zsofia Juhasz

This research explores my grandmother's memories of home dressmaking in the Hungarian socialist era. I conducted an interview with my grandmother, Julianna, in 2016, when she was eighty-eight years old.[1] At this point she had early-stage dementia, which meant she could not recall certain events and people that she may have once remembered. However, her memories of her profession and her self-made clothes were clear and vivid. After conducting and analyzing the interview, the goal of the chapter shifted from exploring the meaning of home sewing in Julianna's life (in the context of socialism) to understanding why her memories of making and homemade clothes were much more resilient to forgetting than other subjects. Julianna passed away in 2021, at the age of ninety-three. By this time her dementia had advanced; toward the end of her life, she did not recognize her surroundings and it had become difficult to have a conversation with her as she forgot past events, people, and places. She passed some of her time going through her wardrobe, trying on clothes she found. When my mum asked her what she was wearing, she declared that "I made this!." The clothes made by her, even with late-stage dementia, were still clear in her memory.

In the first half of this chapter, I outline the historical background of home dressmaking in the socialist countries of the era, placing my grandmother's recollections in a wider context. In the second half of this chapter, I take a closer look at memories of making. Clive Baldwin (2006) argues that this is particularly poignant in the case of people with dementia, as the illness, by making remembering harder, weakens narrative agency and continuity. I consider how, through remembering her homemade clothes, Julianna was able to not only recall past events but also maintain continuity in her sense of identity.

Historical Overview of Fashion and
Home Sewing in the Socialist Era

After the Second World War, Hungary remained under Soviet occupation and later under Soviet control. The country was officially proclaimed the Hungarian People's Republic in 1949 and became a socialist state closely controlled by the USSR.[2] To investigate fashion in the context of socialism, we have to look at the tensions between the Soviet regime's propaganda and how people chose to dress in their everyday lives.

In the socialist regimes of Eastern Europe, efforts to make social differences disappear through the distribution of wealth were to be "complimented by internal changes within each member of society. The goal was to create a 'socialist personality' with new needs, habits, and values that would be in harmony with the needs of society as a whole and thus help to create a communist utopia" (Stitziel 2005: 1). The intention to change consumer behavior was key for the socialist regimes, as they tried to shift citizens' habits from consumption motivated by the desire to look fashionable to shopping only to satisfy one's basic needs. In her essay on gender and consumption in the Soviet Union, historian Philippa Hetherington (2015: 418) examines the Stalinist turn toward consumerism in the 1930s, to "buy and sell in a 'cultured' and refined manner." Her writing considers a "cultured and socialist" mode of commerce and consumption, and how these are "paradigms for correct Soviet behavior" (Hetherington 2015: 418). In her book on fashion in socialism, Djurdja Bartlett (2010: 7) discusses Khrushchev[3] launching a new aesthetic in the Soviet Union in the late 1950s characterized by "modest prettiness and conventional elegance" combined with traditional proletarian simplicity—the aesthetic of socialist good taste.

Fashion theorist Judd Stitziel (2005) discusses consumer culture and fashion in the German Democratic Republic (GDR). He explains the importance of the cultivation of a socialist personality, where consumer practices would ultimately match socialist ideologies. The aim was to create a socialist form of consumption by promoting the value of desiring only the essentials for living regardless of social class, education, occupation, wealth, or the changing of times. Once the years of postwar austerity subsided, fulfilling the population's basic needs became more complex as they became harder to define. Stitziel (2005) points out that even though the definition of basic needs in East Germany shifted throughout the state's existence, the so-called basic needs themselves were always defined by the state rather than the consumers themselves. "By its own definition, the regime's political success or failure depended in large part on its ability to supply its citizens with consumer goods that satisfied not only their 'basic needs' but also their desires. Clothing was on the front line of everyday relations between the citizens of the GDR and their state" (Stitziel 2005: 20).

In his essay on the changes of urban fashion in socialism, Hungarian historian Tibor Valuch (2009) describes the transition to socialist fashion after the Second World War. Satisfying the needs of the "working woman" did not require fashion in the sense of uniqueness or beauty; the goal was producing and advertising practical, modest workwear. After the 1956 Revolution this hardline ideology softened,[4] and "expectations regarding political-ideological dress lessened" (Valuch 2009: 111). By the beginning of the 1960s, consumer demand for fashion grew, which necessitated changes in official attitude. Stitziel posits that the meaninglessness of East German citizens' votes at the ballot box "heightened the political meaning of purchases: consumers' decisions to buy or reject GDR-manufactured goods or to shop in West Berlin served as an indirect plebiscite on the GDR's economic system and the regime's promises and policies that were inextricably intertwined with it" (Stitziel 2005: 19). If the ultimate success of socialism could be measured through the satisfaction of working classes, the ideology had to change in line with public demand. Valuch (2009) cites a book on housekeeping advice for working women from 1961 emphasizing the importance of fashion: "What dress to choose for a particular occasion used to concern only a few hundred thousand women, whereas now it concerns millions. Now that they have the means and opportunity to have fun, it is appropriate to dress up for the occasion" (Valuch 2009: 113). Even when official communication softened toward fashion, the selection and quality of garments were still poor in state-run stores. Fashion historian Ildiko Simonovics (2015) presents a multifaceted analysis of the reasons behind the unsatisfactory clothing offered in state-run shops. Interviewing designers of state-approved clothing lines, she identifies that the ultimate choice in what to produce was in the hands of bureaucrats, and designers would have to fight for each style with some degree of originality. Moreover, this inefficiency was exacerbated by the lack of raw materials, the clothing factories' obsolete machinery, and poor organization of production within the Hungarian planned economy (Simonovics 2015: 169). Valuch (2009) notes that throughout the 1960s and 1970s the proportion of clothes made through employing seamstresses was still significant.

Dress and fashion theorist Katalin Medvedev (2009) examines the relationship between socialism and fashion-related crime. When unraveling the contradictory nature of fashion in socialism, she notes an interesting and significant tension between ideological and material life, "the study of fashion in the era also highlights that in spite of the efforts made by the system, the material world didn't become insignificant in people's lives. On the contrary, to counterbalance an overly ideologized existence, its value largely escalated" (Medvedev 2009: 130). In all of the studies mentioned earlier, the importance of "educating" the population is essential in order to implement deep-rooted changes in society toward the acceptance of communism. This tension between ideology and the material world explains why it was highly important for the socialist state to educate the population in order to control their desires and hints at the reason why it failed, thus forcing regimes to modernize across Eastern Europe. As opposed to the capitalist West, where the free market and the abundance of choice allowed for fashion to evolve rapidly and organically, in Eastern Europe the material shortages and state-controlled design directions and production limited the natural evolution of style. The state's aims to control people's desires failed, thus creating an opposition between official and unofficial discourse around fashion. "East Germans' actual consumption practices differed drastically from the promoted 'socialist consumer habits' that were supposed to mark the new 'socialist personality'" (Stitziel 2005: 144). Throughout the GDR's existence, the planned socialist economy failed to meet or satisfy consumer's needs through ideological education. Stitziel distinguishes several methods of achieving self-expression and nonconformity to social norms in the GDR. Striving to achieve the desired look changed shopping habits and encouraged home sewing, and obtaining Western contacts gained significance.

The widespread practice of smuggling clothing from the West was also rooted in the disconnect between the official ideology and the reality of everyday fashion. Stitziel (2005) mentions the existence of smuggling between East and West Germany. In her essay discussing crime and socialism, focusing particularly on clothing, Medvedev (2009) discusses smuggling practices extensively through interviews with past smugglers and uncovers the significance and motives of smuggling. As the goal of smuggling was to obtain the means of self-expression through access to a wider variety of clothing, for many people the goal justified the means, and criminal activity involving smuggling became widely accepted within the general population (Medvedev 2009). The aforementioned desire to dress as a form of self-expression despite the confines of socialist ideologies, which restricted dress beyond practical necessity, and the subsequent means of obtaining fashionable clothing across socialist countries appear throughout my grandmother's accounts.

A Personal Narrative: Home Sewing in Socialist Hungary

In this section I map out my grandmother Julianna's life and profession through her recollections, more specifically memories of her profession and homemade creations, and understand how memories of her life are unique as well as formed by the culture she lives in. Understanding personal narratives makes it possible to uncover truths about people's everyday lives, but even the most personal memories are embedded in a social context (Hoskins 1998; Misztal 2003; Baldwin 2006; Riessman 2008). In Julianna's case, the ideological nature of fashion in socialism and consequently the high demand for professional tailors and seamstresses had an impact on her career and subsequently her recollections of it. We construct the self through telling stories about our lives (Hoskins 1998; Misztal 2003; Riessman 2008); the purpose of these stories is to maintain continuity in our identity. Barbara A. Misztal (2003) explains that the biographical self constructs itself by creating memories and therefore autobiographical memory changes over time as we change. As a result, autobiographical recollections are not accurate; however, they are consistent with one's self-knowledge and sense of self. The construction of the self created through the telling of stories becomes problematic with the onset of dementia. Marie Mills (1997) argues that "a narrative identity, which is supported by personal knowledge of one's individual biography or life history, presupposes two fundamental conditions. Firstly, that one has accrued a life history and, secondly, that it is remembered" (Mills 1997: 673). To be able to recall the past is essential for biographical continuity. Baldwin (2006: 101) describes how people with dementia gradually become "narratively dispossessed"; they lose narrative agency (the ability to tell their story) because they become less able to create conventional narrative structures.

Baldwin (2006) investigates possibilities to give back narrative agency: narrativizing other, symbolic means of expression (like artistic expression), as well as possibilities of joint authorship, where a fragmented story can be complemented by recollections of people that know the person with dementia. Julianna's dementia was in its early stages at the time of the interview, but her recollections were noticeably less consistent than in the past. The aforementioned possibilities outlined by Baldwin proved helpful to understand my grandmother's recollections in light of her illness. On the one hand, choosing one's appearance through dress, as well as making clothes, can be read as a narrative, symbolic means of expression and played a significant part in Julianna's memories. On the other hand, Julianna wasn't able to recall numerous past events from her life. My mother, Mariann, helped to complement the interview as Julianna couldn't recall the second half of her career.[5] Accepting the more fragmented properties of her narrative, therefore not expecting a linear story, meant that the episodes she was able to recall clearly became the central focus of this chapter.

I conducted a single interview with Julianna with the use of a family photo album (see Figures 3.1 and 3.2). I chose this method as her homemade clothes were not readily available; therefore, I used the photographs as memory prompts. Annette Kuhn (2002), writing about exploring memories through family photographs, explains:

> Memories evoked by a photo do not simply spring out of the image itself, but are generated in a network, an intertext, of discourses that shift between past and present, spectator and image, and between all these and cultural contexts, historical moments. In this network, the image itself figures largely as a trace, a clue: necessary, but not sufficient, to the activity of meaning making. (Kuhn 2002: 14)

Understanding photographs as a clue or trace, as objects that don't have set meanings by themselves, highlights the usefulness as well as the problematic nature of using photographs as memory prompts. Later on in the chapter I will look at the collaborative nature of creating meaning in an interview using photographs, as well as the possibilities of generating "false" memories. I asked my grandmother to look through this family photo album with me. In the interview I let her know that I was interested in talking about clothes she made, and the stories about being a seamstress, but I chose not to pick out certain pictures and just show her those—we looked through the album together, allowing her to comment on any photo she found interesting. I didn't arrive with a list of questions; I intended to allow her to talk about aspects of her past that she wished to highlight.

Interviewing is a collaborative way of meaning-making. Bornat et al. (2000) describe the experience in the following way: "People bring their own agendas and interests to the interview, consequently interviewer topics may well be

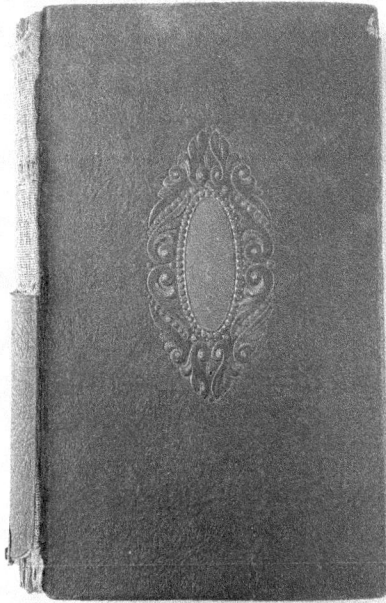

Figure 3.1 Family photo album used in the interview. Author's own photograph.

Figure 3.2 Family photo album used in the interview. Author's own photograph.

reinterpreted, managed or straightforwardly resisted by the interviewee" (247). As we looked through the album, Julianna took more interest in photos where she was depicted, paying special attention to clothes worn by her and others. She also chose to talk about her profession and creative process, and the interview really came to life when she described her professional successes. Why did she choose to talk about certain aspects of her life while leaving others out? My questions led her to talk about these topics, but she also steered the interview her way, bringing up subjects she was interested in and sometimes ignoring my questions. In writing this chapter I wanted to understand why Julianna remembered certain things more than others and how she created meaning out of her autobiographical memories in a way that was coherent with her sense of self. In Julianna's case, a lot of her stories were told through her past as a seamstress and tailor, as well as through particular clothes she wore in the images we looked at. Even though the aim of my research was not to describe Julianna's life story and profession as it actually happened, I found that contextualizing recollections added another layer of meaning to her memories. For this reason, I will roughly outline Julianna's life story as she remembered it with my mother, Mariann, filling in the gaps.

Julianna was a student at a technical sewing school and a tailor's apprentice in Budapest starting in 1945, after returning from Austria, where she spent months separated from her family as a refugee during the late Second World War. After finishing her apprenticeship, she returned to her hometown of Nagykáta (a town about 37 miles from Budapest, the capital) where soon she began to work unofficially as a self-employed seamstress.[6] She continued to practice for years, gaining recognition for herself in her town. After getting married in 1956, the family moved to Budapest, where she kept up her practice working unofficially from home until the mid-1970s. In addition to working on commissions, she also made her own and her children's clothes. Mariann clarified that Julianna apprenticed at Irén Sugár's salon on Dohány Street in Budapest city center, which, by my mother's account, was quite an exclusive salon frequented by a wealthy, highly situated clientele. During her time as a practicing seamstress, unofficial home dressmaking practices flourished due to clothing shortages in state shops. According to Bartlett (2010), "the institution of the dressmaker belonged to the vast unofficial field of everyday dress that the state was unable to completely control" (255). Mariann described Julianna's daily routine in the 1960s and early 1970s. As Western fashion imagery was rarely accessible, customers ordering dresses from my grandmother drew their ideas from local fashion magazines or publications from other socialist countries, such as *Praktische Mode*.[7] Ultimately, her home-sewn creations stemmed from the officially proposed fashion, but by altering them and adding her and her customers' own touch to the designs, these dresses also served as a criticism of fashion published and encouraged by the state. According to my mother, Julianna's sewing practice in the 1960s and 1970s was opposed by my grandfather on the basis of being illegal. Moreover, as she was working without any kind of permit, she kept the prices very low and only practiced in the circle of wider family and acquaintances. She retired in the 1970s, but she continued to make clothes for her family until she was no longer able to.

Memories of Making

Throughout the interview, Julianna's memories of making as well as memories of her self-made clothes have been easier for her to recall than other biographical events. Christina Buse and Julia Twigg (2016) describe clothes as "particularly potent memory objects because they are not just owned, but are worn by the person" (1118). In this case, they are also made by my grandmother, which seems to add another layer of complexity to her memories of clothes. Janet Hoskins (1998) posits that objects are "entangled in the events of a person's life and used as a vehicle for a sense of selfhood" (2), where "the object becomes a . . . mnemonic for certain experiences" (4). There are two types of memories that stood out from the interviews. First, Julianna's autobiographical memories of making—her apprentice years and making practice. These memories are not related to a particular piece of clothing, but they are recalled looking at images of self-made clothes. Second, when it came to particular clothes depicted in photographs, her memories of the material garment were surprisingly detailed. She recalled the feel and color of the fabrics, as well as repeatedly mentioning regretting not having kept these garments, as they would still fit her now.

I will now attempt to unravel why certain memories were more resistant to forgetting than others, and how my grandmother constructed and maintained her identity through these memories. Joanna Bornat (2010) points out that "emotion may determine what is available in memory narratives" (48–9). Numerous researchers argue that emotional life experiences could be more available for recall (Mills 1997; Misztal 2003; Woodward 2007; Slater 2014; Buse and Twigg 2015). Mills (1997) found that memories related to meaningful, emotional life events were generally easier to recall for dementia patients she interviewed. Mills argued that even as dementia progresses emotional memories in which the informant is the protagonist are more available for recall and are more resistant to forgetting than other memories related to the world outside the person and not closely attached to strong emotions. Throughout the interview, my grandmother recalled her apprentice years several times, as well as having frequently told stories about this period in the time I have known her. I believe that Julianna's profession is an aspect of her identity that she feels very strongly about, and in recalling these memories she is asserting her identity in the present as the same person she was at the time of her professional successes.

> Zsofia: I wanted to ask you about the story when you went to Austria with your cousin . . .
>
> Julianna: Oh, that's when I wasn't married yet.
>
> Z: Yes, at the end of the Second World War.
>
> J: Wait a minute . . . I'm not so sure about the order in this story. Well in Budapest my cousin and I were at the same Jewish family, a dressmaker, her shop was across the Synagogue [main synagogue in Budapest, in the city center], we learnt our profession there. And then when we finished, we returned to Nagykáta, and both my cousin and I, we were like, now we have finished, and you know, the family was big back then, so we were sewing for them. And then we were always worried that someone might get jealous that we have a job, and they don't—we had a job because we studied in Budapest, we knew what was fashionable.

Here she changes the subject to talk about her apprentice years. This is one of a few examples where, completely unprompted by me, she steers the interview to talk in detail about her apprenticeship and the start of her career as a seamstress.

The event I asked Julianna to recount in the previous excerpt refers to a period of her life which I assumed she would remember, as it is a significant historic event, and she had previously shared her memories of this period with me in great detail (she was a refugee in Austria fleeing from Russian troops, separated from her family as a minor). The story she recalls instead is that of her apprenticeship. It is clear that dressmaking is a fundamental aspect of Julianna's identity, and she becomes emotional and animated recalling her professional success and creations. In the following excerpt she tells me about her way of working in detail.

> Z: Did you have a lot of customers?
>
> J: Well not to praise myself, but my relatives and my parents told me as well . . . my aunt Anna was the biggest critique, she knew best where we stood professionally. She told my mom, "listen Julcsa," she says, "this girl" she says, "she's learnt it really well, she is really accurate and precise." And then people started coming to me, like I was a professional with a lot of experience. But I just finished then! They came to me, bringing fashion magazines and such.

... Imagine, it was a hard task! And I pushed myself until, even in my sleep, so I couldn't even go to sleep before I finished it, before the problem wasn't solved for the next day. . . . And I thought to myself, oh my god, as a beginner, what if I mess it up or something. I was constantly stressing! At the beginning. And then later I was praised by everyone. I really wanted to prove myself, you know, because I had the passion for it, it was courage I didn't have, initially. I was so hard on myself then! Sometimes I looked at the clock, I wasn't asleep at midnight, because someone picked a model, and I was pushing myself at all costs, to figure that out. And I didn't want to spoil the fabric.

My questioning here was trying to establish the scope of her practice through eliciting factual information about the number of customers she had. Instead, she recalled the praise of her talent and professional commitment, emphasizing her sleepless nights striving to achieve perfection. These memories are full of emotion as she relives how hard it was to live up to her family's, her customers', and her own expectations, as well as a sense of pride in her success. Talking about her feelings toward mass-produced clothing of the era reinforces this point.

Z: So you didn't really buy yourself anything in shops at that time?

J: No, not back then. Nothing at all!

Z: Why, the quality wasn't good, or was it expensive?

J: Because I was really critical of who made it, and I had my own idea . . . and nothing was good enough, I found mistakes in everything.

Z: It wasn't nicely sewn, or maybe the fabric was not good?

J: Well it could be the fabric, or I slept on it, then I changed my mind, because I didn't want to be like, copying someone, you know, that's not like me at all to copy, to not come up with it myself, that was part of it.

Julianna talks less about what mass-produced clothes lack as opposed to her desire to emphasize her own creative ideas.

As mentioned earlier, clothes serve as memory objects, and their potential to elicit powerful memories could be attributed to how close they are worn on the body. Misztal (2003) points to the embodied nature of memories, describing "the importance of the body and its habitual and emotional experiences as both a reservoir of memories and a mechanism for generating them" (79). Richard Ward and Sarah Campbell (2014: 67) discuss that "embodied history" is biography on an embodied level. In their study conducted with persons living with dementia, they found that people found it easier to recollect "lived and embodied experiences of appearance" (Ward and Campbell 2014: 67) and that these memories were multisensory in nature. How it felt to wear a particular garment helped recall sensory experiences of the past. In this case the clothes in the photograph are not only owned and worn but also made by my grandmother. The tactile experience of working with fabrics, manipulating them to create an object that lived up to her expectations of style and precision, could reinforce the intensity of the memories prompted by looking at these garments.

The following excerpt from the interview exemplifies how looking at photographs of garments she made elicited detailed memories of the materiality of the dress depicted. I argue that alongside the embodied experience of wearing this garment, the emotional and embodied experience of making it also contributes to the intensity of these memories.

J: And how come I didn't keep this dress? [see Figure 3.3] It was "piqué canvas."

Z: What was it like?

J: It's not like silk, not like canvas. . . . Think of something that feels like this [touching the tablecloth], but a bit thicker, with horizontal grooves next to

Figure 3.3 Julianna (left) wearing a dress made in piqué canvas. The other clothes in this photograph were also made by her. Left to right: Julianna, Jutka, and Mariann (her daughters), and Gabriella, her niece, 1968 © Mariann. Reproduced with permission.

each other, it was woven like that. So it kept its shape, you know? You didn't
have to iron it. It had ruffles at the bottom, and on the edge the binding, the
same color the print was, the base of the print, it was one of those colors,
the darkest, I don't know which was the darkest in that fabric. There was a
bias binding sewn around the edges that you could buy in the shop. . . . It
was fashionable then!

While Julianna's vivid recollections of texture, color, and minute details based
on a black-and-white photograph can't be verified, as the original dress is lost,
her recollections are indeed persuasive due to the detailed, sensory description
she gives. Alison Slater (2014) argues that "the remembered materiality of
clothing feels as real to the wearer as the physical material garment; materiality
persists in memory long after the garment's material life and is central to the
past, current and future identities of the wearer" (11). As Buse and Twigg
(2016) explain, discarded and remembered clothes "evoke images of . . .
aspects of the self which the teller wished to recall and draw to attention"
(1127). As she recalls the materiality of the dress in the photograph as if it
were there, reinforced by touch as she handles the tablecloth, Julianna recalls
her past embodied experiences of wearing her self-made clothes, the making
process she took pride in, and through this her identity as a tailor. All of these
recollections are aspects of herself from her past that she wishes to be known
by in the present. The following excerpt powerfully demonstrates the evocative
nature of memories through clothes:

> J: Interesting, that I could wear this for such a long time, and the top as well.
>
> Z: Really?
>
> J: Yes, and if you look at it, it is like, how to put it, you can recognize me, after
> so many decades.

In this particular case, Julianna is overwhelmed by emotion about time passing
and remembering her youth, and this is triggered by looking at old photographs
of herself wearing clothes that she had made. It is worth noting that these
memories are elicited by a photo of Julianna wearing the aforementioned dress
in a family album rather than the dress itself, which also has an impact on how
memories are evoked. Kuhn (2002) explains that family photographs may show
us our past, but how we use them is about today. "These traces of our formal
lives are pressed into service in a never-ending process of making, re-making,
making sense of, our selves—now" (Kuhn 2002: 19). Here, Julianna asserts that
she is still the same person depicted in the photograph.

Pointing out how long she was able to wear the clothes depicted and the desire to be able to still have these garments comes up on several occasions. Julianna explained that some clothes might not be in her wardrobe anymore because her daughters took them; they have been remodeled into something new or been discarded for some reason.

> J: And how come I didn't keep this skirt? It would still fit me. . .
>
> And
>
> J: There I am! And that skirt, have I not kept it? Because these skirts, they never go out of fashion, and the tops as well [see Figure 3.4].

Clothes, whether they are kept physically or in memory, allow women to maintain a continuity of self (Banim and Guy 2001; Woodward 2007; Twigg 2010) and to identify "with who she used to be and therefore that she has the capacity to be this person" (Woodward 2007: 62). The significance of these recollections is not whether they are historically accurate but that they signify and maintain the identity of the self.

As Hoskins (1998) explains, narrative devices (in this case clothes) don't necessarily reflect the truth but "construct it in a particular way" (4), and as we recall and tell our stories based on these objects, we perform our memories to a particular audience. Julianna's strong desire to talk about her profession and self-made clothes is performed to me, and my role as an interviewer has an effect on her recollections in several ways. As we have a close relationship, she finds it easy to talk to me about personal memories. I also have some background knowledge about the photographs and garments depicted within them that come up in the interview. The following instance demonstrates the problematic nature of cooperative meaning-making in an interview. As identified by Mariann in one of the photographs (Figure 3.4), my grandmother is wearing a skirt she made herself from a fabric that was a gift from a distant relative who emigrated to America. Even though Mariann did not care much about fashion at the time or what fabrics her mother used in her sewing practice, she seems to be able to recall this particular American skirt. When this skirt came up in the interview with Julianna, I asked her about the skirt's origins.

> J: Oh, I sewed this! It's a fabric that I bought, and as I was a seamstress by profession, and it was the fashion at the time . . . and you know, I thought that, no one will have the same skirt, and this fabric is not from Hungary. This skirt, well, this fabric is not Hungarian.

Figure 3.4 Skirt, made by Julianna in fabric from America © Mariann. Reproduced with permission.

When I asked, Julianna didn't remember the exact origin of the fabric, and she mentioned buying it, in contradiction to stating that it is not Hungarian. She seemed to be assertive about the fact that she made this garment and mentioned her profession, as she had often throughout the interview.

Kuhn (2002) posits that forgetting and misremembering is an essential part of memory. It "calls into question the transparency of what is remembered; and it takes what is remembered as material for interpretation" (157). In this case, by asking about the origins of the fabric, and therefore suggesting that this fabric might be foreign, I could have influenced my grandmother to recall this fact. Even if this was the case, she emphasized the fact that due to its foreign origins no one would have this same skirt. Apart from her previously mentioned striving for originality, this memory sheds light on how the personal and political meet in shaping what is remembered. Misztal (2003) states that even the most personal memories are embedded in social context. Although, in the case of this particular photograph and skirt, my questions as the interviewer might have influenced Julianna's memories of this garment, this skirt illustrates a sense of longing for something that no one else would have due to its Western origins. Bartlett (2010) explains that "western clothing acquired the status of a fetishistic commodity in socialist societies due to its rarity" (266). When talking about the aforementioned skirt, in the discussion with my mother following the interview with Juliana, Mariann reflected on the fascination with foreign fashion:

Mariann: At the time the fact that it was a foreign fabric, it was a treasure.

Mariann explained that a possible reason why Juliana could be able to recall the origin of this skirt could be its foreign origins. Even though the skirt's origins cannot be confirmed by either Julianna or Mariann, the importance given to the garment's possible Western origins is revealing and symptomatic of the times in which these memories originate.

Conclusion

The history of home sewing under socialism, like any other history, can only be fully understood by examining micro- and macro-narratives through interviews and personal accounts. Although they are not always factually accurate, they are significant as they provide an aspect of the past that is not quantifiable and can't be described through analyzing large-scale historical events. During my interviews with Julianna, she often did not remember the wider historical context, but when it came to recalling how a fabric feels, her memories were vivid. Dress, in this sense, is bridging a gap between personal and historical narratives. Recalling a homemade dress or a fabric conjures up memories within a historical context; here, this is a resistance to socialist propaganda. It also conjures up memories of the past, connecting to a sense of self, for Julianna, as an acclaimed dressmaker.

Memories of making bring together several layers of memories of clothes, and thus are possibly stronger, and stay with the person even after the onset of dementia. Cheryl Buckley (1998) argues that "the process of making and designing, the clothes themselves, and the ways in which they were worn, reveal aspects of women's identities" (157). The clothes evoke emotional memories of Julianna's profession, the woman she once was, but as she also wore them, the embodied, sensory memory of the fabrics figures as a memory object, even when no physical item is available. Through interviewing Julianna, I found that the tactile nature of making, as well as the wearing of clothes, creates memories more resilient to forgetting.

Notes

1 Julianna (2016), interviewed by author, November 12.
2 Hungary was one of several nations converted to USSR rulers' visions of communism after being occupied during the Second World War. Any, even cursory,

examination of what the USSR called socialism or communism or how it came to exist in Hungary is outside the scope of this chapter. In brief, leaders in Moscow held comprehensive political power over the Hungarian people initially through military force, then by nationalizing and centralizing most of its industries, banking and trade, and enacting sweeping social reforms (Borhi 2004).

3 Nikita Khrushchev (1894–1971) was the first secretary of the Communist Party of the Soviet Union (1953–64) and premier of the Soviet Union (1958–64). Khrushchev set out on a policy of de-Stalinization of the Soviet Union, denouncing its former leaders' crimes and enacting "sweeping changes in the organization and management of the economy, in the shop floor position of industrial workers, and in agricultural conditions. But Khrushchev and the people around him saw that in order to improve morale and with it labor productivity, they would have to liberalize and reform wider aspects of Soviet life" (Filtzer 1993: 10).

4 "The Hungarian Revolution was the greatest challenge to Soviet hegemony in post-World War II Eastern Europe and at the same time a widely visible symbol of the bankruptcy of Soviet-style socialism" (Lendvai 2008: 3). Unrest and discontent in Hungary evolved into a popular uprising in October 1956. On November 4, the Soviet Union invaded Hungary and reasserted control. Regardless, Stalinist hardline policies were shelved and thereafter Hungary's internal autonomy increased slowly over time.

5 Mariann (2016), interviewed by author, November 12.

6 In our interview, my mother recalls Julianna's sewing practice, which was conducted under the radar of the authorities: "In my childhood, I remember this, when I was really little, that customers were constantly coming to our house. Your granddad kept on nagging her, that it makes no sense that she is sewing, mostly for people she knew, but because she was working illegally, she didn't dare ask for a fair price. She was really precise, but she didn't charge nearly enough for it!"

7 *Praktische Mode*, translated as *Practical Fashion* and later called *PRAMO*, was a monthly women's fashion magazine based in the GDR from 1948 that contained dressmaking paper patterns (Stitziel 2003).

4

Nostalgia, Myth, and Memories of Dress

The Cultural Memory of Madchester

Susan Atkin

"Madchester," on its surface, describes the reaction in Manchester, England, to the "rave revolution" which was the focus of British youth culture from the mid-1980s to the mid-1990s (Haslam 1999: 142). Madchester is now seen as a seminal period in the city's cultural history, though there is much debate about exactly when it began and ended.[1] Manchester, located in northwest England, is a postindustrial city that in recent years has had a strong popular leisure sector built upon associations with urban youth, street style, market stall entrepreneurship, and counterculture.[2] These characteristics reflect a rebellious stance toward mainstream society that appear to be infused with working-class, left-wing cultural and political roots. Madchester is central to Manchester's, the contemporary city's, civic identity; beneath the surface of its popular memory rave-related image, it references its working-class heritage and opposition to the mainstream. Subsequently, Madchester itself has contributed to the city's mythology fed by continued popular media attention and local legend. This chapter focuses on the inception of Madchester where groups of people, including football fans, fans of particular bands, and regular attendees of particular clubs, began to hang out in particular locations and show allegiance to them through their dress.[3] Oral history has been used as a method for this research, gathering testimonials from key members of Madchester on their memories of dress from 1986 to 1996.

Madchester was a turning point where there was a shift in attitude away from traditional subcultures, identified by the Centre for Contemporary Cultural Studies (CCCS) as a form of working-class resistance, due to a less tangible dominant culture and lack of a need to resist it (Atkin 2016).[4] Despite this shift from traditional subcultures, there is agreement by cultural theorists that an alternative to mainstream culture remained, albeit with more eclectic style and taste sensibilities, and is still relevant in the actions of establishing individuality while needing to belong to a group. Sociologists Diana Crane (2000), Sophie Woodward (2008), and Jennifer Craik (2009) perceive a tension between the desire to display individuality alongside belonging to a social group as inherent in our human psyche. Joanne Entwistle (2000: 133) uses the term "connective tissue" to describe the heightened sense of connectedness to a particular group, distinguishing it from other groups and the dominant culture. Madchester straddled the change from subculture to post-subculture. A number of alternatives to "subculture" have been proposed within post-subcultural theory to reflect the shift away from its traditional definition.[5] The term "movement" is preferred in this chapter to define the less tangible, loose social coalitions, with shared activities and geographies that reflect the fluid, multifaceted, dynamic, and rapidly shifting culture of Madchester—and of postmodern culture as a whole (Jenks 2005). "Movement" also acknowledges the relationship with political, economic, and sociocultural contexts that, it has been suggested, post-subcultural theory sometimes overlooks (Ogersby 2014). These contexts, and the advance of creative industries, were all integral to a thriving youth culture that was inherent in Manchester from 1986 to 1996.

In a series of photographs of four men showcasing their flares on the pages of the style magazine *i-D* (see Figures 4.1–4.3), photographer Ian Tilton captures the dress of a group of friends (Steve Cressa, Lee Daly, Martin Prendergast, and Al Smith), who were central to the beginnings of the Madchester music scene in the mid-1980s. The four are presented as initiators of a specific sartorial look comprising of loose tops and flares that the London-based magazine recognized as originating in Manchester with links to the city's music and burgeoning club scenes.[6] In an air of swagger, confidence, and defiance—Cressa is eating a chocolate bar (see Figure 4.2), Prendergast is smoking (see Figure 4.3)—all are making a deliberate statement of group identity by showcasing the flared trousers (see Figure 4.1) that eventually evolved into the "Baggy Look" synonymous with the "Madchester" era (Atkin 2016).

A combination of factors encouraged the relaxation of traditional boundaries of subcultural dress and styles in the Madchester context: coming together in opposition to Thatcherism,[7] the rise of the recreational drug Ecstasy, the egalitarian attitude promoted through the eclectic music choices available, and the open door policies of nightclubs such as the Haçienda and Venue.[8] Hence, an amalgamation of looks arose at local sites where styles were broken down and recombined which marked a shift in attitude: the point at which

Figure 4.1 Baldricks, Martin Prendergast (left), Lee Daly (back center), Steve Cressa (front center), Al Smith (right), the Haçienda, Manchester, by Ian Tilton © Ian Tilton, 1988. Reproduced with permission.

Figure 4.2 Steve Cressa, the Haçienda, Manchester, by Ian Tilton © Ian Tilton, 1988. Reproduced with permission.

Figure 4.3 Martin Prendergast (left) and Lee Daly (right), the Haçienda, Manchester, by Ian Tilton © Ian Tilton, 1988. Reproduced with permission.

identities became less fixed. In earlier research, photographer Ian Tilton used his own photography of a Haçienda organized road trip to Paris to highlight the varying looks and their reference points (see Atkin 2016). Rather than mere eclecticism, emphasis was placed upon the clothing items' origins and how they were combined, bought or acquired because of their meaning to the individual and their local networks.[9] This referencing of multiple cultural sources reveals cross- and countercultural ideals, a more tacit understanding that was inspired by locale, tastes still associated with class background (Bourdieu [1979] 2004), and a continuing interaction with the commercial environment.

Oral History: Spoken Memories of Dress

This chapter utilizes oral testimony collected through active interviews (Gubrium and Holstein 1995, 2002) to gather memories of dress during the Madchester movement. The research recognized the value of oral history as a research tool for accessing firsthand experience of fashion while also having the potential for uncovering hidden, neglected, or marginalized aspects of the past (Lomas 2000; Taylor 2002). Though such material is often undervalued, interviews can capture information that might otherwise go unrecorded, bringing into view areas of experience from respondents with a variety of backgrounds and finding in their recollections rich evidence, in this case of dress. In this study, interviews were sought with figures judged to have played key roles in the interplay of Mancunian fashion and music,[10] including fashion label owners, employees of fashion firms or retail outlets, band managers, and photographers. Participants had to have been directly involved in creative output in Manchester during the time period studied and contributed in some recognized way to the look and style of Manchester from 1986 to 1996. The interviewees' responses highlight experiences from everyday life in a rich and immediate way. Their spoken recollections highlight and reflect important social and cultural experiences, both individual and community based.

It is important to note that "oral histories are works in progress, as individuals cognitively and emotionally grapple with the contradictions and complexities of their lives" (Green 2004: 41), regardless of how many times they have recounted their memories. Overall, nine interviews with men and women took place that involved thirteen interviewees in total. Some of the interviewees for the wider research project had been interviewed many times prior to this research for television, books, and magazine articles and reshaping had taken place on numerous occasions as they reviewed their memories each time.[11] The three interviewees cited in this chapter were not as familiar with sharing their memories of the subject and by contrast presented a tone of reflection where they revealed fresh accounts that they had not discussed or perhaps even thought about since the event occurred. When using interviews as a source of historical evidence, the uncertainty of the individual's memory and the articulation of that memory in the present are concerns identified by oral history researchers (Suterwalla 2013). In the case of this project, interviewees were recalling events from the recent past (1986–96), which made some aspects more verifiable. However, the use of alcohol and recreational drugs no doubt affected the interviewees' memories in some circumstances.

There is also the possibility that the interviewee may try to embellish or overplay their role in a situation. This is an issue that Shehnaz Suterwalla recognized in her interviews with women who were part of sub- and countercultural movements, in particular British Punks and Greenham Common protestors, where

> the self-reflective perspectives of the older self can romanticize the younger self, and that as one grows older the tendency to over-invest or over-connect with particular experiences of youth can become stronger, creating a web of deeply subjective emotional memories. (Suterwalla 2013: 28)

The term "mythologizing" is applied by historians Raphael Samuel and Paul Thompson (1990) to indicate memory that is continually reshaped to make sense of the past from the perspective of the present. However, as the creative reshaping of the past within memory is an inherent part of human experience, this cannot be seen as a fault as if there existed a single objective viewpoint. Samuel and Thompson posit that even while the facts being recalled may be true, the omissions and shaping of the stories told are what develop them into myth. Thus, even recent history can be mythologized with certain facts being omitted, displaced, and reshaped as they are recalled both individually and collectively. As fact and fiction become blurred, active searching for corroboration between independent sources becomes an essential part of the research process to ensure academic rigor.

Paolo Jedlowski describes collective memory as "a set of social representations concerning the past which each group produces, institutionalizes, guards and transmits through the interaction of its members" (2001: 33). Vik Loveday (2014) made links from her participants' individual stories relating to their working-class roots while working in an academic environment to collective forms of nostalgic remembrance with a common set of cultural reference points that formed a key role in articulating their current classed identities. Taking her cue from Susan Buck-Morss (1999), Loveday (2014: 732) uses "cultural memory reservoir" to describe a metaphorical collection of myths and symbols that is used to construct identity. This chapter explores the clothes worn by initiators in the Madchester movement and the collective memories portrayed in the style of clothes themselves that the movement's members used to preserve traditional working-class identity and also to reflect a love of 1960s psychedelia.

Working-Class Identity

The male interviewees in this research all self-identified as working class. As Alison Slater (2011) remarked in her PhD thesis on working-class women in the northwest of England, the term "working class" is both ambiguous and complex.[12] This is particularly so for the time frame of this research as Britain in the 1980s saw deindustrialization under successive Conservative governments (1979–97), which resulted in the loss of traditional working-class occupations in steelworks, mines, and factories. Sociologist Ken Roberts' (2011) study of class in contemporary Britain clarifies the term in relation to work and social arenas and shows insight into the appeal of associating with or claiming to belong to the working class.

According to Roberts (2011), in urban, industrial communities a culture of working-class comradeship originated in the interdependence of the workers which was necessary to ensure safety in the workplace. With the exception of the textile industry, the workforces were mainly male and involved arduous, and at times dangerous, labor. This spilled over into leisure time as workers lived side by side, close to their places of employment, frequenting working men's clubs, pubs, and football grounds. In contrast, the home and neighborhood were domains of women with an equally strong but different sense of community (Roberts 2011). This traditional pattern of women at home and men either going to work or "hanging out" in their leisure time reflects the academic discourse on subcultures.[13] There is an appeal, particularly for men, to associate with the sense of comradeship and community instilled in traditional working-class identities. Despite changes, including the decline of skilled manual (mainly male) jobs and trade unions, this identity has been kept alive in the present by remaining rooted in the past (Roberts 2011; Loveday 2014). Nostalgia, when integrated with the creative process of remembering, actively synthesizing memory and imagination, defined by Emily Keightley and Michael Pickering (2012) as "mnemonic imagination,"[14] can be "associated with the desire for engagement with difference, with aspiration and critique, and with the identification of alternative ways of living in modernity or of the ways of living which modernity lacks" (137). They go on to propose that nostalgia also "represents an attempt to grapple with discontinuities and abrupt shifts in time" (2012: 137). A nostalgic attachment to the past, such as that experienced by members of the Madchester movement, fusing memory and imagination ensures working-class identity is recognized and valued (Loveday 2014).

Football Terrace Culture

It is widely agreed that music and sport play an essential part in Mancunian culture: Haslam (1999) marks Manchester's pop music and football heritage as engaging, inspiring, and often obsessing people. This he expresses in terms of a collective consciousness: "the dreams and imagination of Manchester people have always needed sustenance" (Haslam 1999: xxvi). Football culture is intertwined within the foundations of northern England's postindustrial identity, its cities allied with strong football fanbases, such as Liverpool and Manchester.

Following such teams, attending football matches on a weekly basis, standing at home games in the same vicinity on the football terraces with other fans,[15] where others had stood before them, formed part of the collective memory of the working class as "a set of social representations concerning the past which each group produces, institutionalizes, guards and transmits through interactions with its members" (Jedlowski 2001: 33). The cultural practice of standing on the terraces and sharing the highs and lows of their club's successes and failures itself contributes to the social communication and exchange of memories (both first and secondhand). Keightley and Pickering explain that "we look to the past of others, particularly family members or members of our community, to explain how we have come to be who we are, or more simply, to construct our personal lineage and the story of our forebears" (2012: 91).

Football culture, class identity, and dress are seen here to be intimately interwoven. This is key to the evolution of the Madchester movement and its dress. Anthropologist Ted Polhemus (1994) states that the northern manifestation of Rave, found in Manchester and Liverpool, came from the football terraces: in Liverpool this group was called "Scallies" (a term to describe a roguish self-assured young person, possibly an abbreviation of "scallywag"), in Manchester, they were "Perries" (derived from the Fred Perry polo tops they wore). Collectively, these groupings were later called "Casuals," a term which appears to have stuck.[16] The dress of Casuals evolved in the 1980s when northern football fans, traveling to Europe to support their teams, returned with European sportswear brands. Steve Redhead (1991: 19), in his work on football culture and football fanzines, sees in the "flash and defiance" of this style of dress a celebration of its working-class roots: a form of dressing for impact.

The Manchester football terraces bore witness to a change in the way Casuals dressed, a new silhouette evolving out of a shift from the smart, clean-cut Casual look toward a more relaxed feel: flares, loose T-shirts, hooded tops, and page boy haircuts. The clothes were a response to the music, dance, and drugs scene found in the nightclubs that they were now attending, such as the Haçienda. Despite what could be superficially perceived as a sharp turn away from the dress of the Casuals, there is a logical connection between the type of detailing found on European sportswear brands and those worn during the Madchester movement where there remained great attention to the detail of dress. Redhead (1991: 87) describes the Madchester bands as "street/terrace models getting on stage." Indeed, many of the musicians came from working-class backgrounds and frequented the football terraces, themselves tapping into the collective memories of those attending matches, woven within the foundations of northern England's postindustrial identity. Noel McLaughlin (2000: 264) defines the relationship between popular music and fashion as one in which the music plays a powerful role in "shop windowing" the clothing. The clothing, in turn, is central to providing an image for the music and there is a sense of empowerment in being able to wear what the musicians and performers (working-class heroes) are wearing.

Interviewee Lee Daly (see Figure 4.3), a Londoner who moved to Manchester in the early 1980s,[17] came to know the city initially through his support of the London football club Tottenham Hotspur, following them across the country to watch them play away fixtures and often remaining in the football towns and cities overnight to partake in their nightlife.[18] When he moved to Manchester in the mid-1980s, he made fast friends with the men he saw on the football terraces and in the nightclubs afterward, including Steve Cressa (seen in Figure 4.2), a main player in his circle of friends that included members of the seminal Manchester-based band The Stone Roses. With an interest in fashion and alternative culture, Daly observed a difference in the way Northerners, in particular Mancunians, dressed and was quickly able to see the wearing of flares as a cultural statement rather than dated fashion attire:

> Susan Atkin: So everyone was wearing flares?
>
> Lee Daly: That's a good question. When I started coming up for football. I'm a Tottenham [Hotspurs] fan. We were more skinheads, but we noticed that some of these lads were wearing flared trousers, to us in London, that's what Northerners did anyway. Look at those Northerners still wearing sheepskins and flared trousers! Then I started realizing that they were kind of like Scallies, what we call the Perry boy, Punk call it Casuals and I realized they were doing it on purpose . . . I thought that's a statement, a guy wearing flares in 1981 and 1982 was daring. . . . There was these kind of individuals but with a common love for garage psychedelic Punk. When I first mentioned it to Steve [Cressa] I said it was a cult statement and he said "you are the first one to get it."

From his encounters with Manchester football fans, Daly identified that rather than wearing an outmoded garment hence reinforcing the stereotypes that Northerners are behind the times, the flared trousers were associated with the Scally or Perry Boy look, broadly termed Casual, and were worn to reflect the wearer's taste in music.

> SA: So you were basically making a statement that you wanted to be different or was it referenced to the sixties psychedelia?

LD: With Steve it was. Phil Saxe sold the flares that the Scallywags used to
wear out of the shop. He had a shop at the bottom of the old Arndale.[19] Carl
Twigg was near Quay Street.[20] Steve first got his trousers from there. When
I first spoke to Steve about it, everything was Hendrix. He was a massive
Jimi fan and I guess it was a culture reference as he was a mixed-race lad.
He was mad for Jimi and that was kind of like seen as mainstream. We were
all into the garage psychedelic stuff, but Steve was true to his belief and he
would ape Jimi, not in his regency dandy clothes, but in his mannerism.
The Manchester scene, fashions, musicians at the time, it was all studied, it
wasn't an innate upsurge or natural momentum, it was something that came
from looking at pictures of The Byrds,[21] bear in mind this was before the
time of internet and before we had access to this kind of media. We had to
go to library to find a picture of Byrds. You had to track down the book in
the library.

As Daly explains, the manifestation of flares can be traced to an interest in the
psychedelic musicians of 1960s America. The sense of nostalgia for this era is
understandable when considering Keightley and Pickering's (2012) stance that
nostalgia and mnemonic imagination together can be linked to a desire for
alternative ways of living while also dealing with abrupt shifts and discontinuities,
such as the changes to working-class identity faced by members of Madchester.
However, many subcultural movements have also looked to the counterculture
movements of 1960s Europe and America for inspiration, a time when being
conventional and participating in the capitalist economy became linked to a
sense of phoniness. This can be interpreted as the beginning of authenticity in
counterculture or subculture, a view that supports Lionel Trilling's (1972: 12)
concept of "originative power," as the foundation of authenticity.

Daly's observations concur with Polhemus (1994) who states that the flared
look came from the football terraces, positioning it as a logical progression of the
Casual movement where "an emphasis on brand labels such as the Manchester-
based Joe Bloggs was clearly in the same aspirational, Dressing Up tradition"
(176). The wearing of flares at football matches identified by Daly as early as
1981 or 1982 is a clear example of individuals communicating allegiance to
a group, which in this case can also indicate a geographically based arena: a
Manchester-based football club who were subverting the Liverpool-originating
Casual subculture. Here, the nostalgic collective memory of 1960s American
counterculture was shared and its memory enriched as it was brought into a
new social context of the football terraces. As football sociologist Dave Russell
(1999: 19) writes, the allegiance to local football teams has provided a "symbolic

citizenship," renewing the sense of belonging to a certain place since the late nineteenth century as towns and cities grew too big to be knowable to their inhabitants. At a time when working-class identity was being undermined by the government, such allegiances became ever more important, with attending football matches tapping into the cultural memory of working-class Mancunians.

Workwear

Daly also acknowledged workwear as an integral part of his wardrobe, worn alongside the flared trousers:

> SA: What sort of things were you wearing with the flares, what did you wear on top?
>
> LD: It was a kind of overlap with workwear and Phil Saxe was kind of responsible for that. I remember I went and picked up this knitted thick cardigan jacket thing, which I would never have worn in a million years, but seeing it in his shop in concept [context] with all the flares it seemed like the best thing in the world. I think I've got it on in that picture that Ian [Tilton] took.

The photograph (see Figure 4.3) shows Daly wearing the thick knitted jacket. It has a button front, collar, and revers joined and rounded to present a kind of shawl collar, rounded shoulders, and a slightly baggy shape, appearing to be tapered or gathered at the top of the hip. While it is unbuttoned in the photograph, it can be assumed from the style that it would billow up slightly at the waist when fastened. The photograph is in black and white and this may be why the characteristics of the jacket do not immediately strike the observer as workwear. However, Daly wore the garment with this interpretation from seeing it marketed in Gangway (Phil Saxe's market stall) as such.

During his interview, alongside Terry Kane, AJ Wilkinson also identified influences of workwear, sold and worn alongside garments inspired by the 1960s:[22]

> AJ Wilkinson: I remember, because I used to work for, do some work for Big Banana [in Affleck's Palace],[23] and he was one of the first people to start to bring in Carhartt when it was workwear.[24] So, workwear was a big thing and everybody used to wear dungarees, dungarees were a big thing. And I used to wear Carhartt. And of course, there was no internet then so you used to have to wait for someone to go to the States and get it for you, you couldn't get it. So, I used to have to wait for someone to come back with bales of workwear which I was quite into Red Wings and all that sort of thing.[25]

SA: So when you say dungarees and workwear, what was the shape of it? Was it fitted?

AJW: No. They were baggy. They weren't like 1970s dungarees, they were like—sort of—you looked like you were in *The Waltons* really.[26] It was that sort of look, you know, check shirt thing and errr dungarees with er. . . . Not everyone did but a few people did, sort of, definitely that wider legged, and I remember I had a few pairs by Dickies,[27] Carhartt, American, I was really into Americana, it was a big thing for me, at that point.

Wilkinson observed the influence of what he termed "Americana": American workwear labels, such as Carhartt and Dickies, together with Red Wing work boots. These were all brands whose products were designed for workers (mainly men) who worked in heavy industry in the United States, such as logging, mining, and farming. When describing the fit of the clothing, in particular the dungarees worn, it is worth noting that the dungarees and checked shirts mentioned by Wilkinson have a loose fit, rather than the baggy fit popularly associated with Madchester, suggesting the baggy look has alternative origins. These workwear references were worn by individuals taking a bricoleurian approach, inspired by cultural references, with subverted and transformed meanings as they were reappropriated into casual wear in Manchester, England, to communicate individuality. Journalist Tim Walker (2008) described an individual's creation of their own look from a range of eclectic influences, rather than buying into one concept or trend, as a DJ remixes music. This is an appropriate metaphor for this cultural movement.

In addition to *The Waltons*, Kane and Wilkinson cite other, more cult American film and television programs as a source when considering their influences for dress during this time:

Terry Kane: The mid '80s. One thing that I would say influenced later on was *Twin Peaks*.[28] Because that's when the jeans went looser, the [Levi's] 501s, the checked shirts . . . I remember buying a black leather biker jacket in '89 after watching *Twin Peaks* actually.

AJW: Yeah, the influences were different. I think the influences came from . . . for me, the same, from film, like all that dungarees thing, it came from film . . . Like with [Levi's] 501s, you'd find out information. It's different because there wasn't the internet so you'd find out about a little something that someone had worn and think, "oh, I like that," like Red Wings. I remember them coming over and it's only because of a certain film and someone wearing Red Wings, it could have been *Deer Hunter*.[29] A semi-cool Di Niro wearing Red Wings. And you had to get someone to get them for you. So the influences were probably very subtle.

The references for Wilkinson and Kane can be interpreted as characteristically American. Wilkinson cites actor Robert Di Niro as his character hunts deer, a popular sport in the northern United States. For Kane, inspiration came from the 1990s television series *Twin Peaks*, whose characters' costumes feature styles that are quintessentially Lynchonian,[30] referencing the local logging community in lumberjack shirts and jackets alongside classic Americana. Such contemporary cultural discourse offers representations of the past as popular memory which the viewer can draw upon. Films and television programs are used as a resource for our imaginations where they work in partnership with our memories, becoming interwoven with our own social and historical experiences, both at the time we are immersed in them and afterward (Keightley and Pickering 2012). Popular memories are not just passively accepted but responded to in accordance with the individual's reflections on their own experiences and memories, and even rejected if deemed inauthentic (Lummis 1987; Mills 2016). Anna Green posits "surely the interesting issue is not that individuals draw upon contemporary cultural discourses to make sense of their lives, but *which* ones, and *why*" (2004: 42 [original emphasis]). The dynamic negotiation between popular discourse and authenticity of personal memory enables individuals to assert where their experiences fit into popular memory, but also where they are different. For Kane, it was the workwear of Lynch's 1950s-reminiscent Americana rather than the Dean and Brando-esque biker jackets featured in the series that resonated,[31] reflecting his identity as a working-class Mancunian male at a time when working-class identity was in a state of flux.

Denim jeans are also traditional workwear garments, although since their origins they have been adopted by various groups, gaining an identity not just of American workwear but also of American counterculture. Hence, for the Manchester scene, the sense of authenticity lies not just in the original workwear but also, as with the wearing of flares, in the links to and nostalgia for American cultures. This nostalgia not only can be understood as part of the gaze across the Atlantic toward American culture through the lens of music, film, and photography but also mirrors British subcultures' and the post-subcultural movement's desire to subvert the mainstream. As Keightley and Pickering (2012) state, "[nostalgia] can be about keeping certain alternatives open within the public domain and keeping alive certain counter-narratives that rub against the grain of established social orthodoxies and political pieties" (116). As mentioned when discussing the influence of *The Waltons*, Wilkinson observed the importance of jeans, in particular, Levi 501s:

AJW: I think for me it was different, I suppose—I remember 501s being a big thing, but original 501's with the red selvedge which were slightly wider on the leg than your standard 501's being quite important at that time. I remember seeing The [Stone] Roses on one of those programs which . . . can't remember who it was now, but it was on one of those late night programs they were on and I remember Ian Tilton photographing them [see Figure 4.4], which they used the photos for the cover of their album and ermmm . . . and John Squire, I was knocking around with Matt Squire, his brother, we were all into looking for those jeans that were a slightly bit different than the very straight legged, horrible late eighties, where all the jeans seemed to be exported over from the Czech Republic, bleached, horrible, you know, that sort of look. Yeah, that look was looking for, sort of a nod to Americana, slightly fifties Americana coming through as well, which was quite interesting.

SA: This is something that you remember John Squire wearing?

AJW: Well I remember John Squire wearing those sort of original 501s, they were all looking for those original 501s shrink to fits. . . . But, original shrink to fits, not the low cut that you could buy—you see you couldn't get—you had to really search for them, you had to get them from London, or wherever you could find them.

Figure 4.4 The Stone Roses on the set of *The Other Side of Midnight* at Granada TV, 1989, by Ian Tilton © Ian Tilton, 1989. Reproduced with permission.

The look of the original Levi's 501s shrink-to-fit jeans was due to a specific cut with higher waist and straight leg, sought out by the members of The Stone Roses, who also appreciated its historical styling. Figure 4.4 shows the jeans worn by lead singer Ian Brown, wearing straight-legged jeans that appear almost flared at the bottom due to the width of the straight leg of the jean. The jeans vary in color/wash, and it can be seen that two of the band members have rolled-up hems, which is explained by Kane below:

> AJW: But 501s and slightly bigger 501s belted up was big. [. . .]
>
> TK: And they were so much harder to get then because there wasn't all the different leg lengths and such that you can buy now. You could get different waist sizes.

The difficulty in acquiring these garments with American heritage and workwear references, identified by both Kane and Wilkinson, was undoubtedly part of their appeal. The limited access of these styles was the opposite of mass market, which was deemed inauthentic. As Kane mentions, sizes were limited. This includes leg lengths, so rolled-up hems would frequently be a feature (as shown in Figure 4.4), but waist sizes would be limited too (imports to Britain were usually only even-sized waist measurements). This led to the style of oversized jeans being worn belted, gathered at the waist, the baggy clothing style being dictated to some degree by availability as much as it was by choice.

The authenticity of "workwear," in particular American workwear, here could be questioned, as the wearers did not undertake heavy manual labor and therefore did not wear the garments and footwear for its original intentions. However, when worn in a city whose heritage is steeped in industrialism and thus a working-class culture, there is a near-mythical status in which workwear has an authentic aura and thus relevance to the Mancunians wearing it. With any cultural artifact or product the memory of how it was made and was/is used is carried in its extended meanings and feelings the user, in this case the wearer, invests in it. Original garments convey ideas of authenticity that can be appropriated to construct a "credible" self, with a status of uniqueness and originality that merges with the wearer.[32] This status is also enhanced by garments that were difficult to acquire, such as footwear from the United States, with the difficulty in obtaining such items undoubtedly part of their appeal. The nostalgia for workwear is helpful for the wearer (Blunt 2003), where what is remembered, while attached to a sense of loss, is worn with a great sense of pride. Alongside this is the need to assert a sense of communal belonging and place in the context of rapid deindustrialization and social change (Smith and Campbell 2017).

Heike Jenss (2004) argues that dressing in garments with history produces a feeling of individuality and sophistication: "distinction" as Pierre Bourdieu proposed ([1979] 2004). Referencing her research on jeans, Woodward (2016) highlights "how the material properties of things are central to understanding the sensual, tactile, material and embodied ways in which social lives are lived and experienced" (359), and it is worth noting, as established in earlier research, that "there is a different wearing experience with original garments as the textiles and cut are different to contemporary garments: they *feel* different" (Atkin 2016: 232). This research has shown that this was the case for those interviewed and their friends, with their memories of dress offering insight into the decisions and contexts of the time of wearing.

Conclusion

Madchester marks the point where there was a shifting in attitude, a point at which subcultural identities became less fixed. This fits with the change from subculture to post-subcultural theory, where subcultures evolved from their traditional sense into less tangible, more eclectic style and taste sensibilities. The term "movement" has been used in this chapter to acknowledge the relationship with political, economic, and sociocultural contexts, as well as the more dynamic, thriving youth culture that was inherent in Manchester from 1986 to 1996. The men interviewed in this chapter were initiators of the Madchester movement. They revealed that rather than mere eclecticism, emphasis was placed on the origin of clothing and how it was combined because of its meaning to the individual and their group, referencing cultural memories of American 1960s psychedelia and workwear to support their stance. The interviews also revealed that this bricoleurian approach brought a tacit understanding to dress choices, arising from shared experiences inspired by locale.

As working-class roles, in particular male roles, changed due to the deindustrialization of the North during the late 1970s and 1980s, previous symbols of class solidarity were challenged. Football culture emerged as the focal point of a new sense of pride in coming from a working-class background with expressions of class solidarity manifesting on football terraces in the unified wearing of flared trousers. This was a Manchester-centric subversion of the Casual subcultural movement with its roots in 1960s American psychedelia. The American workwear that was a popular look during this time was a nostalgic combination of mythology and lived experiences, where garments associated with workwear were adopted as tokens of cultural memory as a strategy for working-class identification. This cultural memory acted to reinforce the pride in working-class origins during the transitional phase of class identity in the 1980s. It is unclear from the interviews why American rather than British references were adapted, but with roots in a sense of cultural authenticity these industrial references were filtered through a nostalgic consumption of American film, television, and music.

The garments worn by the original members of the Madchester movement transport ideas of authenticity that can be appropriated to construct a "credible" self, with a status of uniqueness and originality that merges with the wearer as part of their post-subcultural capital (Bourdieu [1979] 2004; Jenss 2015; Miles 1995; Thornton 1995). This is also the case for garments that have been appropriated in the spirit of history (here, the case of psychedelia and original workwear) satisfying the wearer's sense of bricolage and nostalgia while referencing the city's cultural memories of working-class heritage and opposition to the mainstream. Utilizing nostalgia, myth, and memories of dress, the cultural memory of Manchester enabled the initiators of Madchester to exert their identity as "Manchester Men" and their symbolic citizenship (Russell 1999) at a time of flux for working-class identity and the city itself.[33] As the Madchester movement evolved, so too did the city, with a newfound confidence, still rooted in its heritage and cultural memories of subversion and creativity.

Notes

1 Haslam believes that it may have begun as the use of the recreational drug Ecstasy became more frequent in nightclubs around 1985, although he also suggests a start in 1987 with the first play in public of The Stone Roses' *Elephant Stone*. Haslam (cited in Robb 2009: 237) confirms that the crucial time was certainly December 1987 to March 1988, with Madchester ending by Christmas 1990. Luck (2002) suggests that there are potentially many dates for the end of the movement: May 1990 (The Stone Roses' concert on Spike Island, Widnes, Cheshire), September 1992 (the release of the Happy Monday's *Yes, Please*), December 1994 (the release of The Stone Roses' second album, *The Second Coming*), or beginning in 1993 with the hiatus in New Order's band activity. He asserts that the end was certainly by the Reading Festival in August 1996. This date coincides to a certain degree with the bombing of Manchester that caused widespread damage to the city center on June 15, 1996. This ambiguity of the period contributes to the mythological sense of Madchester, and historical accuracy may no longer be possible, nor even welcomed

by former participants in the scene but for the purpose of this research 1986 marks the start, reflecting when the scene was firmly established in nightclubs and 1996 the end at the time of the Manchester bombing.

2　Manchester was the world's first city of the industrial revolution with machine-based cotton manufacturing at the heart of its industry from the mid-eighteenth century. With the decline of the cotton industry after the First World War and other manufacturing industries declining from the 1950s, Manchester was unable to revive its economic base in an increasingly competitive postwar world despite the introduction of service and technology industries (Williams 1996). Williams, writing in 1996 at the end of the period studied, notes Manchester's renewed optimism and confidence as the regional capital and an international city as it embarked on a number of regeneration initiatives and civic and cultural enterprises in partnerships with the private and public sector. This reflects the city's cultural timeline as it moved from the grayscale, industrial-inspired late 1970s through the psychedelic-inspired late 1980s and early 1990s to the confident, European city of the late 1990s.

3　Woodward (2009) and Wenting, Atzema, and Frenken (2011) highlight the importance of this act to be part of a vibrant local scene.

4　Seminal work on subcultures at the CCCS by Hall and Jefferson ([1976] 2006), Melly (1972), and Hebdige (1979, 1988) established the traditional notion of subculture being a form of working-class resistance against the previous generation's conformist attitudes seen against the dominant culture in postwar Britain.

5　For example, Straw (1991) suggests "scene," Crewe and Beaverstock (1998) and Woodward (2009) use "taste constellations," Woodward (2008) also suggests "creative of individuals." Polhemus (1994) uses "supermarket of style," Maffesoli (1996) both "neo-tribes" and "aggregations." Evans (1997) suggests "lifestyle," Jenks (2005) "standpoints," and Hall (2007) "syntagms." Halberstam (2003) also suggests "alternative temporalities," and Maria and Soep (2005) use "youthscape" to describe what subcultures have evolved into.

6　The plural is used here to denote that Manchester had more than one music and club scene, including those that came together as "Madchester," existing in tandem with one another during the period, 1986–96: see Atkin (2016).

7　Thatcherism is a political ideology named after Conservative leader Margaret Thatcher, who was prime minister for the UK from 1979 to 1990 (BBC 2013).

8　The Haçienda was a nightclub and music venue on Whitworth Street, Manchester, which was intrinsic to the inception and evolution of the Madchester movement. It is also central to the cultural memory of the movement. The Venue was another nightclub on Whitworth Street.

9　See Hebdige (1979), Evans (1997), Calefato (2004), and English (2007) based on the work of Lévi-Strauss ([1978] 2001) and de Certeau (1988). Although limited to what these items will signify because of their history and original use, the heart of subculture bricolage is where the original meanings are subverted, to represent their own ideals and place, in opposition to the dominant culture.

10 Mancunian is an adjective or demonym of Manchester that refers to anything that is from or relates to the city.

11 For example, interviewees Phil Saxe and Leo Stanley have both been interviewed on and around the subject of Madchester in a number of popular discourses such as Haslam's *Manchester, England* (1999), and Robb's *The North Will Rise Again: Manchester Music City 1976–1996* (2009).

12 See also Slater's chapter in this book.

13 Polhemus (1994), Woodward (2009), and Wenting, Atzema, and Frenken (2011) highlight the importance of the act of hanging out with particular people in a particular location.

14 See also Jenkinson and Webb in this book.

15 A terrace is part of a football ground that is used by spectators to stand and watch the game. Terraces are the cheaper end of the price range within the ground and as such defines class-watching of live football.

16 The origin of the umbrella term "Casual" is unclear. It includes subgroups, with subtle differences in their look according to their geographical location and football loyalties. The Casuals wore expensive designer sportswear, which could be seen as a means of both disassociating themselves from stereotypical football hooligan looks and subverting perceptions of wealth by wearing expensive designer garments for working-class activities, such as football and fighting (Hewitt 2002).

17 L. Daly (2012), interviewed by author, May 7, 8.00 p.m., The Bar, Chorlton-cum-Hardy, Manchester, UK. Daly was a friend of band members from The Stone Roses and the Happy Mondays. Daly is credited with initiating the Baldrick/Madchester look and was one of a group of young men photographed by Ian Tilton for the *i-D magazine* photo shoot in October 1987 (Figures 4.1–4.3).

18 A football fixture is the schedule of games to be played in a championship which informs when each game is to be played and whether the team is playing at its home pitch or away at its opponent's.

19 Phil Saxe co-owned Gangway, a market stall on the Arndale Market, Manchester, which sold casual wear. He was also the first manager for seminal Manchester band the Happy Mondays and the head of Artist and Repertoire (A&R), a role that scouts for and develop musical talent at record labels, at Manchester-based music label Factory Records during the 1980s.

20 Carl Twigg was an independent clothing store in Manchester at the time.

21 The Byrds were a 1960s American psychedelia band.

22 A. Wilkinson and T. Kane (2012), interviewed together by author, April 10, Mid Cheshire College, Northwich, Cheshire, UK. During the time period studied, AJ

Wilkinson was a photographer for *City Life* magazine, and Terry Kane was a disc jockey (DJ).

23 Once the department store Affleck and Brown, Affleck's Palace is an indoor market in Manchester with independent stalls, small shops, and boutiques selling music, music memorabilia, clothes, and accessories. The vendors range from traders of secondhand goods to designer-makers selling their own wares. Affleck's Palace has a reputation for being a center of countercultural retail experience (Butler 2016).

24 Carhartt was established in 1889 in Detroit, Michigan, producing denim and cotton duck workwear. During the late 1980s, Carhartt goods found their way to Europe in small imports by independent companies. A distribution network for Europe was not formed until 1994 (Carhartt 2022).

25 Red Wing was established in 1905 in Red Wing, Minnesota, producing leather work boots.

26 *The Waltons* was an American television series (aired 1972–81 and continued by film sequels) set in rural Virginia between 1933 and 1946. Chopra-Gant notes that *The Waltons* offered an "anodyne" (2012: 3), tapping into traditional American family values, countering unease of the social and political volatility of the time (e.g., defeat in Vietnam and political corruption). During the time period studied, reruns of the series were aired in the UK on Sunday mornings on Channel 4 where watching it may have been a soothing source of comfort, this time easing hangovers and comedowns from substances taken the night before.

27 Williamson-Dickie Manufacturing Company was established in Texas in 1922, making workwear and uniforms. In 1989 Dickies (UK) was formed. The brand became popular with skateboarders as well as several top music acts (Dickies 2022).

28 *Twin Peaks* (1990–1), [TV program] American Broadcast Corporation. American television serial drama by Mark Frost and David Lynch, aired 1990–1 and followed by a feature film in 1992. Twin Peaks is a fictional small logging town in Washington State.

29 *Deer Hunter* (1978), [Film] dir. Michael Cimino, USA: EMI Pictures.

30 Film and television director David Lynch is renowned for a unique cinematic style with recurring themes, including surrealism, violence or the criminal underbelly, industry and Americana reminiscent of the 1950s. These themes are reflected in the costumes worn in *Twin Peaks*.

31 Images of the American actors James Dean and Marlon Brando wearing leather biker jackets in influential 1950s films such as Dean in *Rebel Without a Cause* (1955, dir. Nicholas Ray, USA: Warner Bros.) and Brandon in *The Wild One* (1953, dir. László Benedek, USA: Columbia Pictures) became iconic imagery representing youth disillusionment and rebellion.

32 "Original garments" is used in this chapter to define authentic clothing from the past, in this case the 1960s.

33 *The Manchester Man* was published in three volumes in 1876 and tells the story of the rise of Jabez Clegg, the "Manchester Man" of the title, mirroring the economic growth of the city of Manchester during the early years of the nineteenth century (Chetham's Library 2022).

Part III

Objects

5

Wardrobes and Soundtracks

Resources for Memories of Youth

Jo Jenkinson

> Marian: I see my little round blue plastic bag that I had when they first came
> out, and it used to fit the records in because it was round. And I remember
> getting on the 89 [bus] to come up to Alan's, and I used to get it in Albert
> Square that, with these records in, you know.[1]

Marian relates a vivid memory while we are listening to "Smoke Gets in Your Eyes"
by The Platters (1958).[2] The seven-inch vinyl record, which she has kept from
her youth, is playing on the record player in her front room. We are surrounded
by photographs of Marian aged between fourteen and eighteen, a pile of records,
and several garments she has kept from that time including a mohair wool suit
from the late 1950s (Figures 5.1 and 5.2). The atmosphere in the room is charged
with emotion as Marian's stories of youth play out through the material artifacts
that are present and the soundtrack that fills the room. These intense moments
of remembering are orchestrated in an interview experience designed to explore
how the clothes we wore, and the musical soundtracks we listened to in our
youth, act as resources for memory. Marian is in her late seventies at the time
of the interview, and yet these moments of recollection are readily recalled and
fluently described in expressive detail.

Marian was one of seven women, aged between forty-nine and seventy-
seven, whose interviews are analyzed in this chapter. Participants were asked
to complete a short questionnaire about their memories of youth in advance of
the interviews, which took place in their homes. They were briefed to compile a
"memory toolkit" to include any kept clothes and accessories from their youth,
photographs of them in their youth (featuring dress), and albums or specific
tracks that were significant to their memories of youth (physical collections, a
digital playlist, or a written list). Also, any other relevant memorabilia, such as,

Figure 5.1 Wool suit jacket, 2018. Author's own photograph.

Figure 5.2 Marian, age sixteen, wearing the suit, 1958. Unknown photographer ©
Marian. Reproduced with permission.

tickets, magazines, objects, and so on, with a connection to the clothes they wore and music they listened to in their youth. This toolkit supported oral narratives which centered on the participants' experiences of youth, as seen through a lens of everyday dress and recorded music. The findings presented in this chapter focus on the interaction between these oral narratives, the images (or items) of dress, and the soundtracks played.

This chapter proposes that both dress and music can be considered "tokens of youth" that play a considerable role in young peoples' participation in youth cultures,[3] becoming intrinsic to self-affirmation in youth and often throughout a lifetime. Youth in the context of this study was defined by the participants, ranging from the age of twelve to beyond thirty years old, framing youth as a transitional stage and a state of mind that goes beyond chronological age (Tebbutt 2016: 3). The participants, who all grew up in the north of England, were selected to ensure that their self-defined "youth" fell after the arrival of the twelve-inch long player album (LP) in 1948 and the end of clothes rationing in England in 1949. Likewise, the younger participants all turned eighteen before access to the internet became commonplace in the early 1990s, and social media and digital technologies for sharing music and photography became available. These boundaries enabled focused analysis on a period within which recorded music and dress, or photographs of dress, were relatively accessible as everyday material objects.

Dress, Music, and Photographs in Context

Dress, music, and photographs have all been found to have mnemonic properties in academic studies,[4] yet they have not previously been considered alongside each other in this context. This chapter scrutinizes how they work together in a multisensory interview environment as described in the previous example. The term "dress" is adopted to include worn garments, artifacts, and body modifiers such as make-up and hair (Roach-Higgins and Eicher 1992: 1), and the evolving content of the participants' wardrobes. "Style" works together with dress to designate the assembling of different looks. This styling activity regularly surfaced when looking at photographs of dress, prompting the participant to recall how they wore a garment or combined items into distinct outfits. Carol Tulloch's (2010) academic framework for the relationship between "style-fashion-dress" in her analysis of "style narratives" of the African diaspora positions dress as a means to articulate personal narratives, as part of "a system of concepts that signifies the multitude of meanings and frameworks that are always 'whole-and-part' of dress studies" (275).

In this analysis the term "music" refers specifically to recorded music, that is, or has been, commercially available in the public domain. Live performances and public events were referenced by the participants, but personally selected music, played in the home, was the focus of the interviews as it prioritizes individual choice above collective music experiences.[5] This is music that has "biographical significance" as defined by Michael Pickering and Emily Keightley (2015: 2) who use the term "self-chosen" music to distinguish between a track purchased and played at home and, for example, music heard on the radio (7).

Photographs, specifically amateur snapshots, have been compared to music as technologies of remembering by Pickering and Keightley (2015), whose theoretical framework aligns music and photographs as communication technologies through which it is possible to access a memory or reflect on the past. They propose that recorded music and photographs are both able to configure or summon mnemonic experiences as "pieces of the past" (Pickering and Keightley 2015: 8). This temporal aspect is what enables music and photographs to act as conduits to memories of youth, as they are often linked to key events, people, or places from a specific time while simultaneously providing fresh experience in the present. Pickering and Keightley (2015: 7) refer to vernacular photography, photographs that take everyday life as the subject, and use the term "self-made" photographs which aligns to their focus on "self-chosen" music. In this chapter the term "snapshots" is used to describe the images of everyday dress included in the "memory toolkit."[6]

The roles dress and music play in our identities as we move through life are performed in private, as intimate personal experiences of dressing or listening to recorded music at home, and publicly as we use these cultural "tokens" to represent our public selves and communicate our interests and preferences to others. It is the personal, self-selected playlists and snapshots of dress (supported by kept items of clothing where available) that are of primary interest in this study. However, personal and collective experience cannot be considered in isolation. David Hesmondalgh (2013) has proposed that although most cultural products have potential to cross personal and social realms, music has a particularly powerful ability to bring together private and public experience. It is suggested that dress crosses a similar scope of experience, categorized by Joanne Eicher (1981) as dressing our private, public, and secret selves. This was evidenced in a previous analysis of dress behaviors in young people, in which I reported a fluid spectrum of experience across the private-public realm (Jenkinson 2020).

Wardrobes and Soundtracks as Everyday Mnemonic Resources

In this project, the focus was on episodic memory and the autobiographical memories described by Martin Conway (2009: 2305) as "summary records of experience." However, the mnemonic qualities of dress, music, and photographs rely on the relationship between the shared public experience of popular memory and firsthand experience of personal or episodic memories, "the mnemonic imagination allows us to connect personal and public remembering as part of the same mnemonic process, with each being implicated in the other" (Keightley and Pickering 2012: 199). Annette Kuhn (1995) described the relationship between her private photograph albums and more public memories of films or art, for example, as "less readily separable than conventional wisdom would have us believe" (4).

The self-edited selection of artifacts in the "memory toolkit" are considered as conduits, access points, or triggers to memory in this research. They provide the mode of access to personal "memory resources," categorized as "wardrobes" (to include snapshots of dress, actual clothing, and dress memorabilia such as dressmaking patterns or magazines) and "soundtracks" (personal playlists and music memorabilia including tickets, scrapbooks, and recorded music in analogue formats such as the compact discs, tapes, and vinyl records included in the toolkits and sometimes played in the interviews). These memory resources act not only as conduits to a memory as part of the remembering process but also as subjects of remembering, often activated by each other in the multisensory interview environment. These resources impact on the "mnemonic spaces" that are accessed and drawn on by the participants through imaginative remembering and re-experiencing. These are conceptualized as the "memory wardrobe" and "memory soundtrack." In the "memory wardrobe" memories of dress are metaphorically stored, whether triggered by tactile or visual stimuli in the present or imagined in the mnemonic process. The "memory soundtrack" includes the musical playlists that accompany an individual through life in the mind, or through analogue formats, or digital technologies in the act of remembering (Davidson and Garrido 2014; Williamson 2014). The communicated content of these mnemonic spaces, accessed through the multisensory interview process, enabled scrutiny of the combined power that dress and music have to support memories of youth. Interviews took place in the participants' homes, guided by the toolkit, playing the soundtracks, and looking at the snapshots and garments where available. This created a space in which narratives from the "memory wardrobe" and "memory soundtrack" were constructed. I undertook thematic and narrative analysis (Riessman 2008) of the verbatim interview transcripts, taking into account descriptions of dress items, musical soundtracks, and snapshot evidence, to consider the trans-temporal experience of remembering in the sensory-rich interview environment.

The interviews evidenced that clothing, music, and photographs are bound together through the relative ease with which they are accessed as tools for remembering; however, accessibility differs for each resource. Although dress is an essential part of everyday life, only three participants had kept garments or accessories from their youth; there are various reasons women may keep clothes that they no longer wear,[7] for example, two participants cited lack of fit as a reason for not keeping clothing. Unlike music artifacts from our youth, often displayed on shelves in shared areas of the home, clothes are not made in compact formats designed for efficient storage, and when they are kept, they are often concealed in out-of-the-way corners (Cwerner 2001).[8] Although accessible in youth as part of the everyday ritual of dressing, clothes are less commonly available as a tool for remembering later in life. However, all participants had distinct memories of what they wore at the time; even in the absence of actual garments there is evidence of strong memory for dress. It is often music and photographs that can support, trigger, or illuminate these memories of absent dress artifacts, as articulated in the example that opens this chapter.

Digital technologies have made music, in the form of personally selected playlists, accessible as a tool for remembering in everyday life. All the participants described buying and owning records, cassette tapes, or compact discs (CDs) in their youth and five included vinyl records or CDs in their toolkit. Swift changes in music listening technology can "trap" music in artifacts: one participant had kept a record gifted by her husband despite having no means of playing it; another described music missing from her toolkit that was on the now defunct eight-track tape format:[9]

> Heather: Well, some of the music is missing because it was all 8-track, a big chunk of time was on 8-track. Some of the clothes are missing because you do get rid of clothes. And I had a friend that always said, "I'll have it, I'll have it, have you got rid of that yet?" so I would hand them over to her.[10]

> Mo: I haven't kept clothing or shoes or anything like that because I've moved around quite a bit and I had a flood in a house where quite a few of my possessions got ruined, and a fire. So, that's mainly why the photographs have survived because I always have those in a really safe place because

to me the photos are something you can never replace. Whereas you can replace a jacket or a pair of shoes, so that's my thinking.[11]

The ease with which photographs are taken, stored, and shared has also been affected by changes in digital technologies. All participants had kept physical photographs, developed from 35mm film.[12] Most of them also had access to digital collections of personal photographs. The research took advantage of this accessibility, with the mnemonic powers of dress being transmitted through the medium of photography. While this was sometimes supported by items of actual clothing, the snapshots played a valuable role in providing a synthesis of style-fashion-dress (Tulloch 2010, 2016), representing the clothed and styled body. While collections of photographs were commonplace, many participants cited chronological gaps in their family albums. Not everyone had access to cameras, before they became part of everyday experience with the introduction of smartphones, and there were often periods of time or events where photographs were not taken. Janet reflects on the gaps in her photo albums, but this does not prevent her remembering what she was wearing at the time:[13]

> Janet: I think I said before that between 14 and 18, I don't seem to have a lot of photographs. I can imagine what I was wearing. And it's not because I didn't want to share it, it's because I just haven't got it, and I would quite like to share it. I can see myself wearing the Perry belt[14] dangling down the jeans and stripy t-shirt, and I can see me in the shirt and the mod tie . . . I will have to try and dig some more out because I think that's the bit that's kind of missing a little bit. And I think the other gaps are, . . . there's a certain time again, where children kind of took over a little bit and all my photographs are like me with the children.

Janet's narrative highlights how changes in life practices, such as motherhood, can impact on how we interact with dress or music. Janet's choice of words is also interesting here as she describes how she can "imagine" what she is wearing and "see" herself back in her youth. This articulation of multisensory and trans-temporal experience is typical in the responses of the participants during the interviews, suggesting a supportive interconnection between experience, memory, and imagination. This is central to the concept of *The Mnemonic Imagination* proposed by Keightley and Pickering (2012), who argue that far from compromising memory, imagination has the potential to synthesize memories and lend new meaning in the present. *The Remembering–Imagining System* proposed by Martin Conway, Catherine Loveday, and Scott Cole (2016) also highlights the relationship between remembering and imagination and the role the past plays in the present and in our future selves, from a cognitive neuroscience perspective. As Keightley and Pickering (2012: 5) explain, "our memories are not imaginary, but are acted upon imaginatively" and this creative practice of remembering was given priority in this study, above concerns about accuracy of memory often evident in scientific literature (Brainerd and Reyna 2005; Bernstein and Loftus 2009).

Pickering and Keightley's approach is further expounded in their text *Photography, Music and Memory* (2015). However, while their view of photographs and music as communication technologies sits comfortably within media studies and memory studies, when using photographs to explore the wardrobe, the focus and hierarchy shift. Keightley and Pickering (2006) described photography and music as "parallel forms of perceptual engagement, as are our own eyes and ears" (150), and here, the inclusion of dress expands this into the realm of touch and tactile perception (Stewart 1999).[15] Kuhn's (1995) writing on the mnemonic power of photographs illustrates this perspective, as she uses the photograph to prioritize the haptic or material, articulating the *feeling* of the clothes she is wearing in an image: "today, as I imagine myself at that moment, inside that dress, my body feels constrained, my chest tight. I can scarcely breathe. The clothes are uncomfortable, restricting. The belt squeezes, the collar chokes. The top half of my body feels cramped and immobile" (Kuhn 1995: 63).

The toolkits that included material artifacts—clothes from the participants' youth, music artifacts, and a range of photographs—elicited strong emotions in the interviews, such as those with Marian and Kate.

> Marian: It's been quite a bit of an emotional trip, hasn't it? . . . And especially that suit, when the photograph that I had, you know, of my friend and I, that was quite, what can I say with that? It was, sort of, the moment there, you know, I was, sort of, in that moment there with her. You know. Yeah, I think if you hadn't have been here and I just brought it out of the wardrobe, I don't think it would have been so emotional. But I think with everything put together it, sort of, brought back everything, you know.

> Kate: So yes, when I was getting stuff out of the box last night, it was just kind of like, "I need the bits that I know are going to be useful," but I'd not sorted anything out. And then when you actually come to talking about it and, "Oh well, there's this, just listen to this, right, this explains why this, this is how we dressed, this is the music." And that's been kind of, making those, making those connections has been really, it's been really nice for me.[16]

The impact of the overlapping visual, auditory, and tactile experience on personal memory intensified these interviews. Bringing together wardrobes and soundtracks as memory resources appeared to enhance imaginative remembering and the "creative regeneration of past experience," creating new meaning and significance in the present (Keightley and Pickering 2012: 50).

Multisensory Mnemonic Experience

William Brewer (1986) found that personal, episodic memories often come to mind as strong visual images. The "memory toolkits" of the participants elicited vivid connections to the past, often accompanied by a mental image. Below Janet relates her memory as if a scene is unfolding in her mind:

> Janet: And it was Suzi Quatro in Tameside[17] . . . and there were people at the front, running to the front, dancing and kind of like bowing to her, because they really like, you know, sort of like, were totally obsessed by her, and that was probably, that's brought back an *image* of me going out with my sister to our first gig.

David Rubin (2005: 79) has proposed that the senses work together as a multimodal system within autobiographical memory to include "vision, hearing, smell, taste, touch, and body sense or kinesthesis," with visual images working alongside auditory and motor images. Scientific evidence suggests that the retrieval of autobiographical memories is supported by multimodal cues. Catherine Stevens (2015: 263) has described music as "multidimensional and multimodal" with auditory, visual, verbal, and emotional dimensions. Likewise, Marie Kirk and Dorthe Bersten (2018) found the use of multimodal objects as cues for remembering past events increased vivid memory recall in adults, recognizing potential for future studies using objects of personal significance. They concurred that objects have significant mnemonic value, yet their study did not evaluate whether a picture of the object could provide a similar effect (Kirk and Bersten 2018). In this study the images of dress present in the snapshots often triggered vivid memories, even in the absence of physical garments.

Johan Willander, Sverker Sikström, and Kristina Karlsson (2015) studied the interaction between different sensory cues, concluding that even when multimodal cues are present, the retrieval of autobiographical memories is largely driven by visual and auditory processes—a hypothesis supported by the results of this study in which the musical soundtracks and snapshots of dress worked together mnemonically. Often it is visual and auditory cues that heighten perception of the tactile object (Spence 2007) and in this study the use of music as a complementary memory resource often intensified the recollection of dress. In this example, "How Can I Tell You" by Cat Stevens (1971) is playing in the background,[18] prompting Helen to go back to her "memory wardrobe" to put together an outfit to go with the song:[19]

> Helen: I'm wearing a sweater from "Way In" in Manchester and I had three, all
> the same style but different colors. And this particular one was grey and it
> had buttons here [shoulder] . . . And I had one in yellow and one in brown.
> I'm not sure what I'd be wearing with it. I don't think it was jeans. Probably
> a brown pleated skirt, *the* skirt.

Instant, involuntary recollections often are considered unique to music, such as the common phenomenon of "earworms,"[20] yet while clothes themselves do not return in the same way as the literal replaying of a song in the mind, memories of dress can be just as spontaneous and unexpected. A song, scent, or photograph can trigger memories of clothing from the past. When interacting with the objects in their "memory toolkits" participants relived the moment worn, evoking strong emotions and meaning in the present; recalling encounters with dress they often referred to "feeling good" in the clothes. The focus on how clothes feel in the present has been explored from both anthropological (Woodward 2005) and cognitive perspectives (Adam and Galinsky 2012), but here the participants were describing a feeling that crosses past and present. This memory of emotional feeling was apparent even when clothes were experienced through an image. Three participants, Heather, Helen, and Mo, used the expression "the bee's knees" when recalling how they felt in the moments captured in snapshots of their youth.[21] Where clothes were present in the toolkit as material resources, visual images were triggered, which in turn provided imagined material feelings as part of the memory. Talking about a suit she has kept from her youth (see Figures 5.1 and 5.2), Marian imagined herself back in the Belle Vue dancehall before describing the feeling of the outfit back then, concluding:

> Marian: I just think when you see these things and you think, "I really felt good
> in that," you know, you had that feel good factor.

The interviews with the "memory toolkit" evidenced this multisensory remembering. When Marian plays "Smoke Gets in Your Eyes" (The Platters 1958) in the example that opens this chapter, she describes a striking visual image. As the music plays in the background, it provides the soundtrack to the materiality of the handbag and its imagined image, integrating visual, auditory, and tactile experience. Much as earworms can be triggered by a smell or visual image, the image of the little blue bag is projected immediately into the foreground, triggered by the sound of the music played and the atmosphere it provides. Dress and music share this ability to act as sensory memory resources, provoking reactions beyond their individual visual or auditory nature. In her interview Mo instantly transposed dress to music:

Mo: As soon as I saw the photograph [Figure 5.3] I thought, "Right, Led Zep."

Figure 5.3 Mo, age sixteen, 1971 © Mo. Reproduced with permission.

The connectivity across memory resources is explicit in these interviews, and it would appear that, through recollections of dress, imagination is vividly at work. In the following example, Helen describes clothes that feature in a black-and-white snapshot (Figure 5.4).[22] The snapshot is acting as an entry point, then once in the memory space, the image becomes technicolor, supported by the mnemonic imagination, and enriched in the retrospective present. This articulation of memory beyond the black-and-white image was common in these remembered experiences of dress; the interview dialogue brought together experience, memory, and imagination.

Figure 5.4 Helen, age fourteen, 1968 © Helen. Reproduced with permission.

> Helen: Let's see what's on my feet? [Studies photograph] Oh pink, pink peep
> toe shoes from Stylo[23] with heels, bee's knees, and a slide just there . . . and
> that handbag was pink and yellow beads, I remember.

Jayne also added color to a black-and-white snapshot of her and her friends
on their way to a mod rally during her interview by describing the Harrington
jacket and button-down shirt that she was wearing in the image:

> Jayne: It was like a pale beigy brown and then when you turned it inside out
> it was dark brown but I never wore it dark brown. I always wore the beige
> color. . . . The shirts I used to buy from Burtons, button down Ben Sherman.
> I had a variety. I had a white one. I had a peach, I think it was a peachy
> color, a yellow one, a pink one, a pale blue one. And if I rightly remember
> that is, I think that is the pale pink one I was wearing there.

Time Travel with Dress, Music, and Photographs

The participants' experiences reflect Sarah Pink's (2015) framework for sensory
ethnography, where she positions sensoriality as "part of how we understand
our past, how we engage with our present and how we imagine our futures" (3).

Dress and music share this capacity to transcend time, making them invaluable as trans-temporal resources that contribute to personal biographies. Experiences of youth accessed through these resources are potentially better understood in the present and have the potential to create future meanings; as Keightley and Pickering (2012: 198) propose "we look backwards in order to see forwards." The meaning we attach to clothes or musical soundtracks shifts over time, and these memories might be translated differently each time they are drawn upon as experience and perspectives change. This is described by Marian:

> Marian: I know how I felt at the time. I thought I was wonderful, but I mean when you see it now, it's, "What a sight!".

This temporality is played out in Jayne's reflection on youth, demonstrating her understanding of the continuity from the past into the future through her "memory wardrobe" and "memory soundtrack":

> Jayne: I think I'll still retain my bob. I always will do. I'm sure I will do. I think Soul [music] will always be a part of me. It's been, it's been too much of a part of me for now, thirty? Since I was fifteen, so what's that? I'm forty-nine now, thirty-four years. Music will always, always play an integral part in my life.

Whereas dress tends to belong to a certain era, due to short-lived fashions or changes in body shape, music travels better. More loosely situated in time, a track or album may be accessed over extended periods of a lifetime. As a resource for memory, music is not always connected to a specific time or place as photographed dress might be; participants linked tracks to the year in which they remembered them, not necessarily the year they were released:

> Mo: The era in which the photograph was taken doesn't necessarily match the music, but it matches the music that was played at that time, if that makes sense. So, it could have been an old tune from the '60s but I've linked it to the '80s because that's when I was experiencing it.

Music can connect experience across time and facilitate an instant plugging in; it has the advantage that it feels the same even though the body has changed. This would indicate that although the wardrobe, specifically snapshots of dress, has more potential to capture a specific moment of youth, a soundtrack often references multiple moments linked together by common emotion. This retrospective application of music to one's own past appears to be a common feature in everyday mnemonic practices.

When referring to snapshots in the toolkit, participants initially referred to the events or experiences captured in the image. Yet, snapshots were often elaborated upon, and literally colored by imagination, suggesting that an image can be translated in diverse ways under the influence of different sensory triggers. The findings suggest that the visually captured moments of a snapshot are more vivid when accompanied by other memory props, such as a music track. Equally the items of clothing, dress snapshots, or soundtracks played in the interview influenced the participants to fit a memory to what they could touch, see, or hear in that moment.

> Jayne: I think looking at my own personal experiences in the photographs linked with the tracks made it easier for specific events to come back.

> Mo: I think the photographs elicit the memories of the music, if that makes sense, because I've chosen, mainly, photographs in social event situations so there was music all happening there.

> Jayne: The older you get, you remember certain things from certain days and certain times in your life, but you don't remember, you can't, you don't remember the minute detail. And I think that when you, like today, when I got the boxes out, you can pick certain things out and you can relate to what photographs they went to, and you remember. You remember a certain incident or a certain song or a certain person. So that's the sort of, the thing that happens when, with the memory thing, I think, keeping the artefacts and the photographs and music.

In music literature "peak music experiences" have been explored by Ben Green (2016). Similarly, wardrobe interviews conducted by Sophie Woodward (2007), and Guy and Banim (2000), referred to dressing for key life events. In this study the participants experienced episodic memories of these peak moments through their "memory wardrobes" and "memory soundtracks." These events included marriage, a special concert or party attended, or more generic periods where memories of youth reach a crest such as the time Helen spent at an American University:

> Helen: I seemed to stop looking [for more items to include in the toolkit] after I'd found my American stuff in the loft . . . I was looking at it myself and hours were ticking by [laughs]. So, I stopped, but I suppose subconsciously that was my, not my best time of life, but a time of life that I enjoyed, and [pause] that I remember.

The participants' mnemonic experiences varied as to whether they remembered particular youth events or a more general era when interacting with the toolkit, for example music genres were sometimes mentioned rather than specific tracks or albums. When Mo was asked if her photograph (see Figure 5.3) reminded her of any connecting events, she recalled the period of time in which the photograph was taken rather than a specific event:

Mo: Not so much particular specific events, but the *time*, the sort of [pause], meeting my husband-to-be, where we used to go, playing Led Zep at his house and my house and that sort of thing, but not a specific one thing.

Focusing on dress, bolstered by personal soundtracks, may support the ability to look beyond the specifics of a snapshot, because the clothing pictured may have been worn on many occasions and triggers multiple memories. In the interview Mo's snapshot (Figure 5.3) and the memory of that time enabled her to rummage even further in her "memory wardrobe," triggering a memory of a green leather jacket she owned around the same time, although no garment or photographs of the garment were available.

Remembering Youth, Remembering Dress

Reflections on youth, experienced through the lens of dress and music, enable memories that endure to take on new meaning across the life span. For these participants, youth was not separated from current experience, and through their "memory wardrobes" or "memory soundtracks" they were able to formulate consistency of self and connection to their youth:

Janet: I think it's interesting, again, how it's come a bit of a full circle, that I feel like I'm in my own youth culture right now, at the moment . . . I'm not sure if I've ever stopped being young or being part of a youth culture.

Working in the field of memory science, Clare Rathbone, Chris Moulin, and Martin Conway (2008) found autobiographical memories relating to self-image are much more likely to be retained in later life. As dress and music support the formation of self-image, they can also enrich our memories and understanding of our youth. There appears to be a strong mnemonic connection to the music listened to during youth (Holbrook and Schindler 1989; Loveday, Woy, and Conway 2020) and vivid autobiographical memories are most likely to be recalled from the period between ten and thirty years of age, a phenomenon known as the "reminiscence bump" (Rubin, Rahhal, and Poon 1998).[24] The events and timescales referenced by the participants suggest that memory for dress *and* music peak in this age range—a time when the participants developed confidence in their appearance and gained autonomy over what they wore, where they went, or what they listened to. Access to cultural events and control over their social lives was cited as a reason these event memories of "youth" hold such significance in the present. Marian described this period as when her "personal life" began. The participant narratives suggest that dress and music have value as "tokens of youth" in our present, remembered, and future experience, and that peak experiences and memories of youth form part of our continuing life trajectory.

In this study "recorded" dress (snapshots) and "recorded" music were prominent in the mnemonic experience. Both provided stable access points to the participants' "memory wardrobes" and "memory soundtracks." The findings suggest that photographs of dress and items of clothing, personal playlists or music memorabilia, and artifacts all have special mnemonic qualities, and when working together they enable a deeper or richer experience of remembering. Pickering and Keightley (2015: 8) propose that it is the ability of music and photographs to act as "an alibi for what we remember" that imbues a memory with deeper meaning. Alison Slater (2011) has also suggested that more trust is placed in memories supported by physical artifacts, such as photographs, and that they may remove doubt. However, the "records" of dress or music referenced by the participants in this study are treated not as evidence but as part of the rich experience of remembering. The wardrobes and soundtracks made combined use of the visual and auditory cues that drive autobiographical memory processes (Willander, Sikström, and Karlsson 2015), a synergy that generated the successful re-creation of vivid memories of youth in these sensory interviews. Yet, multiple memory resources were not always required to activate strong memories; encounters with just one artifact or image from the wardrobe or a singular track triggered vivid, multisensory visual, auditory, tactile, or olfactory experiences. Often it is sight or sound that evokes touch as physical feelings are imagined or re-experienced in the present, in response to an image or musical track. In the multisensory interview environment, rich, textured memories were reported even when the physical dress or music artifact were not present. The snapshots played an important role, as they provided access to the "memory wardrobe," supported by the soundtracks, and sometimes the material artifacts, providing multisensory triggers which served to illuminate and expand the image or dress memory. While instant access to memories through music is upheld by scientific literature, to date there is no equivalent science-based evidence of how similar "snapshot" memories of dress are formed. However, while the scientific approach may go some way to providing hard evidence of access to memory through music, it often lacks the focus on personal experience, emotion, and meaning that is more common in dress research. This suggests scope for further cross-disciplinary research investigating how memories form through multisensory interactions with dress and music.

The interviews and "memory toolkit" were found to be effective methods for reflecting on youth, as dress and music acted as conduits or "tokens of youth" through which the participants re-experienced their past. This led to insights into the significance of music and dress practices during youth and how those memories endure. The combined sensory power of the dress images and artifacts with the musical soundtracks created a sensory-rich environment, impacting on the act of creative and imaginative remembering. The "memory wardrobe"—conceptualized in this study as a space where imaginative remembering brings together the tactile, visual, or imagined memories of dress—expands the possibilities of dress research where original garments are absent. Unlike the content of the physical wardrobe, the "memory wardrobe" contains all potential imagined aspects of dress including memories of hair, bodily sensations, and emotional connections to our clothing. In the "memory wardrobe" intangible aspects of dress can be accessed, where memory and meaning are created, as opposed to the physical wardrobe where garments tend to lie dormant until they are worn. Working hand in hand with the "memory soundtrack" these metaphorical wardrobes store the peak experiences and memories of youth that illuminate our present and accompany us into the future.

Notes

1 Marian (2018), interviewed by author, March 13. Born 1942 in Greater Manchester. Influences include rock and roll. Her memory toolkit included vinyl records, photograph albums, and clothes from her youth.

2 The Platters, "Smoke Gets in Your Eyes." [7" Vinyl Record] Mercury Records, UK, 1958.

3 Youth cultures in this context refer to the everyday cultural practices of young people, not specific subcultures or groups.

4 For dress, see Buse and Twigg (2016), Hunt (2014), Slater (2014); for music, see Baird and Samson (2015), Green (2016), Schulkind, Hennis and Rubin (1999); for music and photographs, see Pickering and Keightley (2015); and for photographs, see Kuhn (1995) and Stewart (1999).

5 Genres of music that the participants related to included rock, rhythm and blues, soul, mod, Motown, punk, indie, pop, and rock and roll.

6 See also Kealy-Morris in this volume.

7 See Banim and Guy (2001) and Bye and McKinney (2007) for studies on unworn clothing.

8 See also Webb in this volume.

9 Eight-tracks were a short-lived tape-recording technology that preceded the cassette tape.

10 Heather (2018), interviewed by author, July 26. Born 1950 in Staffordshire. Influences include rock, R&B, and soul music. Her memory toolkit included music memorabilia (vinyl records, compact discs, cassette tapes, scrapbooks), photograph albums, and clothes from her youth.

11 Mo (2018), interviewed by author, March 24. Born 1955 in Cumbria. Influences include Motown and pop. Her memory toolkit included a digital soundtrack, photograph albums, and digital copies of photographs from her youth.

12 Color or black-and-white photographic film used in single-lens reflex cameras (also known as SLRs).

13 Janet (2018), interviewed by author, February 21. Born 1965, in Greater Manchester. Influences include mod, punk, and indie. Her memory toolkit included music memorabilia (records, CDs, tapes) and photograph albums.

14 Woven webbing belt with a sliding buckle that allows the excess belt to fall free. Inspired by similar military designs and made popular as a fashion item in the early 1980s, usually worn with denim jeans.

15 Research into everyday dress and memory within the academic field of material culture includes studies by Buse and Twigg (2016), Chong Kwan, Laing, and Roman (2014), Hunt (2014), and Slater (2014). Pickering and Keightley (2015: 5) referenced Batchen (2004) and Edwards and Hart (2004) in recognition of the tactile, material qualities of photographs, yet in their own work the communicative value of these visual and audio "technologies" dominates over the haptic.

16 Kate (2018), interviewed by author, January 7. Born 1967 in Derbyshire. Influences include indie (previously a professional drummer). Her memory toolkit included music memorabilia (vinyl records, CDs, scrapbooks), photograph albums, digital copies of photographs, and clothes from her youth.

17 Tameside is an area in Greater Manchester.

18 C. Stevens, "How Can I Tell You," *Teaser and the Firecat*. [Played on iPad through Spotify] Island Records, UK, 1971.

19 Helen (2018), interviewed by author, July 16. Born 1954 in Greater Manchester. Influences include mods, Motown, and the Beatles. Her memory toolkit included music memorabilia (vinyl records), a digital soundtrack, and photograph albums.

20 Earworms or involuntary musical imagery (INMI) are defined as "the experience of a short section of music that comes into the mind without effort" (Floridou et al. 2015: 29).

21 See also Slater in this volume.

22 Jayne (2018), interviewed by author, October 15. Born 1969, in South Yorkshire. Influences include mod (founder https://soulandmod.com). Her memory toolkit included music memorabilia (tickets and flyers), a digital soundtrack, photographs, and digital copies of photographs from her youth.

23 Stylo was a Bradford-based, UK, shoe brand founded in 1935.

24 See also Çili and Slater in this volume.

6

Ken Tynan's Tommy Nutter Jacket as "Materialized Memory"

Ben Whyman

Figure 6.1 Wool and mohair jacket, by Tommy Nutter, T.514-1995 © Victoria and Albert Museum, 1970. Author's own photograph.

This chapter interrogates the complex and dynamic relationships between memory and the biography of objects. It focuses on one object, a safari jacket[1] by British designer Tommy Nutter,[2] that belonged to Kenneth Tynan (1927–80) and is now housed in the collection of the Victoria and Albert Museum (V&A), London.[3] Tynan was a theater critic and writer for publications, such as the *Observer* newspaper and *New Yorker* magazine, and literary manager (*dramatürg*) at the National Theatre in London. He was known for his writing on musicians, actors, cultural, and political players. From an early age, Tynan strove to dress stylishly, and his dress was influenced by mid-twentieth-century jazz musicians (Whyman 2019: 75). Later the revitalization of the UK cultural scene, sparked in "cool" swinging London in the 1960s,[4] encouraged him to wear brightly patterned shirts and ties. Tynan's stylish suiting, the way he allowed himself to be photographed in a very studied manner in magazines like British *Vogue* (with cigarette held between third and fourth fingers),[5] and contemporary descriptions of him as a "character"[6] strongly suggest he was purposefully using clothes and demeanor to construct a representation of a mid-twentieth-century *bon viveur*. Using Tynan's jacket, I explore how such an object becomes evidence of "materialized memory" (Krasner 2010: 41; Abel 2013) and a carrier of personal biographies and histories. I consider Tynan's jacket as a form of material biography—a package of memories (Belk [1995] 2001: 92), a transmitter of experience, and a legacy of a life.

My research analyzes the memory of materiality inherent in clothing that has physically taken on the shape of someone's body over time. The relationships between surfaces interact with the surfaces of memories. The materiality of our clothes is tangible memory, lying somewhere between the surfaces of skin and cloth. Relationships between our worn clothes and our physical bodies stain and crease materials, and this physical evidence marks each garment we wear, telling stories about who we are as individuals. Using the material culture analysis research method, outlined in Jules Prown's (1982, 2001) and Ingrid Mida and Alexandra Kim's (2015) work, I analyze the concept of materialized memory found *on* and *in* the jacket worn by Tynan. The triangulation of embodiment between bodies, memory, and clothes is also sketched out for contemplation.

Materialized memory as a concept has its foundations in archaeology, but since the early 2000s has appealed to researchers whose interest in memory as a tool for locating meaning and connections between objects and humans has aided understandings of the complex dynamics of these relationships. Within the context of this chapter, I define materiality as the constituent parts, the stuff and fabric making up an object, its wear and tear, and state of repair. It is well documented that the wearing of clothes leaves physical imprints, marks, stains, creases.[7] Body and clothing rub against each other, leaving patination, the imprint of embodied presence as a tangible record of biography on and within the object (see Baert 2017). These material qualities are evidence of the relationship between the wearer and the worn object. The coexisting nature of textures, forms, skin, surfaces, and other surrounding objects influences our interpretation of them. Artist Janis Jefferies (2007: 283) uses the notion of "labored cloth" to materialize these interpretations. It is an evocative phrase with which to encounter our feelings toward clothes: from production to everyday use, perhaps altered over time, and finally discarded (thrown away, or, like Tynan's jacket, accessioned in a museum collection).

In the parlance of fashion studies, the notion of "the memory of cloth" has taken on rich metaphorical meanings.[8] Memory in this context refers to the wrinkles left behind after clothes have been worn—the creases in the elbows and behind the knees molded in the cloth (Stallybrass [1993] 1999). This is a symbolically rich mine to source for allusions to the memory of a life, past and present. The physical evidence of a life lived within a garment is important to reflect on when discussing fashion and memory. We form memory through physical touch and bodily actions, we form attachments, establish dependencies, and develop knowledge, which, conflated with metaphors and symbols, blossom "into trees and forests of connections and meanings" (Amato 2013: 37).

It is worth remembering that, as Susannah Radstone states, "memory means different things at different times" (2000: 3). Our sociocultural perspectives influence how we approach, critique, and use memory in our daily lives, in research, and in our approaches to the study of cultural and material memory. What is worth noting is that "memories *continue to be* memories" (Radstone 2000: 11 [original emphasis]): as in, they continue to exist, if recorded in some way, as a form of proof of lives lived. Annette Kuhn states how "the past is unavoidably rewritten, revised, through memory; and memory is partial: things get forgotten, misremembered, repressed" (2000: 184). Intangible memories are interpreted through their tangible, physical materiality; our individual sociocultural perspectives influence the application and analysis of those memories.

So, what can constructing biographies of a subject's clothing reveal that wasn't known before? In 1928, Virginia Woolf reflected in her novel *Orlando*: "vain trifles as they seem, clothes have, they say, more important offices than merely to keep us warm. They change our view of the world and the world's view of us" (Woolf 1928: 92). Claudia Mitchell's (2012: 43) notion of the importance of investigating the "dressed stories" of someone's life is apposite to this argument. Russell Belk (1994: 321) also refers to personal possessions as personal archives reflecting the self, source material for us to reflect on our personal histories and place in culture and society.[9] I develop these ideas in this chapter, encouraging biographical researchers and curators to approach a subject's clothing as evidence of their life, to examine the tangible signs of materiality with which to expand an understanding of the subject's biography.

In 1995, the V&A accessioned a number of garments and accessories of Tynan's that had been forwarded by the British Library (which had been gifted a trunk full of paper ephemera from his family after his death, including clothes the library did not wish to accession). I propose Tynan's clothing, as a group of objects that once formed part of his personal wardrobe, be described as a *post-wardrobe*, now they are stored in the museum. They have left the domestic, private space of home and become part of a museum fashion collection, where opportunities for biographical research, curation, display, and interpretation are possible. The wardrobe in the collection is a fragmented, incomplete reflection of Tynan's wardrobe, including twelve suits, three overcoats, four jackets, nineteen shirts, thirty-five ties, one dressing gown, and one wallet. My aim is to suggest the rich evidence clothing as material artifact contributes to life stories and memories. How did Tynan wear his clothes? What could the materiality of his garments reveal? What could this analysis, alongside interrogation of his paper ephemera and associated archives, uncover that might amplify our understanding of his life?

How Tynan Saw Himself

Exploring things like Tynan's Tommy Nutter jacket is an opportunity to analyze the effectiveness of constructing a biography of an item of someone's clothing.[10] It also highlights the use of informed assumption as a method within life-writing practices, reflected in my use of the image of Tynan sitting (on the left) with actor Laurence Olivier (1975; Figure 6.2). Was Tynan wearing the Nutter jacket in this image? The silhouette is similar, there appear to be buttons at the cuff which correlates to the row of buttons on the Nutter garment. Throughout this chapter, informed assumption plays a role in the construction of biographical narrative.

Figure 6.2 Photograph of Tynan and Laurence Olivier, September 12, 1975 © BBC Archive. Reproduced with permission.

In order to explore Tynan's construction of style, I analyze the Nutter safari jacket (Figure 6.1) to begin a biography of this object and reflect on how it can enhance our understanding of his personal life story.

Tommy Nutter Black Wool and Mohair "Sharkskin" Safari Jacket

A work ticket sewn into the inside right breast pocket states in faded blue, handwritten ink the number "423" alongside Tynan's name and "12 May

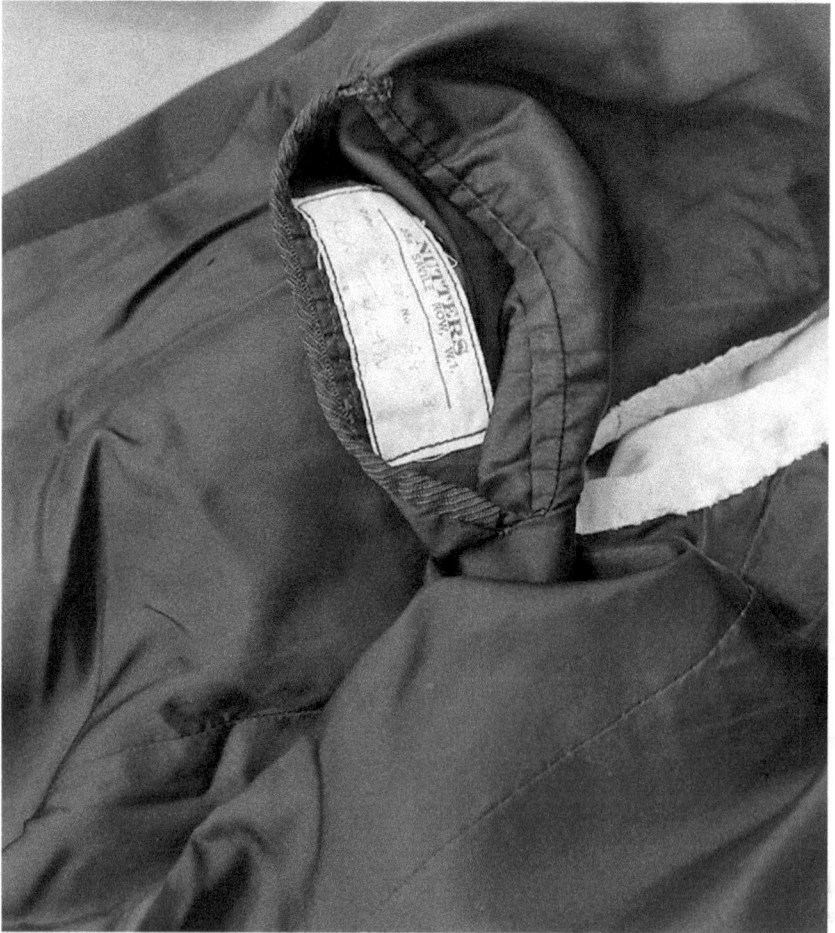

Figure 6.3 Detail of work ticket, wool and mohair jacket by Tommy Nutter, T.514-1995 © Victoria and Albert Museum, 1970. Author's own photograph.

1970"—likely indicating the date he received the coat (Figure 6.3). The extensive wear and tear on this expertly tailored garment made of good-quality cloth strongly suggests Tynan wore this jacket over an extended period of time. It can be assumed that he saw this as, if not one of his favorite garments to wear, then certainly an everyday garment worn with a variety of outfits and accessories. The finely woven material would probably also have been suitable for the warmer Los Angeles climate, where Tynan lived from 1976 until his death in 1980.

Tynan ordered this coat when Nutter's business had been open little more than a year, at a time when the designer's work was perceived as stylish and fashionable. Nutter's provocative design vocabulary reflected Tynan's own incendiary nature, as a writer, *dramatürg*, and in his often confrontational personal and professional relationships. Tynan's choice of clothing was a reflection of his personal identity. His writing, the (at times) controversial choice of plays he programmed at the National Theatre (Tynan 1988: 225–9, 303), and the wearing of striking Nutter clothing suggest he was willing to provoke responses from people.

The jacket is made of a very popular suiting fabric of the mid-1960s, a two-tone sharkskin. It is a very hard-wearing wool and mohair blended twill weave material with a slight sheen. A vent is cut long into the back center seam, almost to the natural waistline, creating a curved, fitted shape to the lower half of the jacket. Darts are machine-stitched, with extra vertical darting in the back panels shaping the coat close to the body from the shoulders to the waist. A broad yoke across the shoulders is a common feature of safari jacket design. Both front panels feature bellows patch pockets and gun-metal buttons, and a wide, flared collar. The buttonholes are hand-stitched on the pocket flaps and lapel hole, cuffs, and front panels. This indicates that the Nutter workshop was consciously spending time on areas of the garment that would receive the most wear. The acetate lining has been sewn in by hand.

There are worn and damaged areas on this coat, some of which appear to have been repaired by professional repairers, perhaps even in Nutter's workshop (Figure 6.4). The right side of the coat is damaged more than the left, including small holes consistent with cigarette burns. The material of the front right bellows patch pocket is heavily worn and, alongside a tear at the top front edge of the pocket, was professionally repaired with hand-stitching. I assume that the heavy use of this pocket indicates it was used more than the left pocket (which shows less wear), suggesting that Tynan was right-handed. He wrote and smoked with his right hand. At the elbow of the right sleeve are two rectangular repairs, one much wider than the other and both approximately five centimeters in length.

Figure 6.4 Right side of front of wool and mohair jacket, showing some pocket repair detail and elbow patch repairs, by Tommy Nutter, T.514-1995 © Victoria and Albert Museum, 1970. Author's own photograph.

These repairs have been made with material cut from the lower front inside lining panel (Figure 6.5) which in turn have been replaced with two rectangular pieces of material, one similar to that of the jacket, the other of a satin-weave finish. Going by the different quality of hand-stitching, the two repairs and replacements were made by different people, perhaps on separate occasions.

In light of this evidence, I argue that the materiality of the garment, analyzed through material culture analysis,[11] tells us something of Tynan's behaviors, nature, use, and demands of his clothing which, conflated with existing material of his life, contributes to his biography. If we did not have preexisting biographical information (his letters, photographs, publications), a jacket like this would tell us about a bias of movement around the right side of his body. The contextual evidence proves Tynan smoked, but if we did not have this material, we would still have the evidence of burn damage on the cloth—which we could say was proof of cigarette smoking. Using informed assumption, we can interpret the wear of this garment—the worn elbows, burn holes, and damaged pocket—to assume that it was regularly worn and potentially a favorite item of clothing.

Memory *in* Cloth

To compare the repairs of one elbow on this garment with the unrepaired material on the other is not only useful for comparative analysis of cloth, design, and manufacture but evocative of materiality and the biography of the object itself. I suggest that we can, working with ideas from new materialism (see Barad 2011), consider the phrase "memory *in* cloth" to explore agency as a protagonist in a two-way relationship between the body and clothing. This informs an understanding of the containment of energy that impacts on the body and on worn clothing.

The importance of studying the everyday action of bodily movement evidenced in clothing can inform our understanding of a life story; where people moved and in what environment; how they moved; what garments they moved in. Heike Jenss (2015) states how memory is imbued in fashion. Memory and fashion are practices that are "material, embodied, enacted" (Jenss 2015: 8). She describes how there is an active relationship between clothing and the body (reflecting new materialist concepts around a two-way relationship of agency, between body and clothing): "this is nowhere more evident than in the material culture of clothing, which imprints itself in all its materiality on the human body, molding its physical shape, affecting corporeality or subjectivity, and the embodiment of dress and style through the wearer" (Jenss 2015: 7).

As described earlier, Tynan's jacket becomes evidence of his life story, using the patterns of wear and tear marked on his clothes: his way of moving, working at a writing desk (leaning heavily on his elbows and wearing the cloth away). The uneven damage to the garment evidences the length of time he must have worn the garment for it to be damaged to the extent that one elbow had to be patched and the other is threadbare, which raises the question of why only one elbow was repaired. Reflecting on the (historically) everyday task of repairing worn clothes is useful here. Victoria Kelley (2015) describes the afterlife in maintenance of cloth and the invisible and ongoing narratives inherent in cloth, and it is a valuable metaphorical direction when analyzing someone's life story through their clothes. I also reflected on the consequences of my assumptions around how this garment was shaped by Tynan's body. Was he repeatedly using the same pocket or was this chance incident, such as him accidently catching and tearing the material of the right sleeve? We cannot assume that the damage was necessarily caused by the wearer's body—but, perhaps, by coincidental external (environmental) forces. I had to treat these ideas and my assumptions with caution and present interpretations and ideas rather than fixed notions.

It is in the repair of Tynan's Nutter jacket as much as the remaining, unrepaired, and worn away cloth at the left elbow that makes the material culture analysis findings so eloquently biographical. He had this garment repaired so that he could continue wearing it. The maintenance and afterlife of the object, and lack of repair on the left elbow, are part of the jacket's story. When, in oral history interviews, I highlighted the material wear and tear and mending to the Nutter jacket to Tracy Tynan, his daughter, by actress and author Elaine Dundy (Tynan's first wife),[12] she was surprised. Her perception of her father's use of his clothes took on new meanings for her, as she realized that her father considered his clothes differently from how she had remembered him wearing them. Her memories of her father centered on a smart-looking man, not someone wearing clothes showing visible signs of damage and repairs. Tracy's altered perceptions of her father's dressing contribute to the garment's biography.

The necessary repairs also corroborate the suggestion that Tynan was wearing his clothes over long periods of time. This commitment to his clothes, his wearing them even in a disheveled state, augments the visual and literary analytical research of his life story that I undertook to expand my construction of a biography of his clothes. He showed commitment to his life's work of writing and dramaturgy, and chose the people he committed to carefully. Many of his clothes were cared for and often repaired—the Nutter jacket on at least

Figure 6.5 Detail of internal panel of replaced rectangle patches, wool and mohair jacket, by Tommy Nutter, T.514-1995 © Victoria and Albert Museum, 1970. Author's own photograph.

two occasions. Even in a state where repairs and damage were obvious, he continued to wear them. A number of assumptions can be made, or at least possible interpretations, not least economic circumstance. It is noted that in the final years of his life, Tynan was seldom healthy enough to write, so his income was much reduced (Kathleen Tynan 1988). This could explain how a damaged jacket could indicate his inability to afford repairs and the need to wear the same clothes for longer. Other interpretations might include Tynan having no time, or inclination, to fix the damage; his wearing clothes for long periods of time, with little interest in what would be considered fashionable menswear; a functional, utilitarian approach to his clothing; and a commitment to caring for the things he lived with. It may also have been a jacket that he loved and wore often, and this pleasure in wearing took precedence over its slightly shabby appearance. This jacket posed enticing questions that were corroborated by object-based analysis and enhanced my understanding of Tynan's approach to life: a snob about people but not about clothes; prepared to purchase good-quality garments and repair them; or continue wearing something even in a disheveled state for the joy of wearing it, something stylish that made him feel fashionable and comfortable. This suggests a complicated and complex personality. It also reflects an object that is infused with materialized memory through being cared for in a museum collection and analyzed by me and potentially other researchers.

Tynan died in 1980. The loss or death of someone impacts our "relationship" to the material objects left behind. Reflection on this is important when considering Tynan's worn clothing and my interpretation of them for this research. The objects are, in a way, released from ownership, to be owned or collected by relatives, or, in this case, donated to and easily accessible in museum collections.[13] The accessibility to these objects in these institutions offers many research opportunities for biographical researchers and curators like myself. Within a museum's collection, fashion becomes "pieces" or "objects" (and, perhaps, more than just "clothes"), for curators and biographical researchers to research and interrogate and make (hopefully) informed assumptions about.

Peter Stallybrass ([1993] 1999) has explored material culture and materiality within a personal context of loss. He describes the coming and going of mortal bodies, and the clothing worn by the deceased remaining behind: torn, damaged, soiled, and yet a physical manifestation of memories of lives lived. Margaret Gibson (2008) continues this thread of thought when describing the impact of clothing on our understanding of someone's life after death. She notes, in oral testimony research into death and material culture, that interviewees focused their grief on objects of the deceased, particularly photographs and clothing. Certain objects such as household items (kitchen utensils, televisions, radios) are not commonly associated with feelings of attachment, specific stories, or memories, whereas personal objects such as photographs or clothes often hold personal resonance (Gibson 2008: 4). I propose that photographs of someone seldom reflect the *physical*, material impact of their bodies lived in clothing, whereas the actual garment itself, imprinted with "the shape, size and odor of the lived body . . . has a power of immediacy that photographs perhaps lack" (Gibson 2008: 111). Photographs and clothes owned and worn by a deceased person are two types of things people in their grief are least likely to give away. This is confirmed by writer and essayist Joan Didion (2006), when she acknowledged her inability to give away her dead husband's clothing, the magnetic pull toward objects retaining for her the memories, symbolic or otherwise, of her husband, and their tangible, physical memories (see also Robyn Gibson 2015). Sherry Turkle describes a Freudian psychoanalytical perspective on loss: "when we lose a beloved person or object, we begin a process that, if successful, ends in our finding them again, within us. It is, in fact how we grow and develop as people. *When objects are lost, subjects are found*" (Turkle 2007: 9–10 [original emphasis]). It is in the retaining of personal objects where they offer access to archives of memory, recollected through lived experience and between the making, and the recapturing, of memory.

Three-dimensional, textural clothing molded to a human body impacts our analysis of its materiality when it is altered beyond its intended construction by the wearer. We imprint our clothing through wearing: clothes "can become imbued with personal scent and bear the marks of wear, from fabric erosion at hem, cuffs and neck to stains that are absorbed or linger on the surface of the cloth" (de la Haye, Taylor and Thompson 2005: 22). The senses are utilized when analyzing clothing, from visual and haptic to smell, and memories created and imbued in the object when closely associated with someone (a relative or partner). The odor of a relative's clothing once they have died or touching the objects "may be more effective in momentarily (although never entirely) bridging the space-time separation that distances the living from the dead" than an image alone might conjure (Gibson 2008: 111). There is a sense of the impact the physicality of an object like an item of clothing can have on our understanding and memories of the wearer, and how memory is entangled in our reading of the thing itself. For instance, Tynan's clothing has been invested with meaning by numerous people: his family and friends (mourning his death and their loss); the public viewer (making sense of this person through viewing their clothing); museum curators and conservators (protecting and contextualizing the objects); and researchers (recontextualizing and interpreting the complexities of someone's life through objects and constructing narratives). How these participants' memories feed into the continuing life narrative of the deceased is reflected in the power of clothing to act as materialized memory.

Gibson (2008) captures the very real sense that objects take on symbolic meanings as much, if not more so, when someone dies than when they were alive.

> When a loved one dies, suddenly their personal belongings and defining possessions come to the foreground of consciousness—they are *truly noticed*. This noticing is complex and often poignant. Death reconstructs our experience of personal and household objects in particular ways; there is the strangeness of realizing that *things* have outlived *persons*, and, in this regard, the materiality of things is shown to be more permanent than the materiality of the body. (Gibson 2008: 1 [original emphasis])

The fact that objects can outlast the life of the owner—the afterlife of a thing—is important to reflect on at this point. Gibson (2008: 2) continues, "for those who outlive a loved one, the objects that remain are significant memory traces and offer a point of connection with the absent body of the deceased" (see also Robyn Gibson 2015). We hold on to the deceased through the objects they owned, surrounded themselves by, and wore (Gibson 2008: 3). Elizabeth Abel (2013: unpag.) reinforces the relationships between "transitional objects" (from a psychoanalytic perspective, those objects that help us transition from one life stage to another, such as the death of parents and guardians) and complex relational negotiations between the afterlife of objects when imbued with memories of the dead. Elizabeth Crooke's (2013) research undertaken with family members of deceased victims of the Bloody Sunday event in Northern Ireland in 1972[14] explores the idea of an object taking on a melancholic symbolism, laden with emotional value and meaning. Her oral history work with these family members, as well as working with the clothing worn by their relatives at the time of their death, brings forth her suggestion that the encoding and production of meanings, through the everyday garments, acted as a means to organize experience, reinforcing a permanence to the relationships with their dead relatives. Crooke (2013: unpag.) described the life stories of the deceased's artifacts as "heavy with consequence."

Clothing carries emotionally charged and symbolic connections and meaning that are imbued in the cloth itself, given it is impregnated with the smell, sweat, and materialized memory, and in the case of some objects Crooke (2013) was working with, blood of deceased Bloody Sunday victims. Working within the boundaries of the museum, where objects can be displayed in a public space, Crooke described how objects are intimately related to the self. In this case, the human beings who wore these garments did not survive to tell their tales; only the clothes remained to bear witness to the events. I reinforce the sense of the memory of cloth found in its materiality—the indentation of the body and the indentations left in the mind—heavy with consequence once someone has died (following Crooke 2013).

As Gibson (2008: 10) suggests, these objects take on another "life," profoundly connected to memories of ourselves and others in death. These connections are often more profound but are usually unarticulated and hidden (Gibson 2008). Noted previously, Tracy Tynan's perceptions of her father's clothing were affected by the record of materiality evidenced in the garments. She was compelled to renegotiate her relationship to these objects once I had pointed out elements of Tynan's dress (the amount of damage, repair, and use on many of the garments) that she had not been aware of previously.

Stallybrass ([1993] 1999) has explored material culture and materiality within a personal context of loss. His article "Worn Worlds: Clothes, Mourning and the Life of Things" has greatly influenced this research. In it, he describes the death of a friend. On being gifted one of the deceased's jackets, he formulated ideas on the power of objects to symbolically reflect a life lived. As he states:

> The magic of cloth, I came to believe, is that it receives us: receives our smells, our sweat, our shape even. And when our parents, our friends, our lovers die, the clothes in their closets still hang there, holding their gestures, both reassuring and terrifying, touching the living with the dead. (Stallybrass [1993] 1999: 28)

Stallybrass describes the "memory" of cloth, a symbolically rich mine to source for allusions to the memory of a life, past and present. It is this palpable, physical evidence of a life lived within garments like Tynan's Nutter jacket which has been important to reflect on during my research.

It is important to note that memories are often clouded by what objects remain of someone's life and people's perceptions of what truth is, or was (depending on the time frames of when they, or their biographers, captured the memories, analyzed them, and crafted a narrative from them), of the things that remain. It is important to remember that in the practice of telling the story of someone else's life, even with evidence to disprove the timing, outcomes, or impact of a life event, it is also necessary to respect the person's right to remember and mis-remember that event of their own life in their own way (Thomas 2013; Phillips 2016).

Memories start from the self, and either remain that way, are studied and analyzed by oneself or someone else, or become part of a wider form of collective memory. Daniel Miller (2008) views memories as artifacts in themselves (see also Dillon 2015). I argue that working with new materialist theory, fashion objects contain agency (movement being the critical element in a physically proximate two-way relationship between body and garment), acting as a constant conduit through the malleable nature of the artifacts of memory (Barad 2011; Miller 2005). Materiality of cloth is evidence that something has happened. In this way, the memories, and the material qualities on the surface of Tynan's jacket, become a kind of recollection. Hugh Haughton (2013), in describing the imprint on paper of a leaf gifted within a letter, questioned how much room for memory an object can have. In the same way, I interrogated the imprint of memory on Tynan's jacket. It literally becomes physically impressed with memory through creases, the degradation of the threads, and stains on the cloth telling their own stories for the researcher to explore. This afterlife of a life, I argue, is the materiality of memory *in* cloth. This suggests the potentially *limited*, and *limitless*, meaning and significance objects can be imbued with and by us: the wearer and the biographical researcher. Given Haughton's descriptions of the imprint of memory, I believe the clothes Tynan wore are imprinted with physical memory.

Traveling Clothes, Shifting Memories

The nomadic, diasporic nature of material culture, specifically clothing, is of particular interest to this research. One needs only to analyze the migration of Tynan's Nutter jacket: purchased in London in 1970; to Los Angeles in 1976; Tynan's death in 1980; a move back to London; and finally, via the British Library to the V&A Clothworker's Centre.[15] As a garment like this shifts and moves through homes, cities, and across borders, regularly worn on his body and moving through many different environments, it takes on different stories. Each narrative adds to its material biography. Paul Basu (2015) describes how all objects are, in a sense, migrant things—constituent materials travel great distances, objects travel with humans, and are handled by other people and placed in different contexts (see also Gibson 2008). Anne Gerritsen and Giorgio Riello (2015: 7) note how no object is stable: "they take meaning in space and time, they change as human thoughts about them change, and it is in the human-object relationship that history is written." Where do objects belong after one biography ends? I argue that dispossession or transition of objects need not be a negative state. Possession by a new owner only acts to extend an object's biography. Like Tynan's jacket, the biography of objects is enriched by the journey from maker, to wearer(s), to museum.[16]

In this way, cultural significance is imbued in the object across time and space by those doing the interpreting, such as a curator or biographical researcher. It can be challenging for researchers to contextualize an object's history, as external forces—contemporaneous cultural, sociological, political, economic, historic events—and personal biases can influence the interpreter's understanding of the thing. Once placed in a museum collection the object is imbued with second, third, fourth (ad infinitum) biographies. Different researchers, depending on their training, background, and perspective, will propose other stories. The object becomes laden with these narratives—remember Crooke's "heavy with consequence" (2013: unpag.). This afterlife is influenced by discourses of continuity when constructing a biography of an object. The resonance of objects is often lost when they are recontextualized in a different environment: in the case of Tynan's jacket, from personal possession to museum collection.[17] I reiterate James Krasner (2010) and Abel's (2013) ideas that objects can become "materialized memory" to reinforce my argument. Very often the presence of an artifact hides an absence. Dispossessed things lapse "into oblivion with every extinguished life," especially if they are no longer useful (Sebald 2011: 24). I concur with Abel's (2013: unpag.) question: if we grant an object a life, do we grant it a death?

Making the capturing of memory even more challenging and enriching, beyond its inherent vulnerability and our personal biases, Adam Phillips (2016) suggests that respecting broken stories—the gaps in memory and information—can be important. Leaving memory alone—the memories hidden from our mind's eye—might be advisable at times for ours', and others', well-being. These gaps can also be, as Woolf described them, the moments of "non-being" in a life, where seemingly not much happens (cited in Schulkind [1976] 1989: 79; see also Strohm 2014). These spaces in a life open up space for interpretation, making a creative place where the reader of a biography or viewer of an exhibition can create narratives in their own minds. The times in Tynan's life when nothing much was happening is ripe with narrative for researchers. Tynan was wearing his clothes during quiet, non-eventful periods in his life, including his Nutter jacket, and it continued to accrue evidence of living, through wear and tear and material change. Now, in the museum collection, slow but sure degradation of material is a continuation of its post-wardrobe life.

Memory and Conclusions

The imprint of Tynan's body on his Tommy Nutter safari jacket is evidential proof of his life story, as well as part of the biography of the object itself. Through material culture analysis and object-based research, the *wearing* of individual garments, from physical adornment to the material degradation of the garment, contributes to life narratives and materialized memories. These memories contribute to the construction of self-identity and biography, our place in social worlds, and the sharing of histories (see Conway 2015). Memory is a form of material energy, embedded within garments like Tynan's jacket. When something like this tangible object is housed in a museum's collection, it becomes an epistemological thing, open to interpretation as well as the construction of object-based biographies. As an increasing number of tangible objects and memories, such as oral history recordings and filmed events, are being stored in museums, future research into biographical narratives of peoples' lives and broader cultural and social histories will transition as our relationships with material objects evolve. The biography of Tynan's Nutter jacket blossoms and continues.

Notes

1   In tailoring terms, "jacket" and "coat" commonly refer to the same type of garment, a sleeved garment worn on the upper body such as this garment. There are differences, however, when describing topcoats and overcoats which are traditionally longer on the body.

2   British designer Tommy Nutter established a fashionable tailoring business at 35a Savile Row, a street renowned for its conservative tailoring businesses, in February 1969. The designer flouted many established Savile Row traditions, creating a vocabulary of high-quality, classic tailoring for men and women, but shifting the silhouette through shorter-length jackets, square shoulders, and narrow sleeves, highlighted with "youthful" touches such as wide revers, flared trousers, and stylish, contrasting fabrics.

3   T.514-1995: man's jacket, black wool with metal buttons, by Tommy Nutter, London, England, 1970. Victoria and Albert Museum, London. Available online: https://collections.vam.ac.uk/item/O234813/jacket-nutter-tommy/ (accessed November 15, 2014; July 6, 2016; March 16, 2018).

4   Journalists noted how the influence of "youth, pop music, fashion, celebrity, satire, crime, fine art, sexuality, scandal, theatre, cinema, drugs, media" modernized the cultural landscape (Levy 2002: 6).

5   Examples of Tynan captured in British *Vogue* include Gross (1962); Anon (1963); Anon (1969).

6   In his published diaries, actor Richard Burton refers unflatteringly to Tynan, comparing his slender frame in fashionable men's dress to German Second World War concentration camps: "Friday 30th [May 1969] . . . Ken has always looked like Belsen with a suit on. Dachau in Daks. Buchenwald in brown velvet" (cited in Williams 2012: 292).

7   See, for example, Stallybrass ([1993] 1999), de la Haye, Taylor, and Thompson (2005), Miller (2005), Gibson (2008), Harvey (2009), and Jenss (2015).

8   The origin of the phrase in dress history and fashion studies is unclear, but there is suggestion it stems from nineteenth-century garment construction (Stallybrass [1993] 1999).

9   See Çili's chapter in this volume.

10   There is always the ongoing issue for biographical researchers and curators working on people's life stories: the availability, or lack, of a subject's clothing to analyze. This research assumes that this access to a subject's clothes is assured by the relatives or museums that store the objects.

11   Material culture analysis is a three-stage research method of description, deduction, and speculation (Prown 1982) or observation, reflection, and interpretation (Mida and Kim 2015) that conflates visual and textual research. It privileges the object and its materiality, focusing on material and its wear and tear, as well as emphasizing textures, colors, surfaces, and construction.

12   Tracy is the eldest of Tynan's children: he had two further children with his second wife, Kathleen Tynan.

13   See also Beale's and Webb's chapters in this volume.

14   Bloody Sunday, January 30, 1972, was when the British Army shot dead thirteen unarmed civil rights demonstrators and injured fifteen more, in the Bogside area of Derry, Northern Ireland.

15   The Clothworkers' Centre is the storage, study, and conservation center of textiles and fashion at the V&A Museum (https://www.vam.ac.uk/info/the-clothworkers -centre-for-the-study-and-conservation-of-textiles-and-fashion).

16   This is further illustrated by Webb in this volume.

17   Reasons for recontextualization can be that garments have been inherited, that we have found, reclaimed, or associated them with a moment in time such as an event and invested in them our own memories; see Çili, Webb, and Beale in this volume.

7

Soft Murmurings

Sensing Inherited Memories in Collections of Dress

Jane Webb

I began researching at the Gallery of Costume, Platt Hall, in Manchester, UK,[1] having never studied a collection of dress before. The gallery had clothing worn in Britain, though not necessarily made, dating from the sixteenth century to the present day. Alongside dress and accessories, there was a vast body of photographs and ephemera dating from the eighteenth century. What I did not expect was how the Gallery of Costume bristled with lives. As I explored the garments within the collection, something of the people that the clothing had been constructed for could be sensed. As I studied more, my own haunted impressions were reflected in the reports of other scholars describing their experience in collections (Hauser 2004). While most of these accounts were used by way of introduction or as an aside, the work of historian Frank Trentmann (2009) offered more insights. In his investigation of the emergence of capitalism and the role of objects, he proposed that clothing offers a physical sense of the individual in a way that few other possessions can. He describes dress as lying somewhere between "inanimate and animate existence" retaining a status as a "half-life" (Trentmann 2009: 288). This description of an almost supernatural object not only reflected my experience but also offered some explanation of it.

Trentmann's account deals with the history of the relationship between wearer (purchaser) and clothing, but in addition I noticed other encounters between people and the garments hanging in the museum. Through the metal-rimmed circular discs, handwritten fabric labels, and printed linen tags, countless curatorial interventions were implied. These important relationships between museum clothing and those who were not its wearers grew stronger as I watched a range of people engage with the Platt Hall collection. Occasionally visitors and regular staff alike would fleetingly hold the historic garments up to themselves and peer down at the effect. This action seemed so natural and were, what the sociologist Saolo B. Cwerner (2001: 80) describes as "wardrobe practices," our most common experience of clothing. Engaging with dress in storage is an everyday activity for us and, even among professional curators and conservators, these vital objects seemed still to convey a personal intimacy that connected to a sense of self. When I added these museum relationships to my reading of the many letters referring to the donations of clothing to the museum (Figure 7.1), I was left with a powerful impression, not only of the original wearers but of the collectors, donors, and curators who had maintained and shaped the collections over many years. I became fascinated by the history of the clothing in Platt Hall

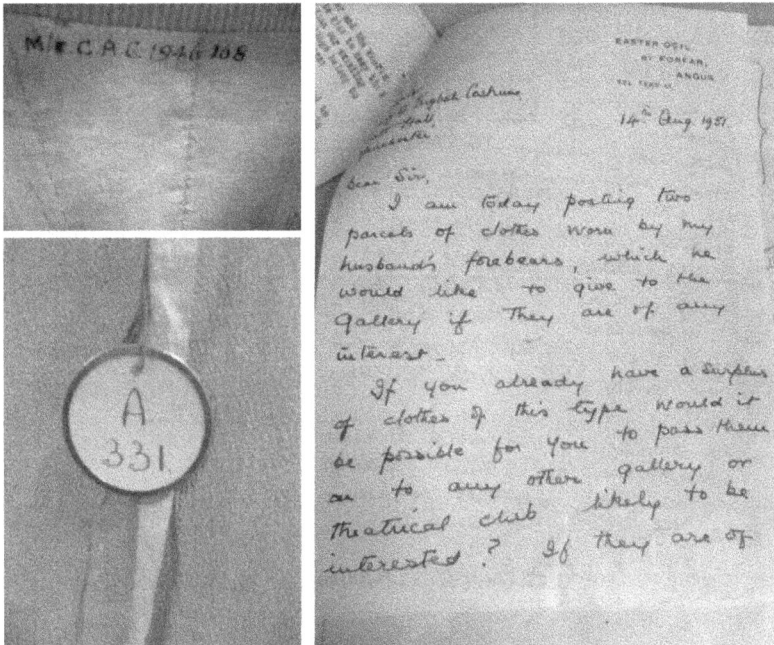

Figure 7.1 Curatorial labeling on clothing from *c.* 1930s (bottom left), handwritten accession number giving year of donation as 1946 followed by number of items donated that year (top left), and an example of a donor letter from Mrs. Naylor, 1951 (right). Author's own photographs, *c.* 2010.

not as a singularly owned object but as one that had passed through numerous hands and that continued to have a life once it was in the collection. But how did all the physical interactions of wearer, guardian, and curator make these objects feel partially alive? Was it just the uncanny nature of their material form—their human shapes—or were they alive with something else? It struck me that this something might potentially be connected to memory. But how might such memory work?

My only encounter with a study that explored the role of donors and memory within the Platt Hall setting was actually a warning against taking too seriously such an account. The textile historian Santina Levey (2010: 31) wrote, in her cautionary "story of a shirt," how easy it was for the "inherited memory" of donors to skew the perception and interpretation of a garment itself. Levey's own brilliant deduction, while reliant on placing the donor family within a vivid historical context, is essentially a meticulous empirical study of the garment's physicality. It is this study that ultimately confirms the actual date of the garment and thus its genuine history (Levey 2010). An empirical approach to an object was not what I had experienced in my own academic background, rather objects were a deeply contested idea, encapsulated by the use of the term "life" in relation to them. From the seminal work of anthropologist Arjan Appadurai in his book *The Social Life of Things* (1986)[2] to later studies such as art historian Peter Mason's *The Lives of Images* (2001), the term "life" when theorizing about objects bound them inextricably to humans, so much so that confidence in something that could be empirically understood was rarely felt.[3] Yet in Trentmann's description of the "half-life" of clothing, I was struck by the idea of an object that was different from other objects. Clothing, it seemed, was neither object nor subject, inert matter or transient flesh but, depending on whether one's glass was half full or empty, seemed to be humanity not quite free but anchored to material object by something. Again, I decided that this something might be memory and so I turned to that which I had been warned off, inherited memory.

The clothes retained at Platt Hall had many different sources.[4] All of the curators to be associated with the collection regularly acquired historic dress directly from professional dealers, liquidated retail outlets, or auctions, but many items were given by individuals who had obtained clothing through bereavement. Some donations came to the museum when the death of a relative had prompted the removal of their clothing directly from where they had existed in life, but other donation stories revealed a more complex history of guardianship. It is within these entangled tales of people and garments that inherited memories were most commonly offered. This chapter will explore the story of a 150-year journey of three dresses to the collection. I will examine whether the inherited memories that these garments came with might help to understand why clothes encountered in such collections as Platt Hall seem to have a half-life. In doing so I will also explore how an item of clothing develops meaning beyond its original wearing through its manner of storage and how this might continue to develop, even within the professional environment of a museum.

In 1951, a large donation was made to Platt Hall which included three dresses. Figure 7.2 is an Indian muslin dress with ornate train, embroidered with detailed tambour work, dated 1806. Figure 7.3 is an equally elegant though simpler gown, dated 1805–10, made from white muslin. Figure 7.4 is a dress of a similar silhouette but made of a rich yellow figured wool and silk with a small train, dated 1810–12.[5] Unaware, at that time, of the relationships between the garments (two of which hung together, one was separated into another wardrobe), it was the second dress (Figure 7.3) that initially fascinated me because of its acroterion design. The acroterion was a decorative feature of many surviving Classical buildings and reproduced in Neoclassical architecture and furniture (Crook 1968: 63; Hope [1807] 1970). I felt sure, recalling Thomas Hope and Henry Moses' *Designs of Modern Costume* (1823),[6] that its original wearer must have been resident within a Neoclassical setting to have such a fashionable item, and I began to investigate.

The dress I had selected was attributed to Charlotte Margaret Martin and according to the correspondence between its donor Mrs. Ruth Naylor and the curator Anne Buck (Figure 7.1), Charlotte had married a John Edwards in 1806.[7] John was the owner of the Ness Strange estate, their union joining two families of local aristocracy that resided in the same village of Great Ness in Shropshire in the UK (see family tree, Figure 7.5). Charlotte was the daughter of the Reverend George Martin and her mother was Lady Mary Murray to whom the third dress (Figure 7.3) was attributed. Charlotte was the granddaughter of John Murray, the third Duke of Athol, Mary's father (Burke 1837: 78). This connection was retained as the inherited memory of the family.[8]

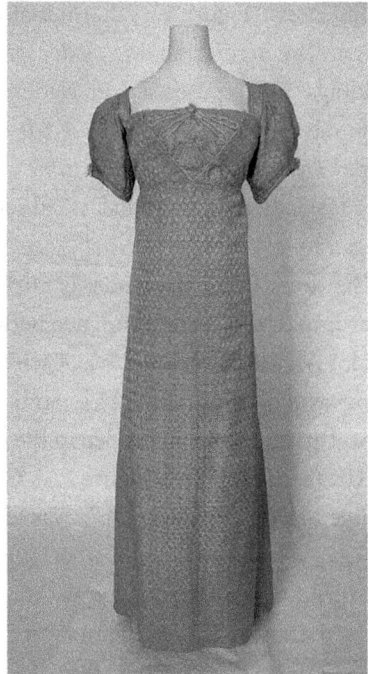

Figures 7.2, 7.3 and 7.4 Wedding dress, 1806, 1951.341 (top); Dress, 1805–10, 1951.342 (bottom left); Dress, 1810–12, 1951.343 (bottom right) © Manchester Art Gallery. Reproduced with permission.

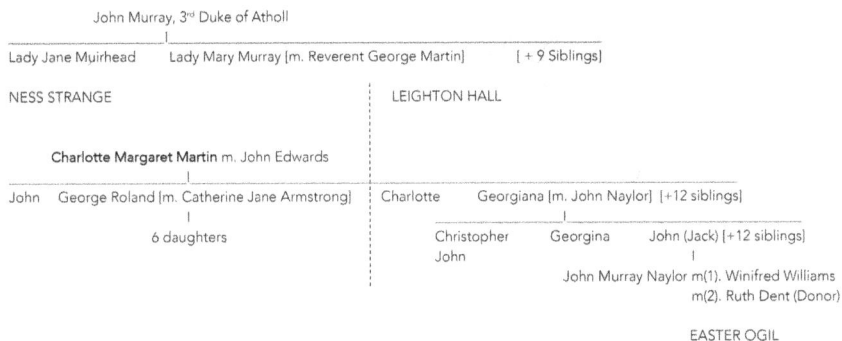

John Murray, 3rd Duke of Atholl

Lady Jane Muirhead — Lady Mary Murray [m. Reverent George Martin] — [+ 9 Siblings]

NESS STRANGE — LEIGHTON HALL

Charlotte Margaret Martin m. John Edwards

John — George Roland [m. Catherine Jane Armstrong] — Charlotte — Georgiana [m. John Naylor] [+12 siblings]

6 daughters — Christopher — Georgina — John (Jack) [+12 siblings]
John

John Murray Naylor m(1). Winifred Williams
m(2). Ruth Dent (Donor)

EASTER OGIL

Figure 7.5 Murray Edwards Naylor family tree © Jane Webb. Reproduced with permission.

Initial research of the Ness Strange manor house suggested some of its features were indeed Neoclassical, as the original 1778 house had been adapted in the early nineteenth century, possibly concurrent with Charlotte and John's wedding (Historic England 2022). The house as it exists today has been transformed repeatedly over the years and now only traces of Neoclassical grandeur can be glimpsed (Figure 7.6).[9] This obvious passage of time and turbulent change initiated the thought that when brick, plaster, and slate seem so much hardier materials than muslin, wool, and silk, three dresses survived to find their way to Platt Hall nearly a century and a half later.

Figure 7.6 Top row (left to right): exterior doorknocker, interior door handle, plaster ceiling rose, at Ness Strange, Author's own photographs, 2019. Bottom: Ness Strange manor house, *c.* 1880–1900, L. Wilding, published postcard, Author's collection.

The donor of Charlotte's dresses was Mrs. J. M. Naylor (Ruth) of Easter Ogil, Angus, Scotland. She was Charlotte Edward's great-granddaughter-in-law and, inspired by a newspaper article, she and her husband, John Murray Naylor, donated a bundle of Victorian garments before suggesting the museum might also want the Murray/Edwards' clothing. This gifting, in which Mrs. Naylor acknowledges that the dresses remained of interest to the family, was done carefully, and Mrs. Naylor was keen to have them returned if they were not of interest to the collection.[10] It is possible that a bereavement may have also prompted the removal of the clothing, as in 1950, Georgina Naylor, who was John Murray Naylor's aunt and the last resident of a place called Leighton Hall, died.[11]

The cultural studies scholar Judith Simpson (2014: 13) has studied the relationship between clothing and bereavement identifying a category of garments that she terms "relic items." These are clothes that stay with the family and help to maintain their connection to the deceased. Significantly, Simpson explains that the clothing kept by the bereaved usually reflects the idealized gender roles that are most valued in life. For a woman, these will typically be a wedding or party dress—the peak of her feminized self—while for a man it will be clothing associated with business prowess or sport (Simpson 2014). Simpson's identification of the types of relic items usually retained match exactly with many of the typical donations made to Platt Hall.

The ritualistic nature of "reducing both the finality of death and the absence of the dead" (Simpson 2017: 8), through the donation of garments to a museum like Platt Hall, enhances the significance of the original owner's identity to the family. In their study of loss and material culture in the UK, anthropologists Daniel Miller and Fiona Parrott (2009) suggest that bereavement begins a process by which an actual relationship with a deceased member of the family shifts to that of a relationship with an ancestor, in which the objects the deceased relative leaves "eventually and effectively turn the deceased gran into a kind of museum figure evocative as much of her period as of herself" (506). In specific reference to clothing and its passage from one person to the next, Simpson (2014: 265–6) explains how garments "modify relationships between the living and the dead . . . facilitat[ing] the transformation of the dead into ancestors." The term "ancestor" is rarely used in the context of social history museums, yet ancestors are precisely what the donors of the garments coming into Platt Hall often understood their donations to be creating.[12] Giving ancestor-status to a person builds on the significance of the deceased individual, but also that of their descendants, as indicated by the careful nature in which the donor Mrs. Naylor wanted to retain a relationship with the garments. They were not to be passed on or destroyed by the curators, rather they were to be returned, even though it is obvious from the correspondence that the donor and closely related family knew very little about the clothing that they sent.[13] Labels on the packaging are briefly mentioned in the correspondence between the donor and Anne Buck,[14] and these must have indicated the lineage that the garments represented. The memory held in these garments in this form is the potency by which they represent a family's or individual's identity shaped by the significance of their ancestors. This ancestral importance is rarely down to their singularity as individuals, but rather driven by the typicality of that ancestor's life and possessions in defining a historical era—they become archetypal.

Reconstructing the Naylor donation from the various categories that it had been dispersed to in the collection revealed that it totaled twenty-one items consisting of the three dresses already described, male clothing including a frock coat and other items owned by a John Naylor and worn by him at his wedding in 1846,[15] male clothing worn later by him,[16] women's clothing from 1850 to 1870,[17] an earlier male under waistcoat,[18] and a boy's dress and undersleeves from 1858 to 1862.[19] Significantly, the clothing had not always been at Easter Ogil but had been removed from Leighton Hall near Welshpool, Wales, at some point.[20]

In 1906, Leighton Hall had passed to John Murray Naylor, the donor's husband. A vast estate, it was an enterprise of the Victorian era, and the economic and social conditions to maintain it grew hostile (Mellers and Hildyard 1989). Published extracts from a letter to his Leighton tenants indicate that it was both increased taxation and huge maintenance costs that forced him to break up Leighton.[21] The estate with its huge grounds, properties, and livestock was sold in 1931 through Morris, Marshall & Poole auctioneers, with Harrods hosting an auction of the contents of Leighton Hall itself. The catalogues for the sale of the estate and hall reveal not only the unwieldy vastness of the estate and its impracticality in the interwar years but also the financial investment and management that it must have taken to create such a property. Of the hundreds of carefully documented buildings, artworks, furnishings, plants, and livestock listed, there is no mention of the three dresses in the inventory or sales of Leighton's contents.[22] For some reason the clothing remained with the family.

The Naylor connection to the Edwards family came through Charlotte and John's fifth daughter. Georgiana Edwards married John Naylor in 1846. In 1856 the couple moved to Leighton Hall which John had rebuilt, a project that was one of Pugin's last works (Pryce 2011: 9). Georgiana's mother and father, Charlotte and John, had died in 1849 and 1850, respectively, resulting in Ness Strange being inherited by their second son, George Roland Edwards. There was an audit of the house contents undertaken just before his return from India, where he resided previously,[23] and although the clothing is not mentioned, it is probable that Charlotte's dresses and other items of clothing were given to Georgiana when she moved into Leighton Hall. I can find no mention of the dresses but Georgiana's sister, also called Charlotte, died in 1851. In her will, Charlotte the younger left various items of memorial jewelry to her sisters including a "bracelet of dear Mamma's hair."[24] It seems likely that sometime between their mother Charlotte's death and the daughter Charlotte's death, the dresses went to Leighton.

When Leighton Hall became the destination for the three Murray/Edwards' dresses and potentially other male garments, these were added to by John Naylor's wedding clothes and what were possibly also those of Georgiana. In the collection only odd garments survive. One imagines that for a time there would have been a wedding dress but this may have been reused by either Georgiana herself or another relative in the same way that the donor Mrs. Naylor had weeded some of the historic clothing, either to discard or to adapt for herself.[25] But whatever it originally consisted of, it is significant that the bundle of clothes from Charlotte and that of the new Naylor family were connected. While they would have also had a very personal connection to Georgiana that I will discuss, seen in the light of her marriage to John Naylor, these items of dress took on an important role for the Naylor family.

Naylor was a partner in the Leyland and Bullins Bank, and, though extremely wealthy, was part of the emerging middle class. It is very probable, therefore, that a marriage match that connected this relatively newly elevated family to one that had derived from the Kings of Wales (John Edwards), and the descendants of Henry VII (Charlotte's connection to the dukes of Athol), however distantly, was very desirable. Even in one of Georgiana's brief obituaries, it is noted that she "was the daughter of the late Mr. John Edwards of Ness Strange, through whom she could trace her descent from the royal Prince of Powys."[26] In the vast space of Leighton's great hall, with its doorway proclaiming "Welcome," a roof frieze with Welsh family shields and other heraldic devices was intended as an obviously public declaration of this lineage—Pugin's Gothic confection, presenting the identity of the new Naylor/Edwards family with a readymade archaism. This emphasis on heritage goes some way to explaining why the clothing got to Leighton. Even though it was no doubt stored out of public sight, its vital presence privately conferred an authenticity to the lineage. Though John Naylor died in 1889 and the property passed down the male line of Naylors, Georgiana remained the figurehead of Leighton Hall and the vast estate, until her own death in 1909. In effect then, even before they entered the museum, the Murray/Edwards' dresses had become ancestor items. But this still does not explain why they had survived so long before being taken to Leighton.

Charlotte and John Edwards married and had twelve children. Like most families in this period, even minor aristocracy like the Edwards, death was a constant in their lives. John, the Edwards' eldest son and heir, died when he was only twenty-six, possibly from complications with either his heart or lungs.[27] The literary scholar Deborah Lutz (2017: 8) describes "secular relics" of death through the Romantic and Victorian periods, noting the prevalence for keeping both first-order (actual parts of the body) and second-order relics (clothing or possessions), by which to memorialize dead relatives and significant others. Lutz suggests that this convention was created through "rising individualism and nationalism," in which identity showed a growing dependence on objects (2017: 31). Trentmann (2009) describes how from the 1770s onward, with the growing sophistication of capitalism, there was an increased sense of ownership where people and their possessions were deemed dependent on each other. Thus "bodies left behind traces of themselves, shreds that could then become material for memories" on such items as clothing (Lutz 2017: 1). The Edwards family had hair jewelry from deceased family members;[28] it is therefore probable that garments were also kept as second-order relics. This might well explain the dress attributed to Lady Mary Murray (Figure 7.4). This dress must have become a relic item for Charlotte after her mother's death in 1814. This is a different type of memory, one that is less abstract than we have seen and is the retaining of a physical remnant of an otherwise absent and dearly missed relative.

Many writers have described the retaining of a dead mother's garments by a child as a very powerful form of remembrance (Dunmore 1998; Picardie 2006; Campbell 2015; Gibson 2015; Vaughan 2015). In her own chapter, "Into My Mother's Wardrobe" within her edited volume, the arts educator Robyn Gibson (2015: 17–21), having acquired two garments from her own mother's wardrobe, writes very poignantly about their role in her bereavement. She ends her chapter by describing how "as I am drifting off to sleep, I hear soft murmurings emanating from my wardrobe. If I listen very carefully, I can hear two special dresses sharing secrets" (Gibson 2015: 21). The terms "murmurings" and "whispering" (Hauser 2004: 299) concur with the haunted atmosphere that I sensed surrounding these semi-animated objects, and it does successfully, I think, convey their odd quality. Clothes of deceased relatives seem to exist both with us and simultaneously elsewhere, they are out of place. For Gibson, there is comfort in this thought—their presence suggests the other that her mother is no longer able to be. But as the literary scholar

Peter Stallybrass ([1993] 2012) describes, there is ambiguity to this temporal and spatial multidimensionality:

> And our parents, our friends, our lovers die, the clothes in their closets still hang there, holding their gestures, both reassuring and terrifying, touch the living with the dead. . . . Bodies come and go; the clothes that have received those bodies survive. They circulate . . . from sister to sister, from brother to brother, from sister to friend. (Stallybrass [1993] 2012: 69)

Looking back at the Naylor donation, at some point, all of the garments would have performed this more intimate role. They did not simply define a lineage but were for individual members of the family, the only tangible link to their loved ones. They, like the garments passed on to Gibson and Stallybrass, murmured and whispered as they were stored. But what is this memory? It seems not to be an impulse contained in the mind of those bereaved but to exist in the qualities of the objects themselves—they are literally an independent presence, a half-life, that one must actively negotiate with in one's present and their past. The answer to this strange vitality lies not just in the basic fact of ownership by the deceased relative but in the manner in which they were themselves worn and stored by their original owner.

Figure 7.7 Portrait in the interior of Ness Strange, *c.* 1862. Accession Number 5358/4/7/16 © Shropshire Archives. Reproduced with permission.

By the time of her death in 1849, Charlotte had already retained her two white dresses for forty years. It is unlikely that she kept all her clothing, as one gets the impression that she was keen on fashion. I believe it is Charlotte who is pictured (Figure 7.7), as an older woman around 1834 (dated with Tarrant 1983), in a portrait that was on one wall of Ness Strange's front drawing room. The dress she wears is ebulliently lacy and highly fashionable for the period, so different from the elegant minimalism of her kept clothing. Letters between herself and her aunt, Lady Jane Muirhead, also suggest that Charlotte regularly commissioned many of her clothes from London.[29] While this does not preclude her storing garments, it does suggest that she frequently reassessed her contemporary wardrobe, and it is more likely that the dresses that survived were kept by Charlotte for a particular reason.

Social scientist Maura Banim and psychologist Ali Guy (2001) have questioned why women keep garments that they no longer wear. Banim and Guy recognized three different types of relationships to an individual's sense of self created through clothes stored. The most common of these being that kept garments helped provide a continuation of the owner's identity from a period or moment in which they were the woman they wanted to be—a reminder of the best version of themselves (Guy and Banim 2000; Banim and Guy 2001). In a study of two stored dresses, one in existence, the other remembered, the dress historian Alison Slater (2014) uses Banim and Guy's ideas to consider clothing stored over a longer period and the intimate interplay between the bodily wearing of an item of clothing and an individual's navigation of their own interpersonal relationships.

Though Banim and Guy and Slater were writing about women from the twentieth and twenty-first centuries, it does not feel anachronistic to ascribe to Charlotte the act of keeping clothing as a symbol of identity because Charlotte was living through the period when selfhood, as we might recognize it, was beginning to emerge. The historian Chris Otter (2008: 11), following Michel Foucault, describes this formation of the "liberal subject"—a model of citizenship that emerged as "a deeply bodily enterprise, a process by which one took the physical attributes of oneself as an object to be worked on." His description echoes that advanced by both Lutz (2017) and Trentmann (2009) in their suggestion that this was the moment that objects began to be indispensable to the expression of identity. Dress was central to this. Early in the nineteenth century commentators had begun to note how important fashion was to define the hierarchical structure of British society.[30] In effect, it was the clothes themselves that ultimately cemented, if not created, one's status. Dress, and the keeping of dress in the manner that many of us do today, might therefore have become a way of developing an individual's "own fund of accumulated experience" in the face of the changes that modernity was bringing about (Keightley and Pickering 2012: 28).

In their study, Banim and Guy suggest that reducing the idea of stored clothing to "memory joggers" is too limiting (2001: 206), and perhaps this is because remembering was considered too static a process or act at the time that they were writing. In contrast, media theorists Emily Keightley and Michael Pickering (2012) propose that there is "no bedrock of memory [that] exists as some permanent and enduring ontological base" (20). Rather, they suggest, memory is entangled with experience and therefore mutable:

> that the subject remembered by the remembering subject alters and shifts from one period of his life to another, along with the meanings and values of autobiographical memories. . . . Consequently, the remembering subject is different from the self in whom the memory was formed, while that memory itself has no fixed form, however precise and vivid it may seem at any specific moment of recollection. (Keightley and Pickering 2012: 20)

This definition of memory-in-action as an ongoing reinvention entangled with the continual shift of lived experience can be overlaid onto the "wardrobe practices" (Cwerner 2001: 80) of Banim and Guy's interviewees. Like the flux of memory that fuels and interacts with identity, the sorting and sifting, retaining, and discarding of garments can be seen to materially and spatially enact this. In this model, clothes are not just "memory joggers" (Banim and Guy 2001: 206), rather clothing is continually working with an individual's memory and is central to how we creatively reinvent our memories and thus our own autobiography. Keightley and Pickering suggest that rather than imagination being understood as in conflict with an authentic memory, instead this continual construction of ourselves is dependent on the ability to imagine in order to rearrange our "hotchpotch of experience into relatively coherent narrative structures" (2012: 43). In relation to our clothes, this is played out by a spatial reordering as we remove some garments and retain others, placing some at the margins of our day-to-day routines (in other rooms or at the back of wardrobes), while others remain more centrally located. While this distancing might seem to weaken the significance of objects for us, the sociologist Sophie Woodward (2015) argues that dormancy, particularly in those objects that have been deliberately put into storage, often makes the status of the object more significant. Like that of the clothing of the dead, this clothing retained for personal reasons must sit elsewhere, slightly at odds to the regular time and space of the domestic home.

Charlotte was a romantic. In the letter dated 1826 from Charlotte to her husband, who was in London at the time of her writing to him, she comments that "tho' I have been married almost 20 years—I shall expect you to fly to me" [original emphasis].[31] They would have been anticipating their wedding anniversary in December of that year, and with this attitude toward her union, it is very probable that Charlotte kept clothing from the period that she was first married. Like so many other donations, it is tempting to imagine that one of these dresses was Charlotte's actual wedding dress but the garments were never described as such by the donor. In the letters they are simply referred to as "[t]wo white sort of muslin dresses (very attractive)" and "Mrs Edwards [*sic*] two white frocks."[32] However, one of them became Charlotte's wedding dress when it entered the collection. This must have been the title assigned to it by Anne Buck who did some confirmatory research to check the date of Charlotte and John's wedding. The *Lancaster Gazette* entry is noted on the original index card and has been transferred to the computer record. This newspaper report does not mention any clothing[33] and so required the use of Buck's experienced empiricism to fill in this gap. Based then on detailed material knowledge, Buck defined this garment as a wedding dress. In this way, alongside family members, the inherited memory of Charlotte's one dress has been extended by the curator and expanded upon by other academics (Sykas 2013). Though I cannot combine an extensive empirical expertise, such as that of Anne Buck and Philip Sykas, with the story of the other Neoclassical dress with the acroterion (Figure 7.3), I do offer a suggestion as to why Charlotte kept it.

Charlotte may have simply loved the muslin dress and felt like the woman she aspired to be when wearing it (Guy and Banim 2000). At the time, magazines like *La Belle Assemblée* claimed that women in such garments were "nymphs."[34] The Neoclassical was promoted from the 1780s by famous figures like Lady Charlotte Campbell who presented themselves as "living statues." This was a style that conveyed a cultured authenticity, honed by Classical artistic understanding for those women who wore it (Rauser 2015). Charlotte was very young in 1806, and this garment would have chimed perfectly with her new home and status—it was a style that seemed to infuse much of the Edwards' lives not only in their architectural surroundings but in small items of personal use.[35] One cannot help imagining that Charlotte must have felt a very particular personal radiance in the garment—one that she might have wanted to retain by keeping the dress with its trace of the best version of herself.

But this feeling of personal positioning, with Charlotte at the focal point of a particular moment in her life, might also have been bolstered by a specific event. It was the dress worn by Lady Mary Murray and dated 1810–12 (Figure 7.4) that made me consider whether there was some connection between Charlotte's Neoclassical dress and this one. Why would Charlotte select that particular dress of her mother's after her mother's death? The garment's manufacture was perhaps too close to her mother's death (1814) to suppose that this had been a long-retained significant garment. I began to wonder if there had been an event that might have linked her own and her mother's garments in some way and during that period there is a possibility—George III celebrated fifty years of his reign in 1809. Though this was actually his forty-ninth year as king, still it was celebrated on October 25 and events took place across the country, including at Great Ness. In this small village John Edwards and Charlotte's father, the Reverend George Martin, were central to the celebrations, as were Charlotte and, it must be assumed, her mother also. The day is described in a handwritten account by an unknown author.[36]

A joyous clamoring of bells began the events organized to celebrate the long reign of George III, and this was followed by a sermon delivered at St. Andrews church by the Reverend Martin. Afterward a procession of the local militia and dignitaries went back to Ness Strange and "a very hospitable and elegantly arranged Entertainment was prepared for the Corps in front of the House, the females and other visitors were received within." Later, "the Corps were formed on the lawn on the West of the House, on horseback, and had the Honor [sic] to receive their Standard in due military order from Mrs. Edwards. . . attended by her Female friends."[37] On the second day when money and food were given to the poor of the district, "some of the Ladies who were the peculiar Ornament of the former day, did no less honor [sic] to the present scene of heart felt Benevolence." The unknown author of the handwritten account suggests that these "scenes of picturesque and benevolent exertion," taking place on that day, would never be forgotten by its participants.[38] Though the clothing of the female group that was led by Charlotte is never described, the dresses at Platt Hall might have been worn at some point during this two-day event. At this moment in her life Charlotte was a new wife, a young mother who was, as one of her relatives described it, fully engaged in the "natural" forms of motherhood[39] that signaled the "reified femininity" of Neoclassical style (Cage 2009: 194). Here was an event that brought together familial and marital relationships, Christian consciousness infused with cultural and societal status, in a way that would have literally placed Charlotte at the center of a public performance of her new identity. I cannot help thinking that if this had all been done wearing the Neoclassical dress, it must have cemented her sense of self at that moment perhaps so much so that, as one of Banim and Guy's informants suggests of her own kept garment, this dress became associated with her feeling "shiny inside and out" (2001: 207).

I began this chapter by exploring the tangible half-life one feels on encountering a museum of historic dress and by taking seriously the idea that selfhood "extend[s] beyond the margins of the body to permeate clothing" even after a wearer's death (Simpson 2014: 256). This led to thinking about clothing as a different type of object, a novel form of possession that is neither subject nor object. When questioning how one might understand this half-alive object, I turned to an examination of the inherited memory that sometimes accompanies garments into collections. This led to considering whether the meaning of a garment might develop beyond its original wearing through its passage from wearer's wardrobe to guardian's attic and even within the apparently sterile environment of the museum itself. Through a case study of one donation that took three dresses nearly 150 years to get to a museum collection, I explored subsequent phases of the memorial role that they might have played, peeling back the layers of interaction between family and garments. Of these, I considered how ancestor-status was conferred on the clothing twice, through their donation to the museum collection and previously, when the garments sanctified the new Naylor family with status based on lineage. This blessing was founded on an earlier period of more personal memorial in which the same garments formed second-order relics whose "soft murmurings" (Gibson 2015: 21) comforted bereaved relatives as multi-dimensional objects forming a bridge between their world and the past. Ultimately, I suggested that each of these acts of remembering was dependent on the original wearers themselves and how significant each garment had been for them.

Through the ideas of Banim and Guy (2001), overlaid onto the dynamic model of memory from Keightley and Pickering (2012), I suggested that it was Charlotte Edwards' storing of her own garments that initiated their life. I proposed that they had been integral to her own sense of identity and were the way she remembered how she felt in those clothes in the past and imagined how she wanted to be and feel about herself in the future. It is this invested life in her clothing, magnified through years of careful guardianship, that I sensed when I came across the dress with the acroterion, on my first day at Platt Hall.

At the start of this chapter, I pitted empiricism directly in opposition to exploring inherited memory. This was not to say that the two approaches are entirely incompatible and scholars like Alison Slater (2014) and Bethan Bide (2017) demonstrate the great potential of these approaches working in tandem. But it was to suggest that too often stories are washed out of clothing when they enter the museum, nowadays not so much the personal biography of the original owner but still those histories of the guardians of garments, who have stored but not worn clothing and who carry with them inherited memories. It is crucial to remember, following Cwerner (2001), Banim and Guy (2001), and Slater (2014), that unworn clothing has a role for us because it is kept, and this should form part of our studies of it. It is also legitimate to explore how this continues through the action of curators whose activities, though obscured by the soft science of archiving, make them new guardians of the garments (Wood 2016; Mitchell 2018). The curator Anne Buck conferred the status of wedding dress on Charlotte Edwards' garment (Figure 7.2) when it entered the museum collection. It had not been understood as this in the most recent family's memory before. This was certainly based on her empirical expertise, but I do wonder whether it was also, in part, her knowledge of what was regularly donated to the collection—those items that typified the idealized gender roles for women—the wedding dress and party frock (Simpson 2014). Finally, it is also important to acknowledge that inherited memories about garments do not cease to exist for the family once clothes become part of a museum. People use museums to remove clothing from their own spaces but not necessarily from their lives, and the stories of those clothes now in the museum remain part of a family's inherited narratives (Gregson, Metcalfe, and Crewe 2007). Other work on museum collections acknowledges that the objects gathered do not cease to have the efficacy they once had just because they are placed inside the institution. Rather they continue to enchant the spaces of the museum (Hill 2007). In the case of historic dress, it is, I think, the very act of passage to the museum that ultimately generates this efficacy and while narratives on production and wear are important, it is the reasons for a garment's continued survival and care that ultimately imbue it with life.

Notes

1   The Gallery of English Costume was first established in 1947 having been developed from a cluster of collections owned by Manchester Corporation, now Manchester Art Galleries. The Gallery of English Costume became the Gallery of Costume in

1997 (personal correspondence with Miles Lambert, July 16, 2021). In the last few years Platt Hall has ceased to be the exclusive home of the dress collection, and it is currently split across a number of sites owned by the Manchester Art Gallery (2019).

2 The full title is *The Social Life of Things: Commodities in Cultural Perspective.*

3 Gell (1998), Latour (1999, 2004), and Ingold (2000) are just a few of the brilliant minds who have tackled the qualities of objects.

4 Manchester's dress collection began in 1922 with donations from the philanthropist Mary Greg (Mitchell 2018). By 1947, through the acquisition of the extensive collection of Drs. Cecil Willett and Phillis Cunnington by public subscription, Platt Hall became the permanent site for the accumulated dress collection as the Gallery of English Costume. Anne Buck was appointed as the new Keeper of Costume (Buck 1972; Jarvis 2009; Wood 2016).

5 Muslin is a plain-woven cotton fabric. Tambour work is created using a small hook to create chained stitches on a fabric stretched on a frame. Figured fabrics are created in the weaving process.

6 Nevinson and Hope (1973). The book was conceived in 1812 but published later.

7 Manchester Art Gallery (MAG) Correspondence File pre-1960 (Correspondence 1), Platt Hall, Rusholme, Manchester, Naylor, August 30, 1951.

8 MAG Correspondence 1/Naylor, August 30, 1951.

9 Thanks to the current owner for showing me around when I made an unplanned visit to the house.

10 MAG Correspondence 1/Naylor, August 30, 1951, and September 22, 1951.

11 Principal Probate Registry (1950), "Naylor," *Calendar of the Grants of Probate*, London: 12; The National Archives (1939), "Forden R. D.," *1939 England and Wales Register*, RG101/ZTCE/004.

12 For example, there are a set of letters from a Mrs. Sharratt, who suggests how "charming" the placement of her mother's clothes at Platt Hall would be as a "way of perpetuating her [mother's] memory" and what "joy to my family and myself" it would be "to come and look at them [her husband's garments] sometimes" (MAG Correspondence 1/Sharratt, November 24, 1940).

13 Ruth Naylor was John Murray Naylor's second wife, and though a cousin of his first wife, they were only married in 1941. Ruth would therefore not have had the familiarity with Leighton Hall and its histories that John's first wife Winifred Williamson must have had. (*The Tatler*, no. 1217, October 22, 1924, includes a photograph of Winifred pictured at Leighton with their three young children).

14 MAG Correspondence 1/Naylor, August 16, 1951.

15 MAG Accession Number 1951.345-347.

16 MAG Accession Number 951.348-356.

17 MAG Accession Number 1951.357, 359–60.

18 MAG Accession Number 1951.354.

19 MAG Accession Number 1951.344.

20 MAG Correspondence 1/Naylor, August 30, 1951, and September 22, 1951.

21 *The Bath Chronicle and Herald* (1930), Saturday August 23: 18.

22 National Library of Wales (NLW), Aberystwyth, Wales, GB 0210/6-11.

23 Shropshire Archives (SA), Shrewsbury, Shropshire, 5358/3/12.

24 National Archives, Public Records Office, PROB 11/2147.

25 Some of the clothing that was donated by Mrs. Naylor had notes on it referring to "fancy dress," and this may have been one of the occasions when the clothing was redistributed within the Leighton household itself (MAG Correspondence 1/Naylor, August 16, 1951). This is also the story of Levey's (2010) shirt and fancy dress may well be the cause of many survivals.

26 *Wellington Journal* (1909), Saturday February 6: 10.

27 SA 5358/4/1/58.

28 SA 5358/4/1/100.

29 SA 45358/4/13.

30 *Lady's Magazine* (1801), Vol. XXXII: 92.

31 SA 5358/4/1/53.

32 MAG Correspondence 1/Naylor, August 30, 1951, and September 22, 1951.

33 *Lancaster Gazette* (1806), Saturday December 13: 3.

34 *La Belle Assemblée,* February 1806: 13.

35 A number of Neoclassical styled and illustrated diaries are contained in the archives belonging to various members of the Edwards' family (SA 5358/4/27/1-3).

36 SA 5358/3/14.

37 SA 5358/3/14.

38 SA 5358/3/14.

39 SA 5358/4/1/31.

Part IV

Practices

8

"The American Look"

Memories of Not Fitting In

Elizabeth Kealy-Morris

This chapter introduces the term "body dressing work" to examine my experience negotiating the social norms and expectations of clothing a suburban American female body with the anxiety of living in a "deviant body" (Grimstad Klepp and Rysst 2016: 79) due to a spinal deformity. At the age of ten I was diagnosed with scoliosis, a curvature of the spine, and by eleven was prescribed a corrective orthotic that I wore twenty-three hours a day until the age of fourteen during the years 1978 to 1981. Memory is engaged with here as a constructed representation of the past which, although unstable and unreliable, is used by individuals and groups to produce meaning and makes sense of the world through signifying practices in the present (Hall 1997). Two disciplines of memory are applied: individual, personal memory (Ricoeur 2006) articulated via photographs and autoethnographic prose, and cultural memory.[1] The interwoven nature of history, memory, and popular culture comprising American cultural memory is examined through an analysis of "the American Look,"[2] the casual American style of sportswear and daywear.[3] Developed by American ready-to-wear garment manufacturers and their designers, this style emerged in the 1930s and 1940s and continues to dominate the nation's feminine silhouette today with the shift dress (Figure 8.1) encapsulating the style.[4] Previous ethnographic analysis of the shift dress' cultural significance in American middle-class suburban culture (Kealy-Morris 2018) is extended into a broader analysis of the style within America's cultural memory as a signifier of female youthful fitness and the cultural expectations of the female body (Arnold 2009). Through this analysis the chapter demonstrates the foundations of America's cultural memory of dress.

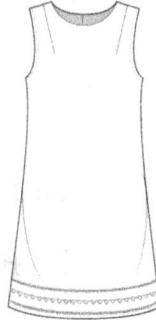

Figure 8.1 "60s shift dress," two-dimensional drawing via computer-aided design of the front of a sleeveless, yoke-necked shift dress © WGSN, 2022. Reproduced with permission.

Existing scholarly work on the links between embodied dress theory and the areas of disabled bodies, excluded bodies, and the psychological consequences of not "fitting in" (Woodward 2005: 24) to the dress of one's social grouping will be further developed in this chapter.[5] Sophie Woodward's ethnographic study (2005) of the internal, environmental, and social motivations for developing an individual aesthetic style that meets cultural expectations is useful here. Through methods of personal memory and autoethnographic practice this concept is extended further, using the terms "fitting in" and "not fitting in" to refer to clothing, culture, and expectations of how a suburban girl's body should look and function. These terms will be linked to the negotiated effort encapsulated in body dressing work with the purpose to actively seek, test out, and find clothing that enables individuals to fit into social settings.

I will explore how a sense of shame (Fredrickson and Roberts 1997; Tangney and Dearing 2002; Mair 2018) and stigma (Goffman 1990a) can be internalized by those unable to wear key styles representing social group identity. This "failure" implies the inability to fit into both the garment and the normative culture it signifies (Goffman 1990a: 152). The concept of "body dressing work" has been developed in recognition that dressing oneself is an everyday embodied material practice comprising a set of actions carried out and decisions made to manage what Fred Davis (1992: 24) terms our "ambivalent social identity"— whom we would like to be perceived as, rather than who we consider ourselves to be. As Davis notes, dress plays a key role in identity management due to its framing of our bodies and therefore its immediate representation of the self. Through memory work and autoethnographic practice, I reflect on the body dressing work I engaged in during the early years of wearing my brace, which encompassed my pursuit of what Daniel Miller and Sophie Woodward (2012: 150–1) describe as "ordinariness" to seek "inclusion rather than exclusion" through my dress choices. I further argue that the memory of not fitting in, and seeking ordinariness to blend in, can develop into learned lived practice via dress and possible numbing behaviors (van der Kolk 2014) as situated work involving the body. Throughout this chapter, the reader will encounter autoethnographic passages of prose that appear in italics. These are interspersed to surprise and startle, and which aim to shift the reader's perception of both linguistic and visual communication.

Cultural Memory of American Dress

Cultural memory is an active process in which memory is produced through cultural products that circulate through popular culture and media; this chapter will focus on items produced within America's commercial fashion market. Specific to American culture and memory, Marita Sturken (1997) proposes, "cultural memory is a means through which definitions of the nation and 'Americanness' are simultaneously established, questioned and reconfigured" (13). Her central point is that there is a shared materiality to this kind of remembering that is meaningful to a group's identity via official memorialization activity (i.e., via statues, parades, museum exhibitions, speeches, days of mourning) and popular culture (i.e., films, TV broadcasts, books, and commemorative souvenirs). I will argue that the shared materiality of the sportswear style of the American Look, and in particular the shift dress style, offers a representation of a national dress style American women and girls ought to fit into.

As this is an autoethnographic study, I am interested in what Sturken (1997: 6) terms the "political nature of memory": Who decides what representations of the past should enter the public domain? The French philosopher and cultural theorist Michel Foucault's ([1975] 1980: 82) notion of "subjugated knowledge" is useful in order to deepen an understanding of what is at stake in defining the function, practices, traditions, and memorializing of my suburban Northeastern American hometown. Foucault (1975, [1975] 1980) was interested in the knowledge of the unheard, unrepresented, and unacknowledged in society such as the patient and the prisoner whose experiences and voices are not included in official records of history or memory. Foucault termed the memory of those without access to official representation as "popular memory" (1975: 25) and noted that power struggles take place between official and popular memory to determine which will be recognized and acknowledged.

I experienced "identity ambivalence" (Davis 1992: 25) and anxiety regarding who I was and where I belonged long before I began wearing the brace. I was a middle-class child from a large extended working-class family living in an upper-middle-class, comfortable, and safe suburb that was known regionally as a representation of "the American Dream" (Adams 1931: 404).[6] I felt odd to my friends—the daughters and sons of professionals—and I felt odd to relatives who lived a long drive away. The town's cultural mythology conveys residents are lucky to live there, and any negative experiences are the fault of the individual; this left me in awe and silence, and anxious to fit in. Aligned with Reed-Danahay's (1997) notion of the counternarrative within the autoethnographic framework is Foucault's (1975: 25) use of the term "counter-memory" to represent memories that resist official memory. I have developed a "counternarrative" (Reed-Danahay 1997: 9) which is expressed in autoethnographic prose through which I analyze my life experiences as self-described evidence rather than a set of archived official truths. In doing so, this practice creates a legitimized space for the voice of my eleven- to fourteen-year-old self.

> *It is a very sunny and hot day in July 1978. I am 11 years old. I am now familiar with the doctor's office in the pediatric orthopedic department in Boston Children's Hospital: it is narrow and long, the view from the equally narrow and tall window is of the back of the hospital where all the exhaust fans have their outlets.*

> *The doctor arrives, he sits on his desk facing my mother and I; he towers over us. He delivers his verdict which at the time is a life sentence: my spinal curve (idiopathic scoliosis) has grown to the unacceptable amount of twenty-three degrees, and I will now be fitted for the Boston Orthopedic Brace (Figure 8.2) to wear twenty-three hours a day to correct this deformity.[7]*

> *I find out that day that I have an untrustworthy body; a body that reflects what I knew all along: I wasn't good enough. I spend the next three years in the brace for twenty-three hours a day. I outgrow one and am given another. It hurts all the time—pinching and poking and causing me welts where the t-shirt I wear to protect my skin from the plastic has creased. I walk strangely. I no longer fit into the clothes of my peers: I wear odd tent pinafores my mother sews at home for me to hide where the brace protrudes (Figure 8.3).*

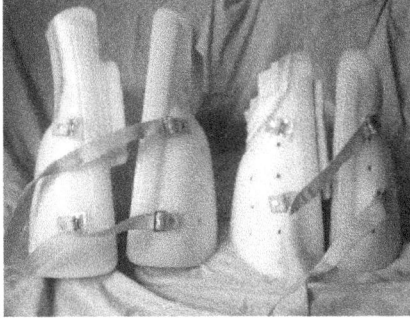

Figure 8.2 The author's braces: right was her first one, fitted at age eleven, 1978; left was her second and final, fitted at age *c*. thirteen, *c*. 1980–1. Author's own photograph.

Figure 8.3 Author (far left) in a home-sewn pinafore, age twelve, April 1979. Author's own photograph. Reproduced with permission.

American Cultural Memory: The National Myths

This section will discuss American national myths that I argue have defined what "Americanness" is and how it is represented. I will show the influence these myths have had on the development of the American Look sportswear style and its enduring power to reproduce itself in contemporary markets. As argued elsewhere (Kealy-Morris 2021), there are four fundamental beliefs held in official history and what Foucault (1975: 25) termed "popular memory" which have impacted on American cultural memory and the development of a national identity and myth. These beliefs have profound implications on the American body politic and the dressed body corpus. These include the analysis of the Myth of Revolution and "the patriot" developed by American historian Catherine Albanese (1976: 8);[8] Manifest Destiny (Scholnick 2005; Walker Howe 2007);[9] the frontier as shaper of the American character (Turner 1893);[10] and the constitutional belief in the Right to Liberty.[11] At the heart of these powerful myths lie the rejection of European influence on American religion, culture, political interference through insurrection and revolution, and later territorial control over much of the North American continent. With these concepts and myths, the development of American cultural memory can be seen through "the interaction of individuals in the creation of cultural meaning . . . [and] cultural negotiation through which different stories vie for a place in history" (Sturken 1997: 1). American historian John Bodnar (1992) notes that the enduring symbols of "pioneer" and "patriot" are both powerful in America because they both serve civic and vernacular interests, negotiated for meaning locally and nationally. Indeed, he notes, the pioneer symbol originated in the attempts of local communities and ethnic groups to mark and remember their cultural origins as more recent settlers. While various interests are bound up in these symbols, cultural negotiation is clearly playing out in the development of cultural memory here.

The stereotype of the pioneer woman, her spirit, and her dress were a great influence on my pre-brace childhood through the popularity of Laura Ingalls Wilder's autobiographical book series *Little House on the Prairie*, first published in 1934 and reprinted in the early 1970s. These were the first novel-length books I owned, and I read them repeatedly. The main character, Ingalls Wilder herself, was smart, curious, spirited, and, as a result, frequently in trouble like me. The book series was later broadcast on national television from 1974, bringing the myth of the pioneer firmly into popular culture, beyond hypermasculine Western battle dramas, to include women, family, and community life on the American frontier (Ingalls Wilder [1934] 1953). Wearing blankets as capes, my friends and I dressed like pioneer girls as best we could while play-acting the stories in each other's houses, each of us taking turns to play our heroine Laura. The Ingalls family's frontier experiences, communicated through popular culture, promoted the myth of pioneer women's spirit, grit, determination, intelligence, bodily strength, bravery, moral fortitude, and resilience. Through my exposure to these pioneer stories, and enacting them through play, I formed a strong sense of the American woman I ought to become.

The American Look: Designing a National Style

The myths and symbols of patriots and pioneers free from colonial rule, forging a new nation and working their own land, are woven into the development of a popular early sportswear style: the American Look. Design historian Rebecca Arnold (2008, 2009) notes that the sensible, affordable, and practical clothing produced by the New York fashion industry matched the informal and active nature of modern American life. While Parisian couture brands Chanel and Patou created sport-inspired fashions for the young elite, it was American ready-to-wear designers who shaped the ideal of simplified, modernized affordable styles for middle- and working-class women with cost-conscious, easy-to-launder fabrics.

Sportswear marketers sought to attribute American principles of democracy, freedom of movement, and healthiness to the New York sportswear style which aligned to the rise of the idealized vision of the independent "Modern Woman" (Arnold 2009: 30).[12] Visuality of the American modern woman was apparent in the modernist aesthetic of 1930s fashion photography, magazines, and popular films. Popular visual culture in the forms of photography, cinema, and fashion magazines encouraged women to train their bodies through dance and exercise (Arnold 2008). As early as the February 16, 1929, issue of *Vogue*, the beauty and grace of dancers' bodies were discussed with encouragement to readers to emulate their silhouette and to explore the shift from private to public space. Arnold (2008: 345) notes, "exercise developed women's figures, and was a part of a cultural shift towards viewing movement as a quintessentially modern aspect of (feminine) identity." As dancers, actresses, and fashion models, young women living in New York City were the first to take advantage of the freedom of movement that modern dance and innovative fashion offered. During the Depression era (1929–38) department stores, magazines, and manufacturers sought to appeal to customers' patriotism to lure them away from French fashions. This was done by creating direct connections between the New York-based sportswear designers and the stores' customers through marketing campaigns and magazine articles, which suggested only American designers would understand the fashion needs and desires of the American woman

(Arnold 2009). The American Look, led by Dorothy Shaver at the Lord & Taylor department store, became such a campaign which was curated through carefully executed marketing during the early postwar period of the mid-1940s.[13] Figure 8.4 illustrates the astute creative direction of the campaign in a

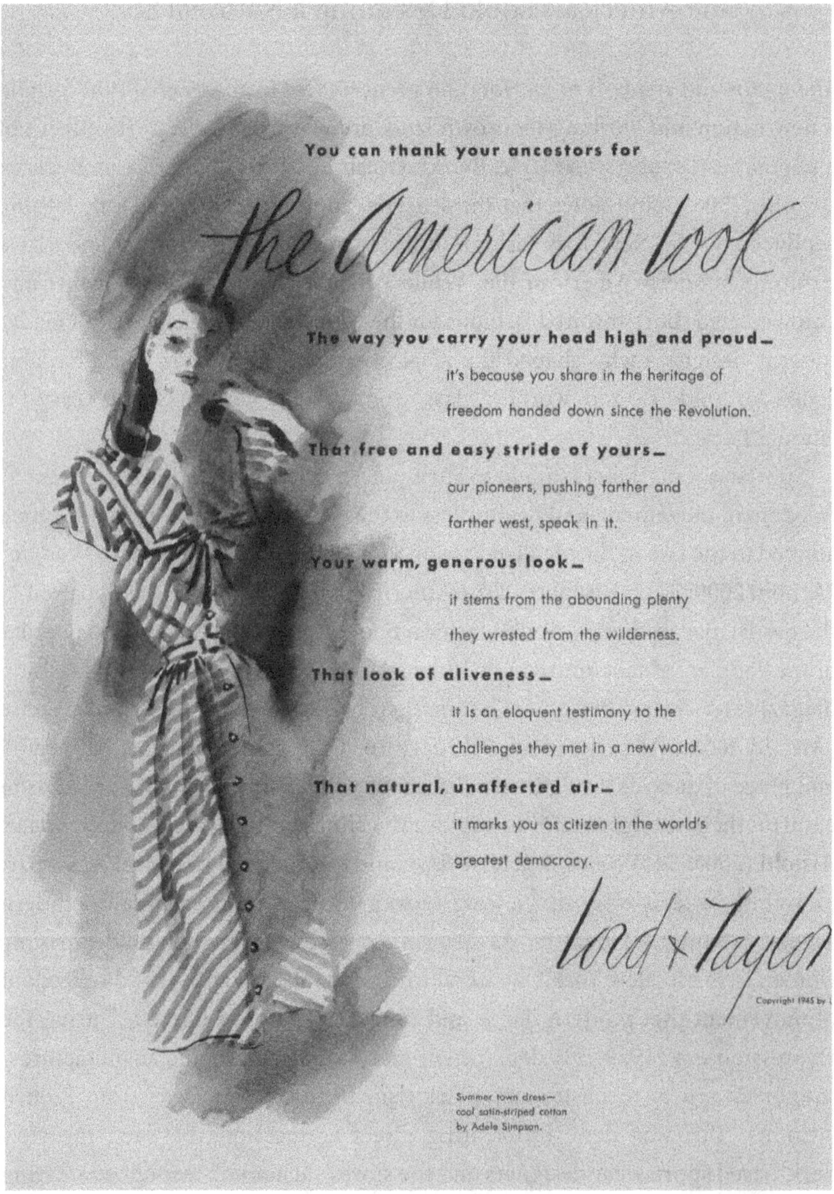

You can thank your ancestors for

the American look

The way you carry your head high and proud—
it's because you share in the heritage of
freedom handed down since the Revolution.

That free and easy stride of yours—
our pioneers, pushing farther and
farther west, speak in it.

Your warm, generous look—
it stems from the abounding plenty
they wrested from the wilderness.

That look of aliveness—
it is an eloquent testimony to the
challenges they met in a new world.

That natural, unaffected air—
it marks you as citizen in the world's
greatest democracy.

Lord & Taylor

Copyright 1945 by

Summer town dress—
cool satin-striped cotton
by Adele Simpson.

Figure 8.4 "You can thank your ancestors for the American Look," Lord & Taylor advertisement promoting the American Look © Lord & Taylor, 1945. Reproduced with permission.

full-page advertisement in the May 1945 edition of American *Vogue*. A warm invitation is conveyed to middle-class American women to see themselves and their lives represented in the style using hand-drawn type, engaging populist storytelling in an easy-to-read modernist sans-serif typeface which is set in the cadence of a poem. The advertisement is illustrated by an informal watercolor in the style of luxury print-based fashion promotions contemporary to the times.

The American aesthetic of natural and unadorned beauty can be located in what is today still recognized as the classic minimalist style of Katherine Hepburn, Audrey Hepburn, Grace Kelly which we see in the contemporary collections of DKNY, Calvin Klein, Ralph Lauren, Halston, Tom Ford, Tory Burch, and Kate Spade. Figure 8.5 is a shift dress worn by the First Lady of the United States, Jacqueline Bouvier Kennedy, the wife of the then president, John F. Kennedy, during a high-level official state visit to India in 1962. Bouvier Kennedy's choice of this new style during a diplomatic tour, as the woman with the greatest responsibility to represent American womanhood, demonstrates the status of the style at the time. The dress has been preserved and archived in the John F. Kennedy Museum in Boston, Massachusetts, as a symbol of his presidency. This is a good example of the cultural memory of dress: the weaving together of culture, history, memory, and the clothing that represents this entanglement. It is this American aesthetic which I lived with from the age of six to the age of eighteen in the 1980s when preppy dress was the dominant style of the suburban town's mothers and daughters: button-down Oxford blouses, chino pants with embroidered d-loop belts, and the shift dress.[14] Even if my family were able to afford the preppy style, I would not have been able to wear it as my brace would have been fully exposed: the shift dress, for example, would have been as revealing of the protrusions of the brace's orthotic restraints as if I were wearing a negligée.

Good American suburban girls have bodies that work properly—they play tennis and swim and play soccer. Their bodies are just the right size for the correct suburban uniform in the early 1980s: shift dresses, chinos, cable knit sweaters, Oxford button down shirts and loafers. This uniform is linear and masculine and hipless. Even when, at sixteen, finally rid of my orthopedic brace and working very hard to self-discipline my body, I have wide hips and big feet that don't fit in the uniform; I am reminded that I don't fit, still.

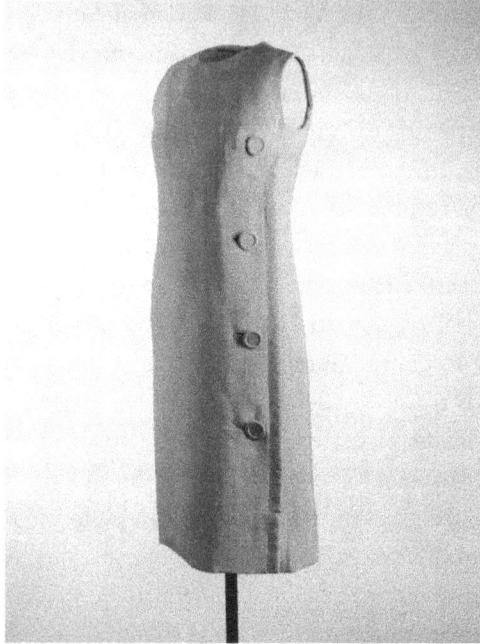

Figure 8.5 Shift dress in pink silk shantung with four large covered buttons down the side, MO 63.1261. Worn by Jacqueline Bouvier Kennedy, First Lady of the United States, 1962. Collection of the John F. Kennedy Presidential Library and Museum, Boston © John F. Kennedy Library Foundation. Reproduced with permission.

The Shift Dress: Memories of Not Fitting In

Two memories of wearing my brace twenty-three hours a day from age eleven to fourteen have stayed with me: being in constant pain from the tightness of the orthotic and the daily anxiety of getting dressed; I couldn't fit into the clothes of my peers because of the shape of my body in the brace and therefore I could not fit in with my peers. Here I consider the body dressing work I engaged in to carefully develop a wardrobe full of what Miller and Woodward (2012: 63) term "ordinary" clothing to seek cover in my quest to fit into an American culture which celebrates strong, healthy bodies that are ready for the frontier, the field, or the dancefloor. Alison Guy and Maura Banim (2000) argue that women have an active relationship between their clothes and their identities. One self-view is "the woman I fear I could be," reflecting the anxieties women reported regarding their wardrobes and their possible sartorial errors which could affect their relationships with others (Guy and Banim 2000: 313). For some women this anxiety culminated into viewing certain clothes as representations of the woman they feel they must hide from view. This supports my own experience: my greatest fear was that the exposure of my brace would mean ostracization from my social group, therefore my body dressing work involved taking great care of which garments I selected and rejected.

The shift dress has evolved to allow for a choice of silhouettes from unfitted loose dresses to more body-conscious figure-hugging styles (Ward 2010). Though updated, it remains an essential part of the American woman's wardrobe as it signifies understated feminine youthful health by accommodating full body movement and casual ease. The shift dress was further embedded into popular culture by the socialite Lilly Pulitzer, who introduced her "Lilly Dress" (Figure 8.6) at her orange juice bar in the upmarket resort of Palm Beach, Florida (Banks and de La Chapelle 2011).

Figure 8.6 "Pulitzer Fashions: The young matrons of Palm Beach, wearing designs by Lilly Pulitzer" © Slim Aarons/Getty Images, 1964. Reproduced with the permission of Getty Images.

The Lilly Dress is noted for its bright colors and playful fabrics and remains a summer staple for female residents, young and old, of upper-middle-class towns like my suburban hometown. Banks and de La Chapelle (2011: 168) write that "Lillys are an eternal reminder that 'it's always summer somewhere.'" Figure 8.6

is an image taken by society photographer Slim Aaron for a lifestyle photoshoot of Lilly Pulitzer's friends and their daughters at poolside in Palm Beach wearing variations of the Lilly Dress. In *Celebrating WASP Style: A Privileged Life*, Susanna Salk (2007: 104–5) captions the photograph as "Ladies in Palm Beach decked out in their Lilly Pulitzer shifts look as youthful as their daughters." A semiotic analysis (following Barthes 1977) of the shift dress as a sartorial sign producing negotiated cultural meaning would suggest its signifiers are a garment worn by females which is manufactured in a light fabric, has a high scooped neck, loose without a waist or any external restraint at the waist, and exposes all limbs to sight. The dress and the lifestyle merge together strongly in this photograph and its captions: what is signified is youthful, active, healthy female bodies, confidently soaking up the sun with their limbs exposed. The sign "shift dress" loses the signifier of "comfort for warm climates" to gain the signified "stylish piece of clothing to wear by body-confident, youthful, healthy, women." Therefore, the signified, connoted negotiated cultural meaning communicated about the shift dress is that the wearer of the dress takes on the signifiers herself: she is full of feminine youthful confidence through the healthy summer activity she engages in.

It's a spring day, my mother and I are shopping in a boutique in the neighboring suburban town. I have just turned thirteen. The trip is not going well. My mother is bored, I am anxious. Tension hangs in the air. She wants me to buy clothes that cover my brace without trace, I want stylish clothes that will allow me to fit in with my friends even if it means the outline of the brace can be seen. I try on garment after garment, and I stand my ground. It is navy blue with a grandfather collar,[15] it is a light rayon-mix fabric and has tinsel-like threads sewn in so that in the light it shines. This reminds me of disco, a music genre I have grown to love, with Donna Summer's Bad Girls *being the first album I bought with my own money.[16] I remember the smell of the blouse and how, somehow, the smell never goes away regardless of how many times it is washed . . . a grown up musky floral scent; I'm not yet allowed to wear perfume, so this smell is very exciting. I think of the boy I like in my Social Studies class; I wonder if he will like me in the blouse. I am hopeful.*

Body Dressing Work: Visibility and Cover

After that July day in 1978 when, at the age of eleven, I was fitted for my first Boston brace, I was never again to achieve the mythical attributes that the shift dress supposedly imbued within its wearer: feminine youthful confidence through healthy summer activity. Carolyn Mair's (2018) discussion of social identity theory is helpful here. Feeling good about membership in social groups is important to a positive self-concept, and clothing enables us to affiliate with our clique and disassociate ourselves from others. Feedback from others influences our self-concepts and self-esteem, and these are interrelated. My body had become "a social barrier . . . a deviant body" (Grimstad Klepp and Rysst 2016: 85) because I was unable to wear a key sartorial staple of my social grouping due to my anxiety at exposing my deformity and the fear of subsequent social exclusion.

Joanne Entwistle (2000) notes that dress can be a source of shame as well as a method for avoiding it. She suggests that the sense of shame is a social one, not simply focused on the garments themselves but rather related to not having met the standards expected within a social space with a defined moral code of conduct expected of participants. My brace did not allow me to "pass" as healthy (Goffman 1990a: 153) and the outline of the orthotic, and the way it distorted my movements was apparent to everyone. I was very aware there was a peculiarity to my body which no cloth could conceal. I sought ordinariness in my dress to reduce visibility and cover my abnormality to minimize the visibility of my stigma so that my deformity did not disrupt relationships with my peers. I carried out body dressing work to fit into the expectations of the clothed body of a suburban girl. Dressing my deformed body and covering my unseen brace were complicated, contradictory, stressful, and worrying because I had few options; the body dressing work had to be deliberate and intentional, and based on trial-and-error testing.

As I had already accepted that I couldn't pass for a normal suburban girl and hiding the orthotic was causing me great anxiety, I wanted my peers to know why I moved so robotically. I had fantasies of wearing the "Milwaukee brace" like the title character in Judy Blume's (1973) young adult novel *Deenie* who had a higher curve on her spine and therefore her brace protruded above her collar for all to see.[17] This is a secret I never told anyone. My curve is mid-spine so I was prescribed the rib-cage crunching "Boston brace" (Figure 8.2). I walked oddly, I sat oddly, I moved oddly, but no one knew exactly why. I imagined the whispers, and I saw the doubt in my classmates' eyes, which, in my mind, said, "Is she ok to be around? Or is she weak and strange and will ruin my chances with other kids in the class?" I remember thinking, "If I wore Deenie's brace everyone would know it is just my body that's crooked, not *all* of me." I sought dress that would allow me ordinariness and cover. Through body dressing work I used dress as "a central part in the on-going, day-to-day negotiation of self" (Buse and Twigg 2013: 328). This involves a process of choosing, negotiating, and wearing clothing for particular purposes that are consciously understood to construct and perform our identities, a "presentation of the self" (Goffman 1990b: 244; see also Entwistle 2000; Buse and Twigg 2013).

By age twelve I rejected the homemade pinafore (Figure 8.3) and the shift dress (Figures 8.1 and 8.5) for the store-bought ready-to-wear separates of the light blue jersey blouse and light blue calico peasant skirt seen in Figure 8.7. This skirt, just visible on the bottom right of the photograph, became one of my most treasured garments. I felt beautiful and grown-up wearing it—when no one was looking I would twirl and twirl, loving the way the skirt billowed out, allowing me to forget my brace for a few moments. This clothing was socially acceptable for a middle-class girl in suburban Northeastern America in the late 1970s and early 1980s. The outline of my brace can be seen in the blouse, but the jersey material was more flexible and thicker than that of a shift dress, fully covered my back, and the longer sleeves meant my protective T-shirt was hidden. I chose not to wear the pinafores, which were home-sewn by my mother, because they were not the style of my in-group, they were not to a retail finish, and I felt childish in them. At the other end of the spectrum, I chose not to wear the shift dress as it would not have closed the shame gap (Entwistle 2000; Goffman 1990a): the high back of my brace (Figure 8.2) would have protruded the thin, stiff cotton/linen mix in very strange ways. In addition, the T-shirts I wore to protect my skin from the orthotic constantly rubbing against my skin would have ruined the clean lines of the sleeveless shift dress style. I remember feeling that my failure to meet expectations of a healthy body would have been the focus of every social encounter if I wore the shift dress; I sought belonging, not exceptionalism. I walked a very fine line in my body dressing work to find clothing that fit my brace, my body, and my peers' sartorial expectations.

June Tangney and Ronda Dearing (2002) note that shame often generates a longing to escape or hide and can be further extended when we link our own negative beliefs of ourselves with the fear of exposure from others (Fredrickson and Roberts 1997). My body was a danger to who I wanted to be (Guy and Banim 2000) so I kept it hidden, out of sight, away from notice. With my choice of dress, I was not concerned with the appearance of my body but rather I sought to perform the social identity and stereotype of what an American suburban girl

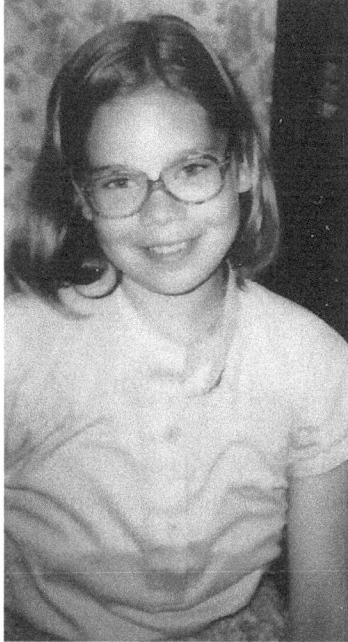

Figure 8.7 Author in store-bought clothes with the outline of the brace evident at her rib cage, age twelve, June 1979. Author's own photograph.

should be. As noted by Davis (1992: 25), because clothing is draped upon the body, "dress . . . comes easily to serve as a kind of visual metaphor for identity, and . . . for registering the culturally anchored ambivalences that resonate within and among identities." This reflects my experience: my memories of shame of my disfigurement, social fear, and anxiety of possible exclusion by my peers are culturally specific within the body discourse of middle-class American suburbia in the late 1970s to early 1980s.

I want to end looking to the future of a productive dialogue and discourse between dress theory and feminist disability theory, where the praxis might be less about the shape of bodies and more about how beautifully unique bodies are engaged in body dressing work, the everyday negotiation of the self. Rosemarie Garland-Thomson (2002: 21) states, "disability is perhaps the essential characteristic of being human. The body is dynamic, constantly interactive with history and environment. We evolve into disability." This mirrors the findings of Buse and Twigg (2013) who have found that the choosing of clothing and the act of dressing remain important for the identities of those living with dementia. Locating clothes that fit and are suitable is key to self-acceptance, self-confidence, and a sense of inclusion into one's social grouping. The experience of identity ambivalence continues for me. I have come to understand that I experienced being braced at eleven, and the acute social anxiety I felt living in a disabled body, as an "Adverse Childhood Trauma" (van ker Kolk 2014: 173). The development of the term "body dressing work" has been important in developing an understanding of the sense of deviance I still feel: we are all experiencing a continuum in our social interactions between our desired and actual selves, and everyday dress practices are key to this negotiation.

Conclusion

This chapter recognizes that dressing the body is an embodied, experiential, situated, everyday practice involving negotiation and purposeful activity. Within dress theory there is much critical analysis of choices made to wear clothing and much less on the exclusion from clothing with physically and socially acceptable fit for the disabled. The purpose of this chapter has been to establish an extension to dress theory to encompass the experience of dressing disabled bodies and to recognize the psychological consequences of not fitting into the dress of one's social grouping. The concept of "body dressing work" has been introduced to recognize the negotiated effort to actively seek, test out, and find clothing that enables individuals to fit into social settings through careful clothing of the body. The autoethnographic prose narrating personal memories of not fitting into the dress of my peers articulates the structures of marginalization that operate within everyday dress practices. These autoethnographic passages bring authenticity and significance to the suggestion that the practice of body dressing work could be further recognized, discussed, and explored within embodied dress theory as well as other disciplines including garment design, product design, prosthetic design, disability studies, and behavioral psychology. More participatory action research and memory-based research projects together with the disabled would enable articulation of memories, experiences, and body dressing work practices to include their voices and bodies in the framing of inclusive solutions to this challenging subject.

Notes

1　For more on autoethnography as a methodology and practice, see Reed-Danahay (1997), Neumann (1996), Ellis and Bochner (2000), Holman Jones (2005), Denzin

(2006). For more on cultural memory, see Nora (1989), Halbwachs ([1950] 1980, 1992), Huyssen (1995), Sturken (1997), Bal, Crewe, and Spitzer (1999).

2 For more on the American Look, see Talmey (1946), Leach (1993), Webber-Hanchett (2003), Arnold (2009). The phrase was developed in the 1940s by marketing executive Dorothy Shaver (Talmey 1946; Leach 1993; Yohannan and Nolf 1999; Breward 2003; Webber-Hanchett 2003) at the upscale department store Lord & Taylor to promote the American fashion industry through encouraging middle-class American women to see themselves in the styles. See Campbell Warner (2010), Millbank (1989), and Yohannan (2010) for more on the ready-to-wear designers of this era.

3 This chapter refers to "sportswear" as distinct from "active sportswear." As Campbell Warner (2010: 650) notes, "sportswear concerns the fashionable aspects of clothing for sport rather than the athletic. Individual items such as jerseys, sweaters, and turtlenecks came directly out of active sports." The separate items of clothing are specifically designed to be mixed and matched in different combinations to create various outfits from the same garments and worn off the athletics field, tennis court, and golf range.

4 The shift dress is cut straight at the sides and unfitted at the waist in straight and A-line styles. It originated as daywear from the early part of the twentieth century known as a "chemise" and became popular in the 1950s when luxury fashion design houses Dior and Balenciaga began experimenting with the style. Sometimes called a "sack" or "sheath" dress, from the 1960s straight-cut dresses have been commonly known as "shifts" and since the 1980s the term has encompassed more silhouettes (Ward 2010).

5 For embodied dress theory, see Davis (1992), Craik (1993), Entwistle (2000), Woodward (2005, 2007), Miller and Woodward (2012). For disabled bodies, see Buse and Twigg (2013), Hirsch ([1998] 2003), Garland-Thompson (2002), Linthicum (2006), Grimstad Klepp and Rysst (2016), Stauss (2020). For excluded bodies, see Rothblum and Solovay (2009), Erdman Farrell (2011), Volonté (2022). For the psychological consequences of not fitting in to the dress styles of your social group, see Fredrickson and Roberts (1997), Guy and Banim (2000), Tangney and Dearing (2002), Johnson, Lennon, and Rudd (2014), van der Kolk (2014), Mair (2018), Volonté (2022).

6 Adams created this phrase in his 1931 populist bestseller *The Epic of America*, which refers to the dream of homeownership. Attached to this socioeconomic status were the attributes of being an upstanding, responsible, respectable citizen. See also Gallagher (2013).

7 The categorization of my type of brace as a "Boston brace" was an official medical typological one referring to an orthotic for a spinal curve in the mid to lower vertebrae. It was coincidence that I was a patient at Boston Children's Hospital when prescribed this type of orthotic.

8 Albanese (1976) writes about the enduring myths that succeeded in the development of a successful army of "patriots" to wage a successful revolution against England which is the basis for the development of "Civil Religion" in America and "patriot thought" which has created a new unique national truth to live by (8).

9 "Manifest Destiny" was a phrase that promoted continental expansion, resulting in a doubling of American territory in four years. It continues to influence popular culture and memory through the notion of the shaping of the nation's psyche via links to the frontier (Walker Howe 2007).

10 The popular myth of the frontier romantically suggests that with the exploration, mapping, and setting down of communication lines to develop new settlements in land west of the original thirteen colonies, a set of American character traits were forged, including "restless, nervous energy, dominant individualism . . . humor, bravery, and rude strength" (Turner 1893 [online]).

11 The Right to Liberty is an American constitutional principle of individual autonomy, which can be summarized as "my body, my choice."

12 For further discussion on cultural memory relating to American dress, see Atkin's chapter in this volume as well as Breward (2003: 110–11) and Fleetwood (2005). For further discussion on the American drive for cleanliness and hygiene as a patriotic duty, see Arnold (2009: 48–9).

13 Talmey (1946), Leach (1993), Yohannan and Nolf (1999), Breward (2003), Webber-Hanchett (2003).

14 The origins of the preppy style dates to early twentieth-century sportswear clothing worn by wealthy young American men at their private preparatory ("prep") schools prior to entering elite male-only colleges (the "Ivy League" colleges). Tuite (2014) notes that by the mid-1930s young American women began to copy and develop their own adaptations to the style at their exclusive female-only colleges (the "Seven Sisters" colleges). For more on the preppy style, see Salk (2007) and Banks and de La Chapelle (2011).

15 This is the American term for the collarless "grandad shirt" (Breward 2004: 178).

16 D. Summer, *Bad Girls*. [Record] Casablanca Records, 1979.

17 Blume (1973). For more information on the Milwaukee brace, see Physiopedia (2022).

9

Black/White/Yellow

Elizabeth Chin[1]

For some time now, I have imagined making a series of quilts that meditates on the question and problem of my daughter's racial makeup. According to the US-based racial reckoning that both calculates racial proportions and measures color, my daughter is half black, one-quarter white, and one-quarter yellow. And yet she is a whole person, seamless. It is a fiction that she is fractions of this and that stuck together. As a person who is half white and half Chinese, I know that to be racially mixed in the United States is to fight for wholeness, to struggle to feel complete as a person. At every turn our wholeness is picked apart, divided into bits. Just as I was confidently told by other people's parents that "you must be adopted" because they could not imagine my dark hair being birthed by the body of my milky white-skinned, blonde-haired, blue-eyed mother, neither could my daughter's childhood friends see me, yellow as I am, as the mother of a Black child.[2] There is a special sort of rage generated by the daily wear and tear on family fabric that too many of those around you snip away at with their pointed ignorance. Some things get worn out and do not survive the thousand cuts.

In the abstract, the concept of the quilt is like my daughter, it is half black, one-fourth white, and one-fourth yellow. For the sake of illustration, let's say two yards of black, one yard of white, and one yard of yellow. The first step is to stitch them together to create a starting place. The process is one of cutting the whole and restitching it together.

One cut, restitch. Two cuts, restitch. Three cuts, reconstruct. Four cuts, make it whole again, continuing like this through twenty-three cuts: the number of chromosomes (a nod to the biology of humanness). Within this process of cutting and remaking, the original proportions stay the same: at the end the resulting quilt will still be half black, one-quarter white, and one-quarter yellow and yet we have no idea what it will look like. I imagined a series, all beginning with the same basic foundation, resulting in many different outcomes.

As I was researching quilts and quilting, I realized that it was essential for me to use the clothing of my own loved ones, my daughter's ancestors. This realization came as I was thinking about African American quilting, specifically, the much-celebrated quilts made by women from Gee's Bend, Alabama.[3] The quilters of Gee's Bend have used quilting—among other techniques of remaking and survivance—as everyday practices of creating lives of wholeness in the afterlife of slavery. Most of the quilts are improvisationally constructed, and the piecing, similarly, tends to be freehand rather than undertaken with the precisely measured templates more commonly seen (and valued) in pieced quilts in the United States. Gee's Bend quilters employ considered practices of composition that "demonstrate the power of needle as pen" (Sohan 2015: 296), both drawing from and contributing to improvisational forms distinctive to African aesthetic production throughout the diaspora.

Mrs. Missouri Pettway was one of the women from Gee's Bend who responded to her husband's death, as her daughter remembers it, by saying, "I'm going to take his work clothes, shape them into a quilt to remember him, and cover up under it for love" (cited in Beardsley et al. 2002: 67). In deconstructing her husband's work clothes, Missouri Pettway was refashioning the garments that had held her loved one's limbs, absorbed his sweat and scent, so that at night she would still lie with him upon her. It was an act of mourning, a stitching through of grief, creating seams between life and death, love, and loss. Sohan's (2015) own analysis of these women's work seeks to trouble the distinction between language and craft, between making and speaking. She argues that the quilts constitute a form of discourse and that they can be understood as compositions that address numerous issues including family life, labor, and racial injustice.

It was at this point that working on the quilt moved from being just quilting to being a much richer, complex project in research-creation. The term has emerged especially strongly in places that have developed new PhD programs in the arts. Because the signature accomplishment of the PhD is the creation of new knowledge, these programs must answer the question: What does it mean to produce new knowledge through creative practice—as a painter, designer, dancer (Barrett and Bolt 2013; Elkins 2014)? What constitutes research in these areas?[4] People wrestling with these questions are generating practices and methodologies that cross boundaries in a way that Natalie Loveless (2019: 59) describes as "polydisciplinamory" in her book *How to Make Art at the End of the World*. Similarly, digging into research-creation asks new and exciting questions about methodology (Sheller 2015; Truman 2021). While research-creation writer-thinkers are savvy about race, the majority are white. The Black feminists Tina Campt (2017) and Alexis Pauline Gumbs (2020) bring distinctively politicized attunements to body politics as they encourage us to "listen to images" or to write in ways utterly outside scholarly boundaries. Saidiyah Hartman (2008), for her part, delves deeply into the dispossessions of slavery in her genre-bending writing. Their work is a reminder that structures of knowledge, and of the academy, have long silenced Black women and seek not simply inclusion but a shifting of the structures of knowledge and the rituals through which it is legitimated.

As a material experiment with ethnographic knowing and writing, the quilt is piecing and memory-work, made by using garments from my own family as the ground of exploration. Working back and forth between constructing the quilt, researching the worlds into which each garment and textile leads, and writing this chapter have involved looping meanders where sewing inspires research investigation and vice-versa. The resulting writing is a patchwork, in part because the material experiments that it has generated alongside have resulted in a patchwork quilt, albeit one that is at this point unfinished. The writing is also a patchwork as a way to take apart and piece together the three historical threads represented by the materials from which the quilt is made. As with the autoethnographic work I undertook in my book *My Life with Things: The Consumer Diaries* (Chin 2016), the method of inquiry is at once deeply personal and broadly ethnographic.

These are fabrics from which the quilt is constructed:

- Black. A length of Swiss lace I bought in London a few years ago in an African textile shop.
- White. The skirt portion of a two-piece Chinese outfit that belonged to my white grandmother, Jessie Gorham Toll.
- Yellow. A cheongsam that belonged to my Chinese grandmother, Lilac Bow Yoke Chin (Figure 9.1).

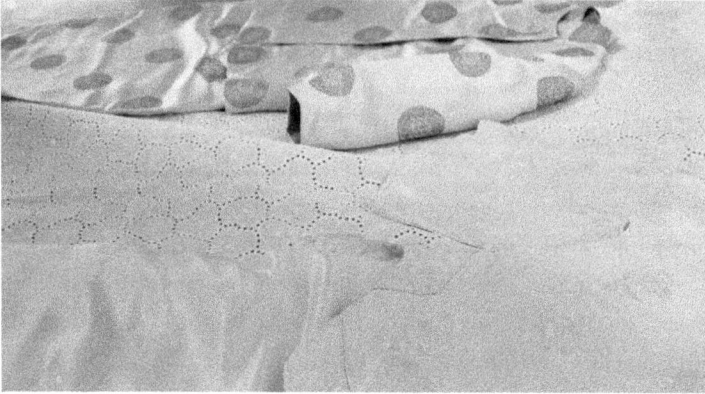

Figure 9.1 Two garments and a textile © Zoë Jackson, 2022. Reproduced with permission.

This project, then, as making/thinking/writing, is a composition that works at the seams of racial histories, racial mixing, family, and notions of belongingness in the United States. What I learned from Mrs. Pettaway is that the project required me to take apart clothing of loved ones in order to properly make my ideas material. Retrograde notions about blood and purity still circulate as a kind of folk wisdom even among people who think of themselves as good and true, as generous and loving, as fair and thoughtful. Education is no protection against entertaining racial beliefs that are, quite simply, wrong. In my experience, education merely provides cover for racist acts under the cover of science, good intentions, or both. A 2016 study asked 418 medical students and residents to evaluate the truthfulness of statements such as "Black people's nerve-endings are less sensitive than White people's nerve-endings" (Hoffman et al. 2016). About 50 percent reported that at least one of the false belief items was possibly, probably, or definitely true. For me this statistic translates into the fervent hope that not one of those medical professionals who believes such things ever lays a finger on my child.

Black

My daughter's father, Robert, born in Washington D.C., remembers going to segregated beaches as a child. When we met, his father had long ago passed away, as had his sister. His mother said, as he recounted it, "If you're going to marry one of them, I don't want to hear from you anymore." My daughter has no mementos, no inherited items from them. Her flesh is her inheritance. In this way, she lives the afterlife of slavery with doubling and redoubling of the losses and dispossessions specific to the descendants of enslaved Africans in the Americas, relatives she will never meet, ancestors whose names can never be known because they were likely never recorded, it's a long, long thread to pull.

The black in the quilt is made up of several yards of Swiss lace, as white as can be, embellished with crystals (Figures 9.2 and 9.3). I bought that fabric in London from an African textiles store. The crisp newness of the white Swiss lace is another visual pun—the black is white. It also is a marker of the absence my daughter experiences, never having met her father's family.

Figures 9.2–9.3 The starting point; First cut. Author's own photographs.

White

The one-fourth white portion of Black/White/Yellow is made of a skirt and top that used to belong to my mother's mother, Jessie (Figure 9.4). It is made in an ivory-colored silk, hand-embroidered with flowered designs. It is possible that the fabric originally came from a journey to China made by my grandmother's great-grandfather in the 1920s or 1930s; he returned to the United States with crates full of treasures. The loose jacket comes to the waist and closes at the front with frogs.[5] An ankle-length, A-line skirt has a yoke at the waist. The skirt has been modified by hand, a zipper installed, and I recognize the competent, yet inelegant, stitches I have seen in other clothes that my white grandmother once owned. She was an accomplished do-it-yourself-er, thrifty as anything, proud to have paid off her mortgage in full.

What was Jessie doing with that Chinese outfit? When or where did she wear it? It could only have been a form of dress-up, a kind of fashion play. There is a visual pun built in: the white fabric for the quilt is, simultaneously, conceptually yellow. Because race is messed up that way.

Figure 9.4 Chinese embroidered jacket © Zoë Jackson, 2022. Reproduced with permission.

Yellow

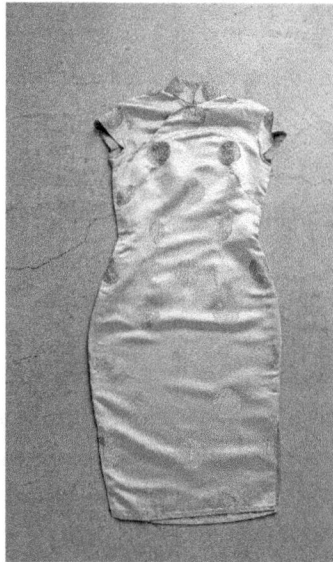

Figure 9.5 Cheongsam © Zoë Jackson, 2022. Reproduced with permission.

For yellow, I use a cheongsam and matching jacket made of a silk brocade with oyster-colored ground and olive green design that belonged to my grandmother Lilac (Figure 9.5). When I was in my early thirties, my Auntie Vi—Lilac's sister

Violet—took me down into her San Francisco basement and gave me a box of clothes that had belonged to my grandmother, and my great-grandmother, some old family photos, and some lengths of fabric. My grandmother Lilac had died in 1974, in an accident with a drunk driver. My grandfather was driving. I don't remember her smell.

The cheongsam and jacket were among the things I received that day, and they brought me close to my long-dead grandmother in a profoundly physical, material way that was surprising in its power. These are custom-tailored pieces from a trip my Chinese grandparents took to Taiwan in the early 1970s. As I take apart the garment, I can see faint sweat stains in the armpits.

White

My grandmother Jessie Gorham Toll was born in Ojai, California, to a well-to-do ranching family. Her lineage stretches back to John Howland, who was one of two indentured servants to arrive in the so-called new world on the Mayflower. At one point on the trans-Atlantic journey, he was washed into the sea during a storm and was fished back onto deck by Miles Standish. I find it endlessly amusing that I am descended from the guy who fell off the Mayflower.[6]

Black

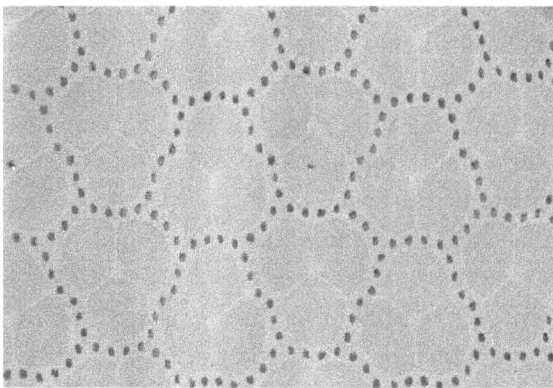

Figure 9.6 Lace detail © Zoë Jackson, 2022. Reproduced with permission.

The white length of Swiss lace, bought in London, holds space; it is a site of blankness, questions, suppositions. It is up to my daughter to dig into the history of her Black ancestors. It is not my task. What does Swiss lace have to do with Blackness? The laces, so iconically African today, are firmly stitched to colonialism, though that history is relatively shallow in the case of lace and begins in the 1960s. Swiss lace may or may not be Swiss. Sometimes it is actually Austrian. Sometimes these textiles are generically called "African lace" (see Figure 9.6). In technical terms they are not lace at all but industrial embroideries. These not-truly-lace-laces (but what is truly anything?) are required wearing at most Nigerian weddings and festive events. This ubiquitous and defining textile, it turns out, only really burst onto the Nigerian scene in the 1960s (Plankensteiner 2013). Like Lilac's cheongsam, Nigerian lace is both a marker of ethnic authenticity and a product of colonialism and global circuits of trade in things and people. The relatively shallow history doesn't make it any less legitimately African. After all, Nigeria itself is a colonial creation.

Yellow

My Chinese grandmother Lilac was born in Alameda, California, in 1919. Her mother was born in San Francisco, as was her mother before her. I searched for records of their births but could find none. The US census from 1900 records only 1,196 US-born Chinese girls and women in San Francisco, a total of 2,101 women and girls overall in a Chinese/Chinese American population of 11,449 (Chan 2005: 44–5). Why so few women and girls?

Chinese began coming to the United States in large numbers beginning in the latter half of the nineteenth century. It was gold rush time, and times were tough in the southern provinces of China, what was then known as Canton, now Guangdong. Nearly all those who came were men, mostly young, hoping to make a fortune and then go back to China. Very small numbers of Chinese women immigrated at this time and most were either wives of well-to-do merchants or prostitutes. San Francisco, like other Chinatowns, was a "bachelor society" (even though many of the men had wives and children in China), and this state of affairs was framed as not just distasteful but downright unnatural by the increasing numbers of people who feared Chinese immigration (Rouse 2009: 2). The "failure of Chinese men to establish families" became one of the tent-poles of anti-Chinese sentiment, as this supposed failure represented a refusal to assimilate and lack of interest in nation-building (Rouse 2009: 16). Cheap "coolie labor" was another target, particularly of trade unionists who argued that Chinese workers suppressed wages for whites (Rouse 2009: 96). The Page Act

of 1875 had a twofold aim: it banned the immigration of both "coolie labor" and barred Chinese prostitutes (Rouse 2009: 9). This gendered policy led to a 68 percent drop in Chinese female immigrants between 1876 and 1882 (Peffer 1986: 29). Chinese women seeking to enter the United States were forced to undergo interrogations that included such questions as: "Have you lived in a house of prostitution in Hong Kong, Macau, or China?" and "Are you a virtuous woman?" (Peffer 1986: 32).

Part of the history of Chinese in the United States is that for many decades, having a family that included mothers and daughters was astonishingly rare. I try to imagine what life was like for US-born Chinese girls in those early days, to be so rare, so precious, so prized, so desired, so vilified, so terrifying that entire laws had to be created to keep them out.

White

In contrast to the spotty and inconsistent presence of my Chinese family in census records, the Gorhams, Tolls, and Joys are everywhere: in each census, in newspapers, draft cards, ship passenger lists, passport applications, telephone directories, deeds, marriage registers, birth announcements, obituaries, cemeteries. There's even a tortoise at the Santa Barbara Zoo whose enclosure bears a plaque in honor of my grandmother Jessie, to recognize her years of service to that organization. The celebrated photographer Walker Evans took a childhood portrait of my white grandfather, Carroll Costello Toll. Carroll's brother, Maynard, was a prominent lawyer and founding trustee of the Los Angeles Museum of Art.

That side of the family has left a trail across the landscape as well as in bureaucratic records. Scripps College, in Pomona, California, has a building named after Eleanor Joy Toll, who would become my grandmother Jessie's mother-in-law. Eleanor Joy Toll also has her very own entry in Wikipedia. The Toll family home in Glendale is on the national historic register. Does their existence in the archive and landscape make their history more real, their impact more meaningful?

Black

The Swiss lace is also made of cotton. The connections between cotton and Blackness are nothing if not fraught. Zoë Jackson, who took many of the photos for this piece, is descended on her father's side from enslaved people who picked cotton in the south. My daughter's ancestors may have worked alongside Zoë's or near them. Who knows? At Zoë's senior photography installation, a branch of cotton fluffy with ripe bolls was placed beneath a table strewn with uncut negatives. I was carrying a plastic cup full of reception-grade red wine and sprinkled a few drops to pay my respects, leaving berry-colored stains behind.

Yellow

There may be a trace of those Chinese ancestors in the census of 1900. Lilac's mother appears in the 1940 census as Ling Lee Quan. There is a household that appears in the 1900 census whose members include "Wong Shee" and her daughter Suey Ling Lee.[7] Could Suey Ling Lee be Ling Lee Quan in the 1940 census? My Chinese grandparents gave me the name Ling Ling and, only as I wrote this paragraph, did I wonder whether that name was as a tribute to Suey Ling Lee from whom I might be descended.

The census record is a tantalizing possibility that my elusive Chinese history has left a documentary trace. The first thirteen lines of the form are taken up by Bow Lee and his household. His wife, Wong Shee, born September 1861, thirty-eight years old, married for twenty-five years, and mother of five living children.

From the information inscribed in those thirteen lines of data, I've pieced together a narrative.

By the time Wong Shee was 17 years old, she had been married for four years and was mother to three young sons. She and Lee Bow had married in 1875, the same year that the Page Act restricted the immigration of women from China. Lee Bow had been born in China, was 20 years older than Wong Shee, and listed as a cannery worker. His job was likely in a salmon canning factory, one of many in San Francisco at the time. The marriage quickly produced three boys and then Wong Shee seems to have had a nine-year break from childbearing. One likely explanation for the break is that, like many sojourning Chinese men Lee Bow returned to China for a spell after the births of those first three boys. Or perhaps Wong Shee had ways to prevent pregnancy, or perhaps she had had pregnancies that did not result in live births. In any case, her two girls, Lucy Sum Lee and Suey Ling Lee, were born nine years after their youngest brother.

In 1900, Wong Shee was a 38-year-old matriarch. She and her husband were living at home with their five children, two daughters-in-law, three grandchildren and a lodger. A total of thirteen people living at 1024 Pacific Street, a neighborhood made of the two- and three-story walkup flats that are still found throughout the city. The youngest son, eighteen, was a cabin boy.[8] The two older boys were cannery workers like their father. They had married, one after the other, and brought their wives to live at Pacific Street. The wives had, one after the other, blessed the family with grandchildren. Though Wong Shee had been born in the United States, she did not speak English, nor could she read or write. Her two daughters-in-law were also born in the United States but the generations were changing: in contrast to Wong Shee who had been a bride at 14, they did not marry until their early twenties, and their husbands were only a year or two older. They could speak English, and could also read and write. Wong Shee's first daughter, Lucy, was eleven years old and attending the racially segregated school San Francisco provided for Chinese children. Suey Ling Lee, the eight-year-old, was not recorded by the census worker as attending school.

This Chinese American family appears only in the 1900 census; I could not find traces of them either before or after. They are unusual particularly because Wong Shee was among the first native-born Chinese and a woman. Although Wong Shee and most of the others disappear from later census records, I know they were there in San Francisco—and that they likely moved to Oakland after the devastating 1906 earthquake. My father says that my great-grandmother remembers being on a boat in San Francisco Bay after the earthquake. I don't know whether it really matters if the Wong Shee in the census is a woman in my family line, if the life I've conjured from the census page is the actual life in my family's history. Whoever she was, I claim her and honor the extraordinary hard work she must have done every single day.

/////

The manner of their arrival: They all came on ships: The Mayflower John Howland and Elizabeth Tilley (white); an enslaved person on an unnamed slave ship (black); a Chinese man and woman, no names, no records (yellow). None of them could help who they were or how they arrived wherever they found themselves, even as who they were and how they arrived made all the difference. If you arrived on a ship, you are a settler.

/////

Black

The popularity of African lace is largely responsible for the continuing survival of industrial lace factories in Switzerland and Austria (Plankensteiner 2013). As China zooms in to out-produce and out-distribute as part of China's "One Belt, One Road" effort, those factories are seeing huge challenges. Launched in 2013, the Belt and Road initiative has involved, in part, Chinese investments in African infrastructure on a massive scale, together with ambitious efforts to forge new and enduring paths for trade. One of the outcomes is that, increasingly, "African" fabric is designed and produced in China.

Black/White/Yellow

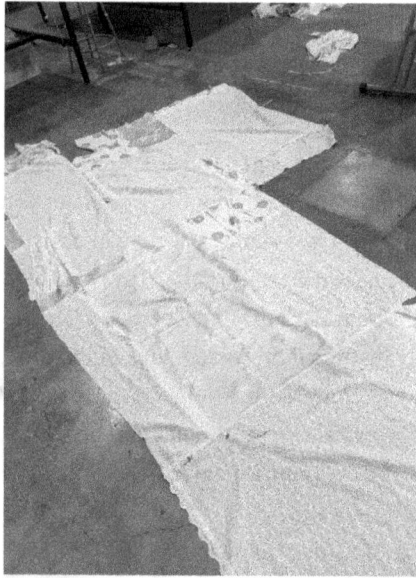

Figure 9.7 Sewn together after three cuts. Author's own photograph.

Settler geographies are baked into the ways we talk. People on the east coast of the United States speak of going "out west," while people in the west speak of traveling "back east" (Figure 9.7). African Americans speak of going "back" to Africa, and those of Chinese, Korean, and Japanese descent are still commonly told to go "back where you came from." Whites rarely speak in this way of going back to their places that lie elsewhere, places where they more properly belong.

These ideologies of out and back trace histories across native lands. We are all settlers if we are not native. In what ways is China where I came from? By what means would my child claim going back to Africa or back to China?

Triangulating Race

Pa-pa (the Cantonese word for "father's mother") was born in the United States; her mother was born in the United States, and her mother was born in the United States. This means that on the Chinese side, my family has been in the United States longer than a great many white people. My colleague, Sean Donahue, has four grandparents who "came over" from Ireland. Nevertheless, even our Chinese students assume his "Americanness," while I appear as fundamentally foreign, new, less-of-this-place than he is. The archaeologist Laura Ng—an expert in Chinese migration between the United States and China—told me to look in the Chinese exclusion files in the national archive. These files, it turns out, are an archive of the ways that the United States has designed Chineseness as forever alien. While the Page Act was concerned with coolie labor and Chinese prostitutes, the Chinese Exclusion Act of 1882 barred Chinese laborers from immigration altogether and required those who had already entered the country to obtain recertification to return. The exclusion files record the dehumanizing process of, among other things, Americans of Chinese descent having to prove their citizenship against the foundational assumption of foreignness. The files are an archive of what Iyko Day (2016) describes as "exclusionary logics" (32–3). The logic of exclusion serves capital by racializing Asian labor as always alien, unassimilable, something to be cast out, returned to sender, go back where you came from. In tying racialization in the United States to labor and capital, the texture of varying experiences becomes more comprehensible. Triangulating race in this way helps to explain why I was often asked "where are you from?" in a way that assumed I was born somewhere other than in the United States, while my daughter is frequently asked "what are you?," a question that has very different assumptions baked into it, assumptions that veer toward a lack of humanity itself.

In the project of nation-building it was important to destroy as thoroughly as possible family, culture, languages, and worlds of the enslaved and the native. Such destruction was not a priority with regard to the Chinese largely because of the persistent idea that they would ultimately go back where they came from. Chinese immigrants maintained exceptionally strong ties to their homelands and even natal villages and ancestral clans. Throughout the 1800s and early part of the 1900s, these ties were maintained through a steady back-and-forth of money and people, but after Mao's 1966 cultural revolution, going home was no longer an option.

Black

Blackness, for its part, stands on a different axis in the triangulation of race, one no less troublesome or fraught but without the assumption of foreignness particular to the Chinese. Swiss lace is full of embroidered holes, carefully stitched absences rigged up as patterns of beauty and elegance. Those absences suffuse Blackness in the history of the United States. Some of those holes are blanks in the archives; others are silences and absences, whispers and secrets. Chinese coolies at least provisionally were recorded in ship manifests with some version of a name, unlike the enslaved who arrived as items of cargo and not as human beings. The pattern is built out of embroidered emptiness. Like Mrs. Pettway, my daughter will need to slash in and through the pattern to make her way through, to craft her own wholeness, to cover up with love.

Yellow

When my Chinese grandparents went to Taiwan in the early 1970s, it was a kind of home-going, but they were far from their ancestral villages, which lay on the Chinese mainland in the Taishanese province of Guangdong. I wonder what it was like for Lilac, who I doubt had ever left the country before that, to find herself in a Chinese nation—was anything and everything even remotely "Chinese" like home to her? Or did she long to place her feet on the soil that her forebears had known and mourn the impossibility of returning to where her family roots lay? Perhaps when she arrived in Taiwan she felt a kind of claim to that place, a belonging unlike the conditional and circumscribed life in Chinatown, with its segregated schools and redlined geography.

The cheongsam is a quintessential Chinese garment in the United States, one that encases stereotypes as much as it also carries culture. Like the Chinese themselves, the cheongsam has migrated globally into different cultures and contexts, resonating differently wherever it finds itself. My grandfather was active in the Six Companies, the family associations that got so much work done in Chinatown.[9] They raised money, gave scholarships, built buildings, promoted business and commerce, and dabbled in mafia-esque shenanigans. In the formally posed group photos from big events, the women wear cheongsam. Out beyond Chinatown, the dress brings up images of the Orientalist and exotic movie character Suzie Wong, dragon lady, images of Asian femininity wreathed in smoke.[10] This image is one created by Hollywood, and by white directors, screenwriters, and actors, to serve the interests of white supremacy portraying Asia and Asians—especially women—as subservient, consumable, and, if mixed race, tragically marooned between cultures at war. (As a mixed-race person, I am especially offended by the whole mixed-person-is-a-tragic-happening trope.)

Black

In an analysis of garments worn during celebrations by the Ijebu-Yoruba of Ogun State, Niger, the author concludes that "Yoruba traditional dress should be promoted in traditional festivals in order to preserve our dressing norms and prevent acculturation of western garments" (Diyaolu 2010: 40). Diyaolu's data show that women wear net lace, voile lace, organza lace, and Swiss lace—that is, their preferred fabrics are very much like the Swiss lace I am using, though undoubtedly finer and more costly, since their cost was more than double what I paid for mine.[11] That these dressing norms arose from and are enabled by circuits of production that are indisputably global does nothing to destabilize the authenticity of the customs Diyaolu seeks to preserve; Swiss lace is certainly part of traditional Yoruba culture. My daughter is named for the kingdom of Benin, a kingdom that had a thousand-year history and whose capital was then brutally sacked and destroyed by the British in 1897. The Oba, or king, of Benin was known to be extraordinarily rich, and the intricately carved elephant tusks and intricately modeled metal objects taken from Benin are legendary for their beauty. Benin was also rich because of its involvement in the slave trade, making for a complex relationship to slavery and its history. My daughter's name, then, tasks her with seaming together and pulling apart complexities and contradictions, past and present.

Yellow

The hybridity stitched into the cheongsam is multilayered and woven into a several-hundred-year political history, involving several Chinese dynasties, colonialism, global migration, power, women's freedoms, and prostitution (Ng 2018). The stereotypical Hollywood cheongsam is hardly Chinese in the sense of being an age-old "traditional" piece of clothing. Rather, it emerged in the early part of the twentieth century in Shanghai and then Taiwan as the result of Japanese efforts to colonialize and modernize China by forcing it to be more western. One instrument of this Japanese-imposed westernization was to change its loose, tubular shape and silhouette. Using an arsenal of English tailoring techniques—precise measurement, darts, zippers, and seaming—ensured that the two-dimensional fabric could be molded closely to the body. The new cheongsam feminized the body and sexualized it, invoking new ideas of women's freedom even as those freedoms were embodied in sexuality and licentiousness, prostitution, and vice.

By the time my grandmother Lilac went to Taiwan in the 1970s, the skilled tailors who made her dress and matching jacket had likely migrated from Shanghai via Hong Kong (where they would have received English-style tailoring training) bringing with them a set of sartorial techniques and sensibilities now thoroughly immersed in a complex web of nationalist projects and increasingly global economic systems. The cheongsam of my grandmother's Oakland Chinatown was not Suzie Wong's cheongsam, nor was it a qipao, the Mandarin version of the dress that became more widespread as a fashion item after the cultural revolution in 1966—which is to say, long after my own ancestors had left China.

White

The Chinese outfit I inherited from my grandmother Jessie is not a cheongsam in its design. The jacket and skirt likely were undergarments in China, not the right against the skin but a medium layer atop the most intimate layer, and beneath the outer, visible garment of a relatively high-status woman. In the United States, in my grandmother's closet, they become a costume of a sort. I imagine that a fashion-conscious woman such as my grandmother might have worn this outfit for an at-home cocktail party, a film noir production with ladies smoking cigarettes and popping out snappy repartee. Very Barbara Stanwyck in *Double Indemnity*, very Joan Crawford in *Mildred Pierce*.[12]

Nothing about anything Jessie wore was ever accidental, and so the "Chineseness" of the Chinese outfit is something of a mystery to me in the sense that I wish I knew what she was thinking. But I have my suspicions. These suspicions spring from some other things I also inherited from her: a richly embroidered silk shawl with long fringes and a couple of bright, floor-length dresses with

Mexican embroidery. The shawls and Mexican dresses were without doubt things she wore to Santa Barbara's annual fiesta, also known as Old Spanish Days. For the Californians who dreamed up fiesta in 1924, fiesta was meant to spur tourism to the area. Fiesta's theme was initially heavily Spanish, with flamenco, toreadors, and lots of sangria. Fiesta is temporally situated in the Rancho Period "taking place from around 1824 to 1864, when Santa Barbara was under Mexican rule and American rule ... but not Spanish" (Graffy n.d. [online]). To put it another way, as Patricia Ann Hardwick (2010) observes, "Official versions of Santa Barbara's past promoted by Santa Barbara's civic leaders and Old Spanish Days Fiesta literature tend to privilege romanticized historical interpretations that submerge and absorb California's hybrid ethnic and cultural histories into an idealized Spanish colonial narrative" (60). The Chinese outfit likely fit into some other idealized narrative but what that narrative might have been is a mystery to me.

/////

Jessie, like many old Californians, pronounced the Spanish words of the state's geography in distinctive ways. Los Angeles, in Spanish, Los **'ahn**-hel-es. In standard American English, it is transformed into Los **'ann**-je-lez (or, sometimes, los **ann**-je-leez). Either way, three syllables. Old Californians pronounce it this way: Los **ayng**-glis. There's something willful about the mispronunciation, the loss of a full syllable, the anglicization and hardening of the consonants. Old Spanish Days was dreamed up by a community of people, who, like my grandmother, said Los **ayng**-glis and wanted their history Spanish (that is white) but not Mexican and certainly not Indigenous or native. Thus, Old Spanish Days was celebrated with, among other things, sangria and a lot of flamenco dancing, complete with fringed, silken shawls. According to Hardwick (2010), these shawls came from the Philippines, colonized by Spain from 1565 to 1898, and their provenance adds an interesting layer to the colonial complexity of Old Spanish Days. My mother's cousin Sally was an excellent flamenco dancer, appearing on stage as "Sarita Diaz." My mother remembers fiesta fondly, even as she now is a bit uncomfortable about the cultural dress-up involved. She also remembers wandering through the grounds of the Santa Barbara mission,[13] across the street from her childhood home, seeing native graves, and being terribly, terribly uncomfortable. She had questions but knew nobody who might answer them. My grandmother Jessie's Chinese outfit lived in that world, costume pieces in a world where these kinds of questions cannot be answered by the people of whom we would ask them.

Black

When trying to find out who the current producers of Swiss lace might be, I came across this heading in Alibaba: "African French Swiss Lace Fabrics Nigerian Party Wedding Dress." China's overseas development finance between 2008 and 2019 is estimated to have totaled $462 billion, rivalling $469 billion in World Bank lending over the same period (Sutter, Schwarzenberg and Sutherland 2021). Producer after producer provides a snapshot of their capabilities. MH Lace, author of the African French Swiss lace headline, boasts an ability to produce the customer's desired number of thirty to forty-five yard bolts of fabric within ten to fifteen days. They own "50 sets of imported Schiffli embroidery machines and 400 sets of Tajima, Behringer and other multi-functional embroidery machines" (MH Lace, no date). No more cotton. Their fabrics are 100 percent polyester.

Black/White/Yellow

The joke's on us: all of these fabrics lead to China and none of us has ever been there. Happy endings? We are whole, frayed here and there, pieced together, hanging in. I always felt like a fraud in Chinatown, when asked a question in Chinese by a shopkeeper and having to answer "I don't speak Chinese." Benin has been race-policed for not being Black enough and I worry that her Chineseness does not feel real or solid. Who my daughter will be is still under construction: Swiss lace pieced with two types of Chinese silk, brocade, and embroidery. Who we are is made up of more than genetic bits and pieces. She's a Black cowboy, an escaped enslaved woman, a mixed-race dancer with marcelled hair and a blue cheongsam. She walks along railroad tracks that scar the land, dances on the gravel verge as honey bees throng among the orange blossoms. We are trespassing, but aren't we all? She has conjured these lives from within, fed by her own wellspring of need and curiosity. Even so, she'll stitch her own quilt, fill in the blanks, wrap herself in memories as yet unknown. It is her work, not mine, that will bring that project to completion. And here are many newly cut pieces, waiting to be fitted into a pattern that, in its turn, fits nobody but her.

It will be beautiful (Figure 9.8).

Figure 9.8 Five cuts. Author's own photograph.

Notes

1 I am so grateful to the editors of this volume for inviting me to write. That invitation sparked this work and brought to life a project that had laid dormant for far too long. An Pan shared thoughts and resources with endless generosity and enthusiasm. Laura Ng, who knows much more about Chinese migration than I do, patiently schooled me with her expertise. Josh Berson gamely assisted with the phonetics for various pronunciations of Los Angeles.

2 It is now common editorial style in the United States to capitalize the words "black" and "indigenous" when they refer to people. The color *black* is not capitalized. For further discussion of this question, see Wong (2020).

3 Gee's Bend, formally known as Boykin, is an isolated area in a large bend of the Alabama River in Wilcox County, Alabama. The quilting tradition of Gee's Bend may go back five or six generations as women slaves used strips of fabric to make bedcovers (Beardsley et al. 2002). Exhibited in museums across the United States, the quilts are seen as a major contributor to African American art, design, and culture (Sohan 2015).

4 In the UK, these PhDs are research by practice, practice-based and/or practice-led research where creative practice forms part of the contribution to knowledge supported by a shorter written thesis.

5 Frogs, also called pankou knots, are decorative fastenings usually in braid with a loop and knot button closure that prevents the need for overlapping seams.

6 John and his wife, Elizabeth, had ten children, all of whom lived to adulthood. Today they have nearly 100,000 living descendants.

7 Wong Shee means, basically, woman from the Wong family who is married. "Shee" is the honorific for marriage. In Cantonese naming practice, women were referred to by their paternal clan even after marriage.

8 Walkup flats are in older apartment buildings with no elevator, accessed by walking up multiple flights of stairs. A cabin boy is a boy who works as a servant on a ship.

9 Formally established in 1882, though beginning activity in the 1850s, the Chinese Consolidated Benevolent Association, also known as the Chinese Six Companies, was a conglomerate of the six most important Chinese organizations in California at the time. The organization was set up to help Chinese people relocate and travel to and from the United States and also offered legal and physical protection. It acted as an authorized spokesperson for the Chinese community nationwide. More information on the Six Companies can be found in Lee (2015).

10 Suzie Wong is the titular character in the 1960 film *The World of Suzie Wong*, directed by Richard Quine, based on a 1957 novel by Richard Mason. The fictionalized tale of Hong Kong's red-light district contributed to the creation of the cultural stereotype of Asian women as hypersexual, yet childlike, duplicitous, and in need of rescue (Hill Collins 2004).

11 Fabric cost ranged from 20,000 to 25,000 naira (about 48–49 USD at this writing); I paid about $25 for the fabric I purchased. I have found that for items that are roughly alike in make, material, and quality, prices are remarkably similar across geographic locations.

12 *Double Indemnity* (1944), [Film] dir. Billy Wilder, USA: Paramount Pictures; *Mildred Pierce* (1945), [Film] dir. Michael Curtiz, USA: Warner Bros.

13 The string of twenty-one missions established by the Spanish beginning in 1769 plays a uniquely important role in the history of California. Founded by Franciscan padres, for about seventy years the missions constituted a "formidable and repressive system designed explicitly to control and indoctrinate their Indian apprentices" (Lightfoot 2005: 80–1). Demographic collapse was one result; few Indigenous people who were born at the missions lived to adulthood (Hackel 2005: 95).

10

Cloth(ing) Memories

Rituals of Grieving

Lesley Beale

Death is universal, as is grief. So much of life is about loss, yet each person's experience of death and each individual's response to grief, mourning, and remembrance are unique. We remember and therefore we grieve, and grief, like death, is anticipatory. For every relationship, there is a separation, for every beginning, an end and "we mourn for tomorrows as well as yesterdays" (Wong 2008: 375). My own very close and personal experience of death and mourning is what set me on this journey. My father died in 2016, at home, looked after by my sister and me. I had never before sat so close with death, held its hand, and moistened its dry, dying lips. My father was a clever, complicated man, full of regret, and had lived what he thought was a somewhat disappointing life. He was a committed atheist, terrified of dying, but in those last few weeks an acceptance and peace came over him as he gave himself up to the inevitability of it all.

Our attitudes to life and death are profoundly affected by our beliefs and assumptions. Using autoethnography as both research method and research process, it is possible to investigate the crossover of the self and society, the personal and the political. Life and death are messy, emotional and uncertain, but through our personal narratives and stories we can make meaning of these struggles (Adams, Holman Jones, and Ellis 2014). Modern dying, like modern living, takes place in an increasingly secular society (Lofland [1978] 2019). Secularism is essentially about rationalism. It is the belief that we must rely on our reason in all matters and this reason takes precedence over tradition. We separate the sacred from the secular, treat the sacred with suspicion, mistrust rituals, and deprive them of any emotional importance (Parkes 1997). No longer is it common practice to hold onto a lock of the deceased's hair, and no one has died in the beds in which the living sleep. David Lowenthal (2015) posits that remembering plays a vital role in forming our identity, and physical remnants from the past can help bridge the gap between the past and the present, the living and the dead. Death destroys our personal memories, but those memories that have been transferred, orally or through artifacts, live a while longer (Lowenthal 2015). Objects that we have an embodied interaction with, such as clothing, hold not only our physical traces but also our emotional ones, making them important as biographical objects and through this material culture we can negotiate some kind of relationship with the dead (Hoskins 2006). There is often the assumption in our society that clothing has limited significance. Sophie Woodward (2005) asserts that within popular discourse, clothing and fashion are often seen to be superficial and unimportant, material objects, situated at the periphery of the body. However, according to Daniel Miller, "we cannot know who we are, or become what we are, except by looking in a material mirror" (2005: 8). If clothes are extensions of the self, and the memory of the self is crucial to perceptions of our identity (Lowenthal 2015), it is no surprise that clothing holds a special place in the ritual of grieving.

Cloth as Memory

Memories, personal and intimate, conscious and unconscious, are "a deeply affective thread of the fabric of one's self" (Brockmeier 2015: 2). If we are what we remember and we are made up of our memories (Brockmeier 2015), then these memories have an agency, which we believe we have a responsibility to, or control of, but memories shift and change over time. In *Philosophy and Memory Traces*, John Sutton (1998) explores the concept that memories are not fixed, not set down independently, but instead they are blended and reconstructed rather than reproduced and are perceptions of the past and importantly a past which was never a reality. Each time we remember, we reframe the memory "in the context of the present and in anticipation of the future" (Hallam and Hockey 2001: 3).

As our bodies deteriorate and die the clothes that held them live on, in wardrobes, attics, and secondhand shops or are passed down "from parent to child, from sister to sister, from brother to brother, from sister to brother, from lover to lover, from friend to friend" (Stallybrass [1993] 2012: 69). When someone dies their empty clothing can offer us a way of remembering them, and a way of trying to make sense out of the senseless, by giving us something palpable to hold on to. Clothes mark the passing of time and are tangible evidence of our bodily existence, helping us locate that memory in an object. Clothes cover our bodies, mold to our shape, and hold our smell, tearing when we fall and staining when we roll on grass.[1] There is always a meeting point between body and cloth. "Clothes shape people and people shape clothes" (Simpson 2014: 3). The haptic relationship between our bodies and cloth recreates these memories, but it is a transformed, changed memory.

After the death of her father, Judith Attfield had the "duty" of going through his clothes and deciding how to dispose of them:

> The shoes under the bed were the most difficult. I've kept his most loved cardigan. He had simple, almost monastic tastes. He hated clothes, especially new ones. He only got to love the cardigan as it grew old and threadbare so I darned the holes and mended the ragged cuffs so it would last a little longer. He died soon after. (Attfield 2000: 149–50)

The cardigan now lies in her jumper drawer, a reminder of "the presence of absence" (Barthes 2010: 69). This familiarity with the clothes of the dead can make us feel safe. They can represent, replace, or replicate both the person lost and the loss itself and function as the "keeper," holding "the sometimes unbearable gift of memory" (Sorkin [2002] 2012: 59).

The iconography of a garment after a bereavement can create a consciousness of absence, particularly in relation to memory (Ash 1996). The look, feel, color, and smell of the clothes that remain after a person has died not only evokes the memory of their presence but also emphasizes their absence. The day after the philosopher Roland Barthes' mother died, he began a diary of mourning. A few weeks later he wrote: "last night, for the first time, dreamed of her [his mother]; she was lying down, but not ill, in her pink Uniprix nightgown" (Barthes 2010: 34). By touching, wearing, smelling, or even dreaming about clothes, memory can be inadvertently stimulated, and we reshape that memory to suit the present and to help us prepare for the future. The presence and absence of a person, within their clothes, means that past-presence and present-absence are located within that item, which becomes the place where memory and memory objects meet (Ash 1996). One knows that the person who once wore the item of clothing no longer exists, but the memory and knowledge of them wearing it is proof of their once physical existence.

While the clothing of the deceased are mostly used as a positive sensory experience to knowingly evoke the dead, unexpectedly coming across a garment can be a different, more unsettling indicia of the person who once wore them and a reminder of not only their absence but also their death. These clothes then become unwelcome prompts and expose the darker side of using clothes for acts of memory making (Hallam and Hockey 2001). This suggests that mourners have a very real sense that people are somehow still present in the clothes they leave behind, as illustrated by Simone de Beauvoir in *A Very Easy Death*; "They found Maman lying on the floor in her red corduroy dressing gown . . . on a coat-hanger there is the red dressing-gown . . . 'I never want to see that dressing gown again'" ([1965] 2013: 9, 48). And Carol Mara (1998), whose son's clothes are the last objects that had contact with his living body, found they held such powerful memories, both painful and precious, that they have to be stored out of sight in the hope that one day they will "no longer hold the terrible potency that they assumed one Saturday in September" (60).

Anthropological studies have highlighted the importance sensory embodied experiences have in memory making. Clothes with their ability to mark the shape and smell of a body have an immediacy and power to temporarily bridge the "space-time separation that distances the living from the dead" (Gibson 2008: 111). After a death we often live with memories that link the bereaved to the body traces of the deceased, and these clothes "live on when living is over for the dead; while death lives with the living" (Ash 1996: 219).

One of my memory objects is a purply blue ballgown, shown in the photograph (Figure 10.1) of my mother and father that used to sit on my mother's dressing table. As a child I often used to put the ballgown on and to me it represented sophistication and glamour. I must have asked her about the dress and why she was wearing it, but I have no memory of her reply. What I remember is that the gown "lived" in a trunk in my parents' bedroom, which I used to call the "dressing-up box." Folded up alongside the ballgown was also her wedding dress and veil (Figure 10.2).

Until I started writing this chapter, I hadn't thought of my mother's wedding dress in a very long time—so much of our past just seeps away—but I remember she let us play in it, so much so, that it became ripped and stained and the dress was thrown away. Remembering can be reconstructive, as we select, and reshape our memories to suit the present, but they can also be destructive. "Memory mangles and transforms its materials, tending to obliterate as well as construct" (Sutton 1998: 18), just like my mother's wedding dress. I really wish she had kept it though, as a memory that not only recorded the marks of our games but as a reminder of my mother, the bride.

I am now "the keeper" of the ballgown, along with her bathing costume, that reminds me of family holidays, and a black crepe cocktail dress, very chic in a

Figures 10.1–10.2 My mother and father dressed to party by an unknown photographer, *c.* 1954; my mother's wedding dress by an unknown photographer, 1950. Author's own photographs.

Breakfast at Tiffany's kind of way,[2] *which I have a very faint memory of her wearing to a party. She gave me the dress many years ago, when I was in my early twenties and I used to wear it out in my clubbing days with black leather jacket, Ray-Ban Wayfarer sunglasses and biker boots, which I also still own. The dress no longer fits, and was passed on to my youngest daughter, who also wore it for a while. It now hangs in her wardrobe, unworn again, a remembrance for her perhaps of both a mother and a grandmother. For me this simple black dress holds many of our collective family memories and has become "intertwined with our histories and identities" (Buse and Twigg 2016: 1115).*

It seems odd to me now that these are the clothes that I kept, as they do not represent my mother at all. The woman I remember was not very interested in clothes and she could not understand my love of dressing up and interest in all matters sartorial. She was often shocked at how much I would spend on clothing. As she fell further and further into dementia, clothing became a source of bewilderment for her; t-shirts became skirts, day clothes and night clothes became intertwined as night and day held no meaning for her. When I would go to wake her in the morning, I would often find her lying dressed in a strange jumble of clothes, a nightie awkwardly tucked into trousers, a knitted cardigan over a jacket.

Being so interested in clothes, I found this incredibly sad, but it probably wasn't so for her.

Maura Banim and Ali Guy (2001) assert that the clothes that women keep, but no longer wear, reveal another dimension of the relationship that women have to their clothes. Perhaps the same is true of the clothes of the dead that we keep. The dresses in my mother's box, and those that I kept, represented another side to my mother; they are a different "narrative in material form" (Buse and Twigg 2016: 1115) to the one she presented daily. I often wonder why her inability to dress herself "properly" in her later life upset me so much. I think that this forced me to confront and ultimately accept her worsening dementia, a change that was so vividly "played out at a material and embodied level through dress" (Buse and Twigg 2016: 1131). Sigmund Freud wrote that it is a natural response to loss for an individual to identify and incorporate in some way the deceased individual into the ego of the mourner (cited in Simpson 2014). When Judith Simpson (2017) put on her sister's coat, she believed that she walked like she did, becoming a more confident older woman. And perhaps the clothes that I have kept of my mother represent the woman I wanted her to be, the woman I wanted to know, rather than the mother I did.

Cloth as Comforter

Anni Albers posited that "we touch things to assure ourselves of reality. We touch the objects of our love. We touch the things we form. Our tactile experiences are elemental" ([1965] 2017: 44), and cloth as comforter can help negotiate the loss of a loved one in many ways. A dead body is often covered with a piece of cloth or blanket creating not only a physical barrier but also a psychological one between the living and the dead. But, do we also cover the body for comfort and is it for the dead, or the grieving, or both? For those who decide on the last thing someone will ever wear, the garments chosen often embody many different emotions and represent many different things. Margaret Gibson asserts "at the beginning of a life clothing is expectant: it represents an absence that is yet to become a presence" (2008: 110). At the end of life, the reverse happens, and clothing represents a departure, instead of an arrival. When we die, like when we are born, our bodies are washed, dried, and wrapped or dressed in cloth. Clothing a dead body can be for practical reasons to help conceal and act as a screen or visual defense against the decaying flesh, but clothes also help to reinforce the body's personhood and place in the moral order of society (Gibson 2008). Emotionally, though, we clothe the dead because we just cannot bear the thought of our loved ones lying naked and cold.

Clothing and time come together as the bereaved contemplate the signs of how a life was spent (Gibson 2008). My father had two distinct "wardrobes." One full of outdated work suits, shirts, and ties, the other full of leisure clothes, slacks and polo shirts, jumpers, fleeces, and walking jackets. Long retired, he still kept the suits, too good to be thrown out, but knowing they would never be worn. As he got older and sicker even the leisure clothes proved too formal, too restrictive and he spent his life in jogging bottoms and sweatshirts. After he died, when the undertakers came to take away his body, they asked my sister and I what we wanted him "dressed in." His best suit perhaps, with shirt and tie? "No," we both swiftly answered as we handed over clean jogging top and bottoms—"These please, we just want him to be comfy." "Who decides what is seemly in death, how much reflects what clothing was most seemly in life, and who is the seemliness for, the departed or the bereaved?" (Davidson 2016: 240). How should we dress the dead and does it matter if they are in the wrong clothes? My mother, lost somewhere deep in the disease that is dementia, was in hospital when my father died, recovering from a broken hip, so when she returned home, he was no longer there. She was initially confused, tearful, and kept asking us where he was. Each time we told her, her face would crumple, but very soon she seemed to forget his existence. For a while she wore a favorite jumper of his that swamped her tiny frame, seemingly unconsciously, but after a while she stopped wearing that too. They had been married for 66 years, but she had forgotten their life together in less than a month, which I suppose was both a blessing and a curse. The jumper and their ashes now "live" in the wardrobe in the spare bedroom at my sister's house, neither of us quite sure what to do with them. As Peter Stallybrass ([1993] 2012) writes, it is sometimes hard to live with the dead and their clothes as they are such a potent form of memory.

Often the garments of the deceased which the living choose to wear are comfortable and comforting, just like my father's jumper that my mother chose to wear. It was warm and enveloping, frayed at the cuffs and smelt of him and then it smelt of her and now it smells of them. These clothes, acting as transitional objects, mediate the void between life and death, presence and absence (Gibson 2008). By wearing the clothes of the deceased, we are bringing the dead and the living into close proximity and through the wearing of their clothes not only can the dead "live on" a while longer, but the living can gain comfort from the dead.

Cloth as Mourning

As Margaret Gibson so poignantly writes, "most of us live with traces of the dead" (2008: 1). The things that we own will probably outlive us and some of the objects that remain will become memory traces for our loved ones. Cloth as mourning explores the conflict between hanging on and letting go. From the cradle to the grave, clothes dominate our lives, they reflect the society in which we live, and shout as loud in death as they do in life. One might think that grief and loss would transcend any sartorial desire, but in fact the opposite is true. In Victorian times what to wear in mourning was a potent indicator of not only grief but also a reflection of society, class, and status. The clothing of grief was a mechanism for assuring the living that their response to the crisis of death was the proper and correct one (Taylor 1983). Is this still true today? Probably not so much, as dress codes throughout much of society have relaxed, so too have the rules surrounding the proper attire for mourning. The ritual of wearing black mourning attire for prolonged periods fell out of practice by the 1920s (Steele 2004), although elements of these traditions remain. Rarely now are curtains drawn in the front rooms of those that have died, or people stand still, heads bowed, in the street as a hearse goes by,[3] but the clothes one wears to a funeral are still significant indicators of loss and mourning, as are the clothes we are buried in. In *I Remain in Darkness*, the writer Annie Ernaux chronicled her mother's decline from Alzheimer's. When her mother finally died, overcome with grief she wrote, "She looked like a sad little doll. I gave the nurse the nightgown she wanted to be buried in—white cotton edged with lace. They won't let me do anything. I wanted to slip it on her myself" (Ernaux 1999: 72). In many cultures the dressing of the dead is performed by family members, whereas in our Western society this is usually done by a third party, such as an undertaker.[4] There is something very intimate about caring for the dead, washing the body, dressing the deceased, but it is a practice that is now alien to us. Dress historian Hilary Davidson describes the act of clothing the dead as "the last tucking-in you ever get" (2016: 240). For Ernaux, she just wanted to participate in the final act of care for her mother, perhaps dressing her as her mother would have once done for her.

My father, who always hated the formality of funerals, said that he did not want us to wear black to his. So, on that sunny day in August, we dressed carefully and colorfully, our bright clothes in stark contrast to the unremitting dull brownness of the crematorium, which looked somewhat like a tired foyer of a Travelodge hotel. My mother, her dementia deepening, was bemused by the proceedings, but she seemed to enjoy the attention she was getting. The dress I chose to wear on that day was a bright pink Rochas silk dress, from their 2015 resort collection, bought from TK Maxx in Birmingham (Figure 10.3). I had bought it, like I buy most of my clothes, on a whim and for no particular reason, seduced by the beautiful material, cut and color and the ridiculous mark-down. In fact, I had bought the dress while on my way to look after my parents for the weekend. I would often "pop in" on the way to or from visiting them and it became a kind of ritual, a way of "treating" myself because I knew that those days would be trying in many ways. This beautiful dress that I imagined wearing to some exhibition opening or evening out, now hangs in my wardrobe, and I can't quite bring myself to wear it again. It has now become the "dress that I wore to my father's funeral," and somehow the sadness and pain of his loss has become woven into its fabric. Planning and presiding at his funeral was an important performance of grief for me, and the dress an important part in preparing me for that role. I remember carefully and purposefully getting ready for his funeral that morning, like an actor dressing for their part. I did my hair, my make-up, my nails. But I couldn't quite obey my father's wishes, which was probably always the way, as I put on a black t-shirt and painted my nails black. It is hard for me to know whether the "stabilizing" of the dress with the color black was an unconscious nod to the expected dress code of a funeral.[5] I'd like to think not. Black clothes have been

Figure 10.3 The author in bright pink Rochas dress, Resort Collection 2015, taken at father's wake by author's daughter, 2016. Author's own photograph.

such a big part of my "usual" wardrobe for such a long time that I think it was a way for me to ground that day in some kind of normality. And that beautiful pink dress now embedded with grief, is a small monument to monumental grieving. "All right, Mr. DeMille, I'm ready for my close-up" (Norma Desmond in Sunset Boulevard*).*[6]

What should we do with the clothes that we mourn in and how do we commemorate the past without becoming slaves to it? Why do we often find the clothes worn to funerals can no longer be worn to any other occasion, have they been touched by death and like Victorian mourning clothes should they be set aside for this specific purpose (Turner 2017)? One day my children will go through my wardrobe and clear out my things that I have so lovingly collected and worn. Will the pink dress still be hanging there, and will it have the same significance to them? Will they remember that I wore it to their grandfather's funeral? I will not know, of course, and it does not really matter as someone else will be wearing the clothing of mourning, and this time it will be for me.

Cloth as Ritual

As an atheist, I don't think I had fully appreciated how important the rituals of death were until being denied them. My mother died at the height of the Covid-19 pandemic. She had not long gone into a care home and the last time I saw her was in March 2020. She could no longer recall my name, or those of her grandchildren, but she seemed happy to see us, then the care home locked down. My mother was a social being, happiest among people and when Covid entered the home all residents were confined to their rooms. In complete contrast to my father's death, where we sat by his bedside and held his hands, she spent her final days in isolation. Not for us the consideration of what she would be dressed in or what coffin to choose. With social distancing in place and only allowed six people at the funeral, we decided to have a direct cremation. No fuss, no funeral, no wake, no memorial, no proper send-off, no final goodbye.

Covid-19 has taught many of us about loss and uncertainty, as we have had to reconfigure our lives, confronting the prospect of death and the reality of dying. In Western society, we have seen a steady decline in collective ritual acts surrounding death and although they can be criticized as falling short, often delivering platitudes that sidestep emotional responses (Rosaldo 1989), they do perform an important function in helping us to accept death as a reality. Old mourning rituals were public expressions of grief that bestowed societal recognition on an individual's loss and although these may seem inappropriate or unsatisfactory today, without the help of rituals to engender memories we have no mechanism for memory making (Hallam and Hockey 2001). If families can no longer "bury" their dead in a way that follows the usual rituals, new ones need to replace the old. With new rituals comes a freedom to explore more informal and individualized rituals that engage more with the body and its materiality (Wouters 2002). The materiality of the body and its connection with other objects are pivotal in these practices that draw upon notions of bodily continuity with material objects, such as clothing, to provide connections between the past and the present. When materials from the everyday world are drawn into ritualized memory making, their resonance and emotional affect are intensified as they become imbued with personal meaning. Cloth, by the very nature of its ephemerality and materiality, and clothes that take on the body's shape and substance situate these rituals firmly in time and to memories, highlighting the transience of human life.

In my grief, as an artist, I continued with my practice, placing ritual at the heart of all that I did.[7] The body of work that I made between the four years that separated the death of my parents was based on the myth of the soul weighing twenty-one grams.[8] When clearing out my mother's things I found two artifacts that resonated with my practice. First, my great-grandmother's christening gown (Figure 10.4) and second my grandmother's hair, but more about that later. Reflecting on the clothes that I kept of my mother, and the gown she kept of her grandmother, I made

Figure 10.4 My great-grandmother's christening gown, 2020. Author's own photograph.

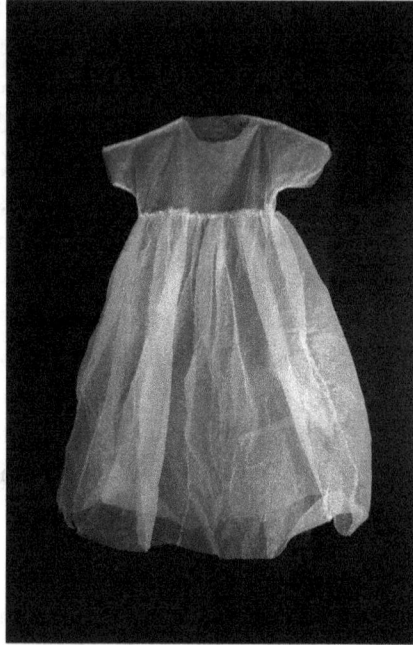

Figure 10.5 *Soul Dress* by Lesley Beale © Lesley Beale, 2020. Photograph by Freddy Griffiths. Reproduced with permission.

a dress that represented life and loss. My Soul Dress (Figure 10.5) is made from four meters of white Japanese Tengujo spider tissue, weighing five grams per square meter, and one gram of red thread. The dress represents the death of the body, but the life of the soul. It is fragile, yet robust enough to be worn; it tears, but can be repaired. It is light enough to float on air, like a soul suspended in space and when photographed it took on a ghostly life of its own.

My rituals of twenty-one gave me rules, repetition, and remembrance. Through the predominate medium of textiles I used repetitive craft processes to question whether it was possible to make meaningful art through ritual practice and practice meaningful ritual through making art. Why should rituals be confined to organized religions and the sacred and the secular be incompatible? My rituals were not about trying to find answers or even hope, but more about acceptance and of learning just to be. Richard Sennett argues that religion and war both function through ritual, but I would add the same applies to living and dying, grieving, and mourning and if rituals can be investigated as a "kind of craft" (2008: 12), then they can also be investigated through craft and its processes.

Janine Miller (2008) claims that disembodied hair is liminal, existing somewhere between the body and the other, life and death. At the bottom of a drawer in my mother's room, wrapped in tissue paper, I found a thick plait of my grandmother's hair, 120 centimeters long and weighing 108 grams. I can only ever remember my grandmother with short, permed hair, dyed black and then silver with a blue or lilac rinse as she got older. This hair is the exact same shade of brown as mine and as I held it, I realized how little I knew about her life and how sad it was that I could no longer ask her about it.

Very soon after my mother's death I made my version of my grandmother's hair (Figure 10.6). I wanted to make something with an imposing sense of scale, therefore my grandmother's plait is twenty-one meters long and weighs 9,525 grams. It is made from sixty-three calico tubes, one meter long, eleven centimeters wide, stuffed with nine kilograms of wool and hand sewn together to make three strands of hair each twenty-one meters long. I used the strands in a performance, where I tangled and untangled, plaited and re-plaited. The strands were unwieldly and heavy: the performance was exhausting, the hair weighed heavily on me and my body, a bit like grief. Domestic, ritualized methods of mourning and remembrance are common, but often not consciously recognized or seen as significant, perhaps because of where they are practiced (in the home) and who practices them (mostly women), much the same as art made with cloth and thread (Parker 2019).

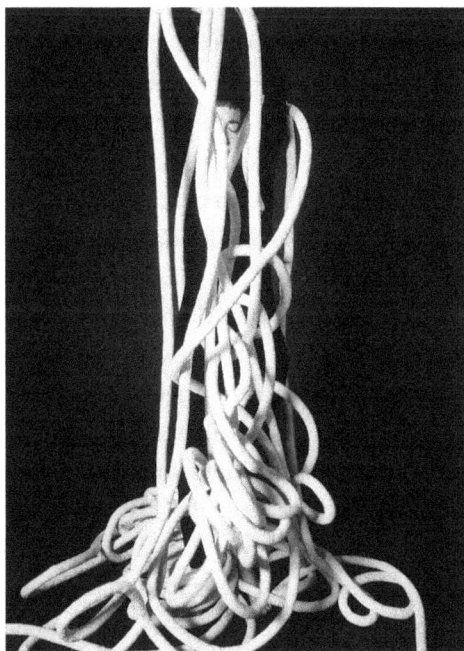

Figure 10.6 *My Grandmother's Hair* by Lesley Beale © Lesley Beale, 2020. Reproduced with permission.

I felt safe in my rituals of twenty-one, like I could control the chaos of life, death, and grief. It not only gave my practice structure, but also my life. Soon the ritual of twenty-one was taking over. I felt confident in the familiar, but like life, of course, each ritual was eventually over and then I would feel lost and adrift, not quite knowing what to do with my hands. Eventually I would move on to a new ritual: unsure at first, but excited by new beginnings and possibilities, then comfortable in the knowing and the doing, then resigned to the inevitable ending and loss. The performative nature of my work gave me a physical outlet for the sometimes stultifying nature of grief. To "perform" these rituals were my way of commemoration, memorialization, and remembrance. My work reflected life, and life was reflected in my work. Through my rituals of making, I interacted with the material world and through reflective practices I found new ways of mourning and memory making. My ritual practices and phenomenological interaction with materials enabled me to reflect on death and interrogate grief and loss through the material object.

Ritual and craft, repetition and craft, ritual and repetition, ritual and remembrance, are all intrinsically linked. Through the process of ritual, the new can be created. If ritual dwells in an invisible reality, a liminal space that separates us from the ordinary, then the act of repetition grounds us in the everyday and the act of remembrance allows us to embed and solidify both the repetitive and the ritualistic act. Ritualized embodied acts of memory can create links between different times and spaces, make complex relationships between the past and the present, and connect between the dead and the living (Hallam and Hockey 2001). Our memories have so much to offer us and through the ritualistic acts of remembering and mourning our lives can be enriched.

If secularism has expedited the end of formalized rituals surrounding death, then Covid-19 is the nail in its coffin. Memorializing the dead in other ways is now more vital than ever and objects, like clothes, that embody the dead can aid the living to grieve and mourn. People grieve with and through objects and "in holding onto and letting go of objects, the grieving simultaneously say goodbye and welcome in a way of living with death and the dead" (Gibson 2008: 193). Penny Macbeth (2019) propounds that cloth imbued with meaning is intimately associated with our rituals around death and that this is almost certainly due to cloth's unique properties to hold our trace and the fact that humans and cloth are fundamentally linked. Cloth as our intimate material of choice can act as a memory, a comforter for the living and a shroud for the dead, a tool for mourning, and a ritual aid. In Western society clothes are so much more than just a covering for our bodies. They not only reflect who we are but also represent our very humanness, even after death. The clothes that have touched our bodies hold memories, of the people who have worn them and the time in which they were worn. Clothes are "chapters" from the story of our lives and can help us "negotiate a path between the secular and the religious, the material and the spiritual" (Gibson 2008: 10). Through death the most mundane of clothes can gain emotional and symbolic meaning.

Although cloth does not have a monopoly on mediating loss, because of its special relationship to the body it is "where we find ourselves" (Barnett 2015: 5). Clothes act not only as the keepers of memory but as a reminder to remember, an obligation to not forget, acting not only as mementoes of the dead or monuments in material form but also as reminders of our own mortality, memento mori, remember you must die. Clothes help keep us rooted in not only our own personal histories and traditions, but our lives and losses can be enriched by using the clothes of the dead in ritualistic acts of mourning and remembrance. Simply put, the dead can be remembered through and in their clothes.

Notes

1 See also Whyman's chapter in this volume.
2 *Breakfast at Tiffany's* (1961), directed by Blake Edwards, is an American romantic comedy adapted from the Truman Capote novella of the same name, starring Audrey Hepburn and George Peppard. In the opening sequence, Holly Golightly (Hepburn) is looking in the window of Tiffany's wearing a black evening dress and sunglasses—obviously it is the morning after the night before.
3 The mostly British etiquette of bowing one's head, to pay one's respects, as a funeral cortege passes by is still practiced in some communities and for high-profile funerals or those mediated by a popularist outpouring of grief, but it is a declining tradition. Funeral directors urged people to revive the tradition during Covid-19, as a way of marking the person's life and showing support for the bereaved in difficult times (BBC News 2020).
4 Defining Western society or culture is a slippery concept, but for this chapter I am referring to the parts of the world where the dominant cultural norms originated in Western Europe, including North America, Australia, and New Zealand, beyond that the lines get blurrier.
5 Connor (2002) writes about stabilizers to counterbalance the femininity of skirts when men wear them, such as the hypermasculinity of the kilt traditionally stabilized with long heavy socks, sturdy brogues, and formal fitted jacket.

6 *Sunset Boulevard* (1950), directed by Billy Wilder, starring Gloria Swanson and
   William Holden, is a film noir about a faded actress' decline into madness. "Alright
   Mr. De Mille" is the final line of the film delivered by Swanson as she steps toward
   the camera, into her imagined stardom again, but is in fact the flashlights of the
   press and the police about to arrest her for murder.
7 By ritual, I mean any symbolic or literal act which allows me (the bereaved) to
   connect to, revisit, or recreate a memory, linking the past to the present.
8 In 1907 Dr. Duncan MacDougall, an American physician, was intrigued by the idea
   that humans had souls, those souls had a mass, and that mass could be measured. He
   weighed six terminally ill patients and recorded their weight at the point of death,
   as the "soul" left their body. Only one patient dropped twenty-one grams in weight,
   but MacDougall believed that this loss was due to the soul leaving the body and
   therefore the human soul weighed twenty-one grams (Mikkelson 2003).

References

Abel, E. (2013), "The Death of the Object," conference paper, *The Lives of Objects*, Centre for Life-Writing, Wolfson College, University of Oxford, September 20.

Adam, H. and Galinsky, A. D. (2012), "Enclothed Cognition," *Journal of Experimental Social Psychology*, 48 (4): 918–925.

Adams, J. T. (1931), *The Epic of America*, Boston, MA: Little and Brown.

Adams, M. (2009), *Slang: The People's Poetry*, Oxford: Oxford University Press.

Adams, T. E., Holman Jones, S., and Ellis, C. (2014), *Autoethnography: Understanding Qualitative Research*, New York: Oxford University Press.

Adler, J. M., Lodi-Smith, J., Philippe, F. L., and Houle, I. (2016), "The Incremental Validity of Narrative Identity in Predicting Well-Being: A Review of the Field and Recommendations for the Future," *Personality and Social Psychology Review*, 20 (2): 142–175.

Ahuvia, A. C. (2005), "Beyond the Extended Self: Loved Objects and Consumers' Identity Narrative," *Journal of Consumer Research*, 32 (1): 171–184.

Albanese, C. L. (1976), *Sons of the Fathers: The Civil Religion of the American Revolution*, Philadelphia, PA: Temple University Press.

Albers, A. ([1965] 2017), *On Weaving*, ext. edn, Princeton, NJ: Princeton University Press.

Alexander, S. (1990), "Becoming a Woman in London in the 1920s and '30s," in (1994), *Becoming a Woman and Other Essays in Nineteenth and Twentieth Century Feminist History*, 203–230, London: Virago.

Amato, J. A. (2013), *Surfaces: A History*, Berkeley and Los Angeles, CA and London: University of California Press.

Anon (1963), "Spotlight on the National Theatre," British *Vogue*, October 15: 37.

Anon (1969), "Vogue's Notebook," British *Vogue*, January: 9.

Appadurai, A. (ed.) (1986), *The Social Life of Things: Commodities in Cultural Perspective*, Cambridge, UK: Cambridge University Press.

Arnold, R. (2008), "Movement and Modernity: New York Sportswear, Dance and Exercise in the 1930s and 1940s," *Fashion Theory: The Journal of Dress, Body and Culture*, 12 (3): 341–358.

Arnold, R. (2009), *The American Look: Fashion, Sportswear and the Image of Women in the 1930s and 1940s New York*, London and New York: I. B. Tauris.

Ash, J. (1996), "Memory and Objects," in P. Kirkham (ed.), *The Gendered Object*, 219–224, Manchester, UK: Manchester University Press.

Assman, J. (1995), "Collective Memory and Cultural Identity," trans. J. Czaplicka, *New German Critique*, 65: 125–133.

Atkin, S. (2016), "Loose Fit? The Impact of the Manchester Music Scene on Youth Fashion 1986 to 1996," PhD thesis, Manchester Metropolitan University, UK.

Attfield, J. (2000), *Wild Things: The Material Culture of Everyday Life*, Oxford: Berg.

Auslander, L. (2005), "Beyond Words," *American Historical Review*, 110 (4): 1015–1045.

Baddeley, A., Eysenck, M. W., and Anderson, M. C. (2015), *Memory*, 2nd edn, New York: Psychology Press.

Baert, B. (2017), "Stains. Trace-Cloth-Symptom," *Textile: The Journal of Cloth and Culture*, 15 (3): 270–291.

Baird, A. and Samson, S. (2015), "Music and Dementia," *Progress in Brain Research*, 217: 207–235.

Bal, M., Crewe, J., and Spitzer, L. (eds.) (1999), *Acts of Memory: Cultural Recall in the Present*, Hanover, NH and London: University Press of New England.

Baldwin, C. (2006), "The Narrative Dispossession of People Living with Dementia: Thinking About the Theory and Method of Narrative," in K. Milnes, C. Horrocks, N. Kelly, B. Roberts, and D. Robinson (eds.), *Narrative, Memory and Knowledge: Representations, Aesthetics, Contexts*, 101–109, Huddersfield: University of Huddersfield Press.

Banim, M. and Guy, A. (2001), "Dis/continued Selves: Why Do Women Keep Clothes They No Longer Wear?," in A. Guy, E. Green, and M. Banim (eds.), *Through the Wardrobe: Women's Relationship with their Clothes*, 203–219, Oxford: Berg.

Banks, J. and de La Chapelle, D. (2011), *Preppy: Cultivating Ivy Style*, New York: Rizzoli.

Barad, K. (2011), "Nature's Queer Performativity," *Qui Parle: Critical Humanities and Social Sciences*, 19 (2): 121–158.

Barnard, M. (2014), *Fashion Theory: A Reader*, Abingdon and New York: Routledge.

Barnett, P. (2015), "Cloth, Memory and Loss," in J. Harris (ed.), *ART_TEXTILES*, 1–7, Manchester, UK: Whitworth Art Gallery.

Barrett, E. and Bolt, B. (eds.) (2013), *Carnal Knowledge: Towards a 'New Materialism' through the Arts*, London and New York: I.B. Tauris.

Barthes, R. ([1957] 2009), *Mythologies*, trans. A. Lavers, London: Vintage.

Barthes, R. (1977), *Image, Music, Text*, trans. S. Heath, London: Fontana.

Barthes, R. (2010), *Mourning Diary*, trans. N. Léger, New York: Hill and Wang.

Bartlett, D. (2010), *Fashion East: The Spectre That Haunted Socialism*, Cambridge, MA: The MIT Press.

Bartrop, P. R. (ed.) (2022), *The Routledge History of the Second World War*, Abingdon and New York: Routledge.

Basu, P. (2015), "Material Culture/Memory/Movement," conference paper, *The Stuff of Memory Symposium*, Wellcome Collection, October 3.

Batchen, G. (2004), *Forget Me Not: Photography and Remembrance*, New York: Princeton Architectural Press.

BBC (2013), "What Is Thatcherism?." Available online: https://www.bbc.co.uk/news/uk-politics-22079683 (accessed February 23, 2022).

BBC News (2020), "Call to Revive Funeral Tradition during Coronavirus Lockdown," April 22. Available online: https://www.bbc.co.uk/news/uk-scotland-edinburgh-east -fife-52370374 (accessed March 12, 2022).

Beardsley, J., Arnett, W., Arnett, P., Livingston, J., and Wardlaw, A. (2002), *The Quilts of Gee's Bend*, Atlanta, GA: Tinwood Books.

Belfi, A. M., Karlan, B., and Tranel, T. (2016), "Music Evokes Vivid Autobiographical Memories," *Memory*, 24 (7): 979–989.

Belk, R. W. (1988), "Possessions and the Extended Self," *Journal of Consumer Research*, 15 (2): 139–168.

Belk, R. W. (1990), "The Role of Possessions in Constructing and Maintaining a Sense of Past," *Advances in Consumer Research*, 17: 669–676.

Belk, R. W. (1994), "Collectors and Collecting," in S. Pearce (ed.), *Interpreting Objects and Collections*, 317–326, London: Routledge.

Belk, R. W. ([1995] 2001), *Collecting in a Consumer Society*, London: Routledge.

Bernstein, D. M. and Loftus, E. F. (2009), "How to Tell If a Particular Memory Is True or False," *Perspectives on Psychological Science*, 4 (4): 370–374.

Biddle-Perry, G. (2005), "'Bury Me in Purple Lurex': Promoting a New Dynamic Between Fashion and Oral Historical Research," *Oral History*, 33 (1): 88–92.

Bide, B. (2017), "Signs of Wear: Encountering Memory in the Worn Materiality of a Museum Fashion Collection," *Fashion Theory: The Journal of Dress, Body and Culture*, 21 (4): 449–476.

Bluck, S., Alea, N., Habermas, T., and Rubin, D. C. (2005), "A Tale of Three Functions: The Self-Reported Uses of Autobiographical Memory," *Social Cognition*, 23 (1): 91–117.

Blume, J. (1973), *Deenie*, New York: Bradbury Press.

Blunt, A. (2003), "Collective Memory and Productive Nostalgia: Anglo-Indian Home-making at McCluskieganj," *Environment and Planning D: Society and Space*, 21: 717–738.

Bodnar, J. (1992), *Remaking America: Public Memory, Commemoration and Patriotism in the Twentieth Century*, Princeton, NJ: Princeton University Press.

Borhi, L. (2004), *Hungary in the Cold War: 1945–1956*, New York: Central European University Press.

Bornat, J. (1989), "Oral History as a Social Movement: Reminiscence and Older People," *Oral History*, 17 (2): 16–24.

Bornat, J. (2010), "Remembering and Reworking Emotions: The Reanalysis of Emotion in an Interview," *Oral History*, 38 (2): 43–52.

Bornat, J., Dimmock, B., Jones, D., and Peace, S. (2000), "Researching the Implications of Family Change for Older People: The Contribution of a Life History Approach," in J. Bornat, P. Chamberlayne, and T. Wengraf (eds.), *The Turn to Biographical Methods in Social Science: Comparative Issues and Examples*, 244–260, London: Routledge.

Bourdieu, P. ([1979] 2004), *Distinction: A Social Critique of the Judgement of Taste*, New York and London: Routledge.

Bourke, J. (1994), *Working-Class Cultures in Britain, 1890–1960: Gender, Class and Ethnicity*, London and New York: Routledge.

Boym, S. (2001), *The Future of Nostalgia*, New York: Basic Books.

Brainerd, C. J. and Reyna, V. F. (2005), *The Science of False Memory*, Oxford: Oxford University Press.

Breen, A. V., Scott, C., and McLean, K. C. (2021), "The 'Stuff' of Narrative Identity: Touring Big and Small Stories in Emerging Adults' Dorm Rooms," *Qualitative Psychology*, 8 (3): 297–310.

Breward, C. (1995), *The Culture of Fashion*, Manchester, UK: Manchester University Press.

Breward, C. (2003), *Fashion*, New York and Oxford: Oxford University Press.

Breward, C. (2004), *Fashioning London: Clothing and the Modern Metropolis*, Oxford: Berg.

Breward, C. and Evans, C. (eds.) (2005), *Fashion and Modernity*, Oxford: Berg.

Brewer, W. F. (1986), "What Is Autobiographical Memory?," in D. C. Rubin (ed.), *Autobiographical Memory*, 25–49, Cambridge, UK: Cambridge University Press.

British Sociological Association (2022), "Auto/Biography Study Group." Available online: https://www.britsoc.co.uk/groups/study-groups/autobiography-study-group/ (accessed March 18, 2022).

Brockmeier, J. (2015), *Beyond the Archive: Memory, Narrative and the Autobiographical Process*, Oxford: Oxford University Press.

Buck, A. (1972), "The Gallery of English Costume, Platt Hall, Manchester," *Costume*, 6 (1): 72–75.

Buck-Morss, S. (1999), *The Dialectics of Seeing: Walter Benjamin and the Arcades Project*, Cambridge, MA: MIT Press.

Buckley, C. (1998), "On the Margins: Theorizing the History and Significance of Making and Designing Clothes at Home," *Journal of Design History*, 11 (2): 157–171.

Burke, J. (1837), *A Genealogical and Heraldic History of the Landed Gentry . . .* , Vol. II, London: Henry Colburn.

Buse, C. and Twigg, J. (2013), "Dress, Dementia and the Embodiment of Identity," *Dementia: The International Journal of Social Research and Practice*, 12 (3): 326–336.

Buse, C. and Twigg, J. (2014), "Women with Dementia and their Handbags: Negotiating Identity, Privacy and 'Home' Through Material Culture," *Journal of Aging Studies*, 30: 14–22.

Buse, C. and Twigg, J. (2015), "Clothing, Embodied Identity and Dementia: Maintaining the Self through Dress," *Age, Culture, Humanities*, 2: 71–96.

Buse, C. and Twigg, J. (2016), "Materialising Memories: Exploring the Stories of People with Dementia Through Dress," *Ageing & Society*, 36 (6): 1115–1135.

Butler, K. (2016), "A Vintage Time for Afflecks as Shopping Emporium Is Full for the First Time in Its History," *Manchester Evening News*, January 15. Available online: https://www.manchestereveningnews.co.uk/news/greater-manchester-news/afflecks -palace-manchester-full-traders-10741564 (accessed February 22, 2022).

Bye, E. and McKinney, E. (2007), "Sizing Up the Wardrobe—Why We Keep Clothes That Do Not Fit," *Fashion Theory: The Journal of Dress, Body and Culture*, 11 (4): 483–498.

Cage, E. C. (2009), "The Sartorial Self: Neoclassical Fashion and Gender Identity in France, 1797–1804," *Eighteenth-Century Studies*, 42 (2): 193–215.

Calder, A. (1969), *The People's War: Britain 1939-1945*, London: Jonathan Cape.

Calefato, P. (2004), *The Clothed Body*, Oxford: Berg.

Campbell, S. (2008), "The Second Voice," *Memory Studies*, 1 (1): 41–48.

Campbell, V. (2015), "The Red Pashmina," in R. Gibson (ed.), *The Memory of Clothes*, 3–6, Rotterdam: Sense Publishers.

Campbell Warner, P. (2010), "Sportswear," in V. Steele (ed.), *The Berg Companion to Fashion*, 648–652, London and New York: Bloomsbury.

Campt, T. (2017), *Listening to Images*, Durham, NC: Duke University Press.

Carhartt (2022), "Outworking Them All Since 1889." Available online: https://www .carhartt.com/carhartt-history (accessed February 22, 2022).

Chan, S. (2005), "Against All Odds: Chinese Female Migration and Family Formation on American Soil During the Early Twentieth Century," in *Chinese American Transnationalism: The Flow of People, Resources, and Ideas between China and America During the Exclusion Era*, 34–135, Philadelphia, PA: Temple University Press.

Change (1941), "Clothes Rationing Survey: An Interim Report prepared by Mass Observation for the Advertising Service Guild," Bulletin No. 1, Advertising Service Guild, August.

Chetham's Library (2022), "The Manchester Man." Available online: https://library .chethams.com/collections/101-treasures-of-chethams/the-manchester-man/ (accessed March 2, 2022).

Chin, E. (2016), *My Life with Things: The Consumer Diaries*, Durham, NC: Duke University Press.

Chinn, C. ([1988] 2006), *They Worked All Their Lives: Women of the Urban Poor in England, 1880-1939*, 2nd edn, Lancaster: Carnegie Publishing.

Chong Kwan, S., Laing, M., and Roman, M. J. (2014), "Fashion and Memory," *Critical Studies in Fashion & Beauty*, 5 (2): 201–204.

Chopra-Gant, M. (2012), *The Waltons: Nostalgia and Myth in Seventies America*, London: I.B. Tauris.

Çili, S. and Stopa, L. (2015), "The Retrieval of Self-Defining Memories Is Associated with the Activation of Specific Working Selves," *Memory*, 23 (2): 233–253.

Çili, S. and Stopa, L. (2019), *Autobiographical Memory and the Self: Relationship and Implications for Cognitive-Behavioural Therapy*, London: Routledge.

Clarke, L. H., Griffin, M., and Maliha, K. (2009), "Bat Wings, Bunions, and Turkey Wattles: Body Transgressions and Older Women's Strategic Clothing Choices," *Ageing & Society*, 29 (5): 709–726.

Connerton, P. (1989), *How Societies Remember*, Cambridge, UK: Cambridge University Press.

Connor, S. (2002), "Men in Skirts," *Women: A Cultural Review*, 13 (3): 257–271.

Conway, M. (2015), "When Memory Works and When It Doesn't," conference paper, *The Stuff of Memory Symposium*, Wellcome Collection, October 3.

Conway, M. A. (2009), "Episodic Memories," *Neuropsychologia*, 47 (11): 2305–2313.

Conway, M. A. and Pleydell-Pearce, C. W. (2000), "The Construction of Autobiographical Memories in the Self-Memory System," *Psychological Review*, 107 (2): 261–288.

Conway, M. A., Justice, L. V., and D'Argembeau, A. (2019), "The Self-Memory System Revisited: Past, Present, and Future," in J. H. Mace (ed.), *The Organization and Structure of Autobiographical Memory*, 28–51, Oxford: Oxford University Press.

Conway, M. A., Loveday, C., and Cole, S. N. (2016), "The Remembering-Imagining System," *Memory Studies*, 9 (3): 256–265.

Conway, M. A., Singer, J. A., and Tagini, A. (2004), "The Self and Autobiographical Memory: Correspondence and Coherence," *Social Cognition*, 22 (5): 491–529.

Coser, L. (1992), "Introduction: Maurice Halbwachs 1877–1945," in M. Halbwachs, *On Collective Memory*, ed. and trans. L. Coser, 1–34, Chicago, IL: University of Chicago Press.

Cox, J. and Dittmar, H. (1995), "The Functions of Clothes and Clothing (Dis) Satisfaction: A Gender Analysis Among British Students," *Journal of Consumer Policy*, 18 (2–3): 237–265.

Craik, J. (1993), *The Face of Fashion: Cultural Studies in Fashion*, London: Routledge.

Craik, J. (2005), *Uniforms Exposed: From Conformity to Transgression*, Oxford: Berg.

Craik, J. (2009), *Fashion: The Key Concepts*, Oxford: Berg.

Crane, D. (2000), *Fashion and Its Social Agendas*, Chicago, IL and London: The University of Chicago Press.

Crewe, L. and Beaverstock, J. (1998), "Fashioning the City: Cultures of Consumption in Contemporary Urban Spaces," *Geoforum*, 29 (3): 287–308.

Crook, J. M. (1968), *The Greek Revival*, London: Country Life.

Crooke, E. (2013), "Autobiography and Contested Histories in Museums," conference paper, *The Lives of Objects*, Centre for Life-Writing, Wolfson College, University of Oxford, September 20.

Csikszentmihalyi, M. and Rochberg-Halton, E. (1981), *The Meaning of Things: Domestic Symbols and the Self*, Cambridge, UK: Cambridge University Press.

Cwerner, S. B. (2001), "Clothes at Rest: Elements for a Sociology of the Wardrobe," *Fashion Theory: The Journal of Dress, Body and Culture*, 5 (1): 79–92.

Davidson, H. (2016), "Grave Emotions: Textiles and Clothing from Nineteenth-Century London Cemeteries," *Textile: The Journal of Cloth and Culture*, 14 (2): 226–243.

Davidson, J. W. and Garrido, S. (2014), *My Life as a Playlist*, Crawley: UWA Publishing.

Davin, A. (1996), *Growing Up Poor: Home, School and Street in London 1870–1914*, London: Rivers Osram Press.

Davis, F. (1992), *Fashion, Culture and Identity*, Chicago, IL: Chicago University Press.

Day, I. (2016), *Alien Capital: Asian Racialization and the Logic of Settler Colonial Capitalism*, Durham, NC: Duke University Press.

de Beauvoir, S. ([1965] 2013), A Very Easy Death, trans. P. O'Brian, New York: Pantheon.

de Certeau, M. (1988), *The Practice of Everyday Life*. Berkeley, CA: University of California Press.

de la Haye, A., Taylor, L., and Thompson, E. (2005), *A Family of Fashion: The Messels: Six Generations of Dress*, London: Philip Wilson Publishers.

Denzin, N. K. (2006), "Analytic Autoethnography, or Déjà Vu All Over Again," in S. A. Hunt and N. Ruiz Junco (eds.), *Journal of Contemporary Ethnography*, 35 (4): 419–428.

Dickies (2022), "Dickies Heritage." Available online: https://www.dickies.com/history .html (accessed February 22, 2022).

Didion, J. (2006), *The Year of Magical Thinking*, New York and London: Harper Perennial.

Dillon, B. (2015), "Opening Comments," conference paper, *The Stuff of Memory Symposium*, Wellcome Collection, October 3.

Dittmar, H. (1992), *The Social Psychology of Material Possessions: To Have Is To Be*, New York: St. Martin's Press.

Diyaolu, I. (2010), "Role of Dress in Socio-cultural Events Among the Ijebu-Yoruba, Ogun State, Nigeria," *Journal of Home Economics Research*, 13 (December): 35–41.

Dunmore, H. (1998), "The Red Dress," in K. Dunseath (ed.), *A Second Skin: Women Write about Clothes*, 61–64, London: The Women's Press.

Edwards, E. and Hart, J. (2004), *Photographs Objects Histories: On the Materiality of Images*, London: Routledge.

Eicher, J. B. (1981), "Influence of Changing Resources on Clothing, Textiles and the Quality of Life: Dressing for Reality, Fun and Fantasy," *Proceedings of the Association of College Professors of Textiles and Clothing Association*, 36–42, University of Minnesota Digital Conservancy. Available online: http://hdl.handle.net/11299 /162458 (accessed May 23, 2018).

Elkins, J. (ed.) (2014), *Artists with PhDs: On the New Doctoral Degree in Studio Art*, 2nd edn, Washington, DC: New Academia Publishing.

Ellis, C. and Bochner, A. P. (2000), "Autoethnography, Personal Narrative, Reflexivity: Researcher as Subject," in N. K. Denzin and Y. S. Lincoln (eds.), *The Sage Handbook of Qualitative Research*, 733–768, Thousand Oaks, CA: Sage.

English, B. (2007), *A Cultural History of Fashion in the 20th Century*, Oxford: Berg.

Entwistle, J. (2000), *The Fashioned Body: Fashion, Dress and Modern Social Theory*, Cambridge, UK: Polity Press.

Erdman Farrell, A. (2011), *Fat Shame: Stigma and the Fat Body in American Culture*, New York: New York University Press.

Erll, A. (2011), "Locating Family in Cultural Memory Studies," *Journal of Comparative Family Studies*, 42 (3): 303–318.

Ernaux, A. (1999), *I Remain in Darkness*, London: Fitzcarraldo Editions.

Evans, C. (1997), "Dreams that Only Money Can Buy . . . or, The Shy Tribe in Flight from Discourse," *Fashion Theory: The Journal of Dress, Body and Culture*, 1 (2): 169–188.

Ewing, E. (1992), *History of 20th Century Fashion*, rev. edn, London: Batsford.

Faulkner, W. ([1951] 1996), *Requiem for a Nun*, London: Vintage Classics.

Ferraro, R., Escalas, J. E., and Bettman, J. R. (2011), "Our Possessions, Our Selves: Domains of Self-Worth and the Possession-Self Link," *Journal of Consumer Psychology*, 21 (2): 169–177.

Filtzer, D. (1993), *The Khrushchev Era De-Stalinization and the Limits of Reform in the USSR 1953–64*, London: Macmillan Education UK.

Fleetwood, N. R. (2005), "Hip-Hop Fashion, Masculine Anxiety, and the Discourse of Americana," in H. J. Elam and K. Jackson (eds.), *Black Cultural Traffic: Crossroads in Global Performance and Popular Culture*, 326–345, Ann Arbor, MI: University of Michigan Press.

Floridou, G. A., Williamson, V. J., Stewart, L., and Müllensiefen, D. (2015), "The Involuntary Musical Imagery Scale (IMIS)," *Psychomusicology: Music, Mind, and Brain*, 25 (1): 28–36.

Foucault, M. (1975), "Film and Popular Memory: An Interview with Michel Foucault," *Radical Philosophy*, 11: 24–29.

Foucault, M. ([1975] 1980), "Body/Power," in *Power/Knowledge: Selected Interviews and Other Writings, 1972–1977*, 55–62, New York: Pantheon Books.

Fredrickson, B. and Roberts, T. (1997), "Objectification Theory: Toward Understanding Women's Lived Experiences and Mental Health Risks," *Psychology of Women Quarterly*, 21 (2): 173–206.

Fredrickson, B. L. (2001), "The Role of Positive Emotions in Positive Psychology: The Broaden-and-Build Theory of Positive Emotions," *American Psychologist*, 56: 218–226.

Fredrickson, B. L., Roberts, T.-A., Noll, S. M., Quinn, D. M., and Twenge, J. M. (1998), "That Swimsuit Becomes You: Sex Differences in Self-Objectification, Restrained Eating, and Math Performance," *Journal of Personality and Social Psychology*, 75 (1): 269–284.

Frith, H. and Gleeson, K. (2008), "Dressing the Body: The Role of Clothing in Sustaining Body Pride and Managing Body Distress," *Qualitative Research in Psychology*, 5 (4): 249–264.

Gagnepain, P., Vallée, T., Heiden, S., Decorde, M., Gauvain, J.-L., Laurent, A., Klein-Peschanski, C., Viader, F., Peschanski, D., and Eustache, F. (2020), "Collective Memory Shapes the Organization of the Individual Memories in the Medial Prefrontal Cortex," *Nature Human Behaviour*, 4: 189–200.

Gallagher, L. (2013), *The End of the Suburbs: Where the American Dream Is Moving*, New York: Portfolio/Penguin.

Garland-Thomson, R. (2002), "Integrating Disability, Transforming Feminist Theory," *The National Women's Studies Journal*, 14 (3): 1–32.

Gell, A. (1998), *Art and Agency: An Anthropological Theory*, Oxford: Oxford University Press.

Gerritsen, A. and Riello, G. (eds.) (2015), *Writing Material Culture History*, London: Bloomsbury.

Gibson, M. (2008), *Objects of the Dead: Mourning and Memory in Everyday Life*, Melbourne: Melbourne University Press.

Gibson, R. (ed.) (2015), *The Memory of Clothes*, Rotterdam: Sense Publishers.

Gillard, D. ([1998] 2018), "Chapter 9: 1939–1945. Educational Reconstruction," *Education in England: A History*. Available online: http://www.educationengland.org .uk/history/chapter09.html (accessed May 3, 2021).

Goffman, E. (1990a), *Stigma: Notes on the Management of Spoiled Identity*, Penguin Books: London.

Goffman, E. (1990b), *The Presentation of Self in Everyday Life*, London: Penguin.

Gosling, S. D., Ko, S. J., Mannarelli, T., and Morris, M. E. (2002), "A Room with a Cue: Personality Judgments Based on Offices and Bedrooms," *Journal of Personality and Social Psychology*, 82 (3): 379–398.

Graffy, E. (no date), "The History of Santa Barbara's Annual Fiesta Celebration." Available online: https://santabarbaravintagephotography.com/fiesta/ (accessed March 5, 2022).

Green, A. (2004), "Individual Remembering and 'Collective Memory': Theoretical Presuppositions and Contemporary Debates," *Oral History*, 32 (2): 35–44.

Green, B. (2016), "'I Always Remember That Moment': Peak Music Experiences as Epiphanies," *Sociology*, 50 (2): 333–348.

Gregson, N., Metcalfe, A., and Crewe, L. (2007), "Identity, Mobility and the Throwaway Society," *Environment and Planning D: Society and Space*, 25: 682–700.

Grimstad Klepp, I. and Rysst, M. (2016), "Deviant Bodies and Suitable Clothes," *Fashion Theory: The Journal of Dress, Body and Culture*, 21 (1): 79–99.

Gross, J. (1962), "The Culture Mongers," British *Vogue*, March 1: 134–5, 186.

Gubrium, J. and Holstein, J. (1995), *The Active Interview*, London: Sage.

Gubrium, J. and Holstein, J. (eds.) (2002), *Handbook of Interview Research*, London: Sage.

Gumbs, A. P. (2020), *Dub: Finding Ceremony*, Durham, NC: Duke University Press.

Guy, A. and Banim, M. (2000), "Personal Collections: Women's Clothing Use and Identity," *Journal of Gender Studies*, 9 (3): 313–327.

Habermas, T. (2001), "Objects: Material," in N. J. Smelser and P. B. Baltes (eds.), *International Encyclopedia of the Social and Behavioral Sciences*, 10797–10801, Oxford: Elsevier.

Habermas, T. and Bluck, S. (2000), "Getting a Life: The Emergence of the Life Story in Adolescence," *Psychological Bulletin*, 126 (5): 748–769.

Habermas, T. and Paha, C. (2002), "Souvenirs and Other Personal Objects: Reminding of Past Events and Significant Others in the Transition to University," in J. D. Webster and B. K. Haight (eds.), *Critical Advances in Reminiscence Work: From Theory to Application*, 123–138, New York: Springer.

Hackel, S. W. (2005), *Children of Coyote, Missionaries of Saint Francis: Indian-Spanish Relations in Colonial California, 1769–1850*, Chapel Hill, NC: University of North Carolina Press.

Hackländer, R. P., Janssen, S. M., and Bermeitinger, C. (2019), "An In-Depth Review of the Methods, Findings, and Theories Associated with Odor-Evoked Autobiographical Memory," *Psychonomic Bulletin & Review*, 26 (2): 401–429.

Halberstam, J. (2003), "What's That Smell? Queer Temporalities and Subcultural Lives," *International Journal of Cultural Studies*, 6 (3): 313–333.

Halbwachs, M. ([1950] 1980), *The Collective Memory*, trans. F. J. Ditter, Jr. and V. Y. Ditter, New York: Harper-Colophon Books.

Halbwachs, M. (1992), *On Collective Memory*, ed. and trans. L. A. Coser, Chicago, IL: The University of Chicago Press.

Hall, S. (ed.) (1997), *Representation: Cultural Representations and Signifying Practices*, London: Sage.

Hall, S. (2007), *This Means This, This Means That*, London: Laurence King.

Hall, S. and Jefferson, T. (eds.) ([1976] 2006), *Resistance Through Rituals: Youth Subcultures in Post-War Britain*, 2nd edn, London: Routledge.

Hallam, E. and Hockey, J. (2001), *Death, Memory and Material Culture*, Oxford: Berg.

Hannover, B. and Kühnen, U. (2002), "'The Clothing Makes the Self' Via Knowledge Activation," *Journal of Applied Social Psychology*, 32 (12): 2513–2525.

Hardwick, P. A. (2010), "The Old Spanish Days Fiesta in Santa Barbara, California: Cultural Hybridity, Colonial Mythologies and the Romanticization of a Latino Heritage," *Humanities Diliman: A Philippine Journal of Humanities*, 7 (2): 60–94. Available online: https://journals.upd.edu.ph/index.php/humanitiesdiliman/article/view/1987 (accessed February 17, 2022).

Hartman, S. (2008), *Lose Your Mother: A Journey Along the Atlantic Slave Route*, New York: Farrar, Straus and Giroux.

Harvey, K. (ed.) (2009), *History and Material Culture: A Student's Guide to Approaching Alternative Sources*, Abingdon: Routledge.

Haslam, D. (1999), *Manchester England*, London: Fourth Estate.

Haughton, H. (2013), "Letters as Objects; Letters and Objects," conference paper, *The Lives of Objects*, Centre for Life-Writing, Wolfson College, University of Oxford, September 21.

Hauser, K. (2004), "A Garment in the Dock; or, How the FBI illuminated the Prehistory of a Pair of Denim Jeans," *Journal of Material Culture*, 9 (3): 293–313.

Hebdige, D. (1979), *Subculture: The Meaning of Style*, London: Routledge.

Hebdige, D. (1988), *Hiding in the Light: On Images and Things*, London: Routledge.

Hesmondalgh, D. (2013), *Why Music Matters*, Chichester: Wiley Blackwell.

Hetherington, P. (2015), "Dressing the Shop Window of Socialism: Gender and Consumption in the Soviet Union in the Era of 'Cultured Trade,' 1934–53," *Gender & History*, 27 (2): 417–445.

Hewitt, P. (2002), *The Soul Stylists: Sixty Years of Modernism*, Edinburgh: Mainstream.

Highmore, B. (2002), *Everyday Life and Cultural Theory: An Introduction*, London: Routledge.

Hill, J. (2007), "The Story of the Amulet: Locating the Enchantment of Collections," *Journal of Material Culture*, 12 (1): 65–87.

Hill Collins, P. (2004), *Black Sexual Politics: African Americans, Gender, and the New Racism*, New York: Routledge.

Hirsch, K. ([1998] 2003), "Culture and Disability: The Role of Oral History," in R. Perks and A. Thompson (eds.), *The Oral History Reader*, 214–223, London: Routledge.

Hirsch, M. (ed.) (1999), *The Familial Gaze*, Hanover and London: University Press of New England.

Historic England (2022), "Listing NGR: SJ3960718897." Available online: https://historicengland.org.uk/images-books/photos/item/IOE01/15347/18 (accessed March 18, 2022).

Hoffman, K. M., Trawalter, S., Axt, J. R., and Oliver, M. N. (2016), "Racial Bias in Pain Assessment and Treatment Recommendations, and False Beliefs about Biological Differences between Blacks and Whites," *Proceedings of the National Academy of Sciences*, 113 (16): 4296–4301.

Holbrook, M. B. and Schindler, R. M. (1989), "Some Exploratory Findings on the Development of Musical Tastes," *Journal of Consumer Research*, 16 (1): 119–124.

Holman Jones, S. (2005), "Autoethnography: Making the Personal Political," in N. K. Denzin and Y. S. Lincoln (eds.), *The Sage Handbook of Qualitative Research*, 3rd edn, 763–791, London: Sage.

Hope, T. (1970), *Household Furniture and Interior Decoration, Executed from Designs by Thomas Hope*, London: Alec Tiranti.

Hoskins, J. (1998), *Biographical Objects: How Things Tell the Stories of People's Lives*, New York: Routledge.

Hoskins, J. (2006), "Agency, Biography and Objects," in C. Tilley, W. Keane, S. Küchler, M. Rowlands, and P. Spyer (eds.), *Handbook of Material Culture*, 74–84, London: Sage.

Hoskins, T. E. (2014), *Stitched Up: The Anti-Capitalist Book of Fashion*, London: Pluto Press.

Howell, G. (2013), *Wartime Fashion*, London: Bloomsbury.

Hunt, C. (2014), "Worn Clothes and Textiles as Archives of Memory," *Critical Studies in Fashion & Beauty*, 5 (2): 207–232.

Huyssen, A. (1995), *Twilight Memories: Marking Time in a Culture of Amnesia*, New York and London: Routledge.

Ingalls Wilder, L. ([1934] 1953), *Little House on the Prairie Series*, New York: Harper & Row; *Little House on the Prairie*, (1974-1982) [TV Series], NBC.

Ingold, T. (2000), *The Perception of the Environment: Essays on Livelihood, Dwelling and Skill*, London: Routledge.

James, W. (1890), *The Principles of Psychology, Volume 1*, New York: Henry Holt.

Jarvis, A. (2009), "Reflections on the Development of the Study of Dress History and of Costume Curatorship: A Case Study of Anne Buck OBE," *Costume*, 43 (1): 127–137.

Jedlowski, P. (2001), "Memory and Sociology: Themes and Issues," *Time & Society*, 10 (1): 29–44.

Jefferies, J. (2007), "Laboured Cloth: Translations of Hybridity in Contemporary Art," in J. Livingstone and J. Ploof (eds.), *The Object of Labor: Art, Cloth and Cultural Production*, 283–294, Chicago, IL: School of the Art Institute of Chicago Press.

Jenkinson, J. (2020), "'Wear Your Identity': Styling Identities of Youth Through Dress—A Conceptual Model," *Fashion, Style & Popular Culture*, 7 (1): 73–99.

Jenks, C. (2005), *Subculture: The Fragmentation of the Social*, London: Sage.

Jenss, H. (2004), "Dressed in History: Retro Styles and the Construction of Authenticity in Youth Culture," *Fashion Theory: The Journal of Dress, Body and Culture*, 8 (4): 387–403.

Jenss, H. (2013), "Cross-Temporal Explorations: Notes on Fashion and Nostalgia," *Critical Studies in Fashion & Beauty*, 4 (1): 107–124.

Jenss, H. (2015), *Fashioning Memory: Vintage Style and Youth Culture*, London: Bloomsbury.

Johnson, K., Lennon, S. J., and Rudd, N. (2014), "Dress, Body and Self: Research in the Social Psychology of Dress," *Fashion and Textiles*, 1 (20): 1–24.

Jones, G. V. and Martin, M. (2006), "Primacy of Memory Linkage in Choice Among Valued Objects," *Memory & Cognition*, 34 (8): 1587–1597.

Josephson, B. R., Singer, J. A., and Salovey, P. (1996), "Mood Regulation and Memory: Repairing Sad Moods with Happy Memories," *Cognition and Emotion*, 10 (4): 437–444.

Kang, J. Y. M., Johnson, K. K., and Kim, J. (2013), "Clothing Functions and Use of Clothing to Alter Mood," *International Journal of Fashion Design, Technology and Education*, 6 (1): 43–52.

Kealy-Morris, E. (2018), "The Shift Dress as Cultural Signifier," in A. Boultwood and S. Hindle (eds.), *Culture, Costume and Dress: Proceedings of the 1st International Conference*, 122–131, Birmingham, UK: Gold Word Publishing. Available online: https://bit.ly/2Iiyubu (accessed February 2, 2022).

Kealy-Morris, E. (2021), "Who Is the Sick One Here: Mask Refusal and Ambivalent Social Identity in COVID America," conference paper, *Face Off: The Provocation and Possibilities of Face Masks and Head Coverings*, Manchester Metropolitan University, UK, January 13–14. Available online: https://fashioninstitute.mmu.ac.uk/faceoff/archive (accessed March 22, 2022).

Keightley, E. and Pickering, M. (2006), "For the Record: Popular Music and Photography as Technologies of Memory," *European Journal of Cultural Studies*, 9 (2): 149–165.

Keightley, E. and Pickering, M. (2012), *The Mnemonic Imagination: Remembering as Creative Practice*, Basingstoke: Palgrave Macmillan.

Kelley, V. (2015), "Time, Wear and Maintenance: The Afterlife of Things," in A. Gerritsen and G. Riello (eds.), *Writing Material Culture History*, 228–234, London: Bloomsbury.

Kirk, M. and Bersten, D. (2018), "A Short Cut to the Past: Cueing via Concrete Objects Improves Autobiographical Memory Retrieval in Alzheimer's Disease Patients," *Neuropsychologia*, 110: 113–122.

Kirkham, P. (1996), "Fashioning the Feminine: Dress, Appearance and Femininity in Wartime Britain," in C. Gledhill and G. Swanson (eds.), *Nationalising Femininity: Culture, Sexuality and British Cinema in the Second World War*, 152–174, Manchester, UK: Manchester University Press.

Koppel, J. and Berntsen, D. (2019), "The Cue-Dependency of the 'Reminiscence Bumps' in Autobiographical Memory and Memory for Public Events: What They Reveal About Memory Organization," in J. H. Mace (ed.), *The Organization and Structure of Autobiographical Memory*, 160–182, Oxford: Oxford University Press.

Krasner, J. (2010), *Home Bodies: Tactile Experience in Domestic Space*, Columbus, OH: The Ohio State University Press.

Kroger, J. and Adair, V. (2008), "Symbolic Meanings of Valued Personal Objects in Identity Transitions of Late Adulthood," *Identity*, 8 (1): 5–24.

Kuhn, A. (1995), *Family Secrets: Acts of Memory and Imagination*, London: Verso.

Kuhn, A. (2000), "A Journey Through Memory," in S. Radstone (ed.), *Memory and Methodology*, 179–196, Oxford: Berg.

Kuhn, A. (2002), *Family Secrets: Acts of Memory and Imagination*, 2nd edn, London: Verso.

Kuhn, A. (2010), "Memory Texts and Memory Work: Performances of Memory In and With Visual Media," *Memory Studies*, 3 (4): 298–313.

Kwint, M. (1999), "Introduction," in M. Kwint, C. Breward, and J. Aynsley (eds.), *Materializing Memories: Design and Evocation*, 1–16, Oxford: Berg.

Langford, M. (2006), "Speaking the Album: An Application of the Oral-Photographic Framework," in A. Kuhn and K. E. McAllister (eds.), *Locating Memory: Photographic Acts*, 223–246, Oxford and New York: Berghahn Books.

Latour, B. (1999), *Pandora's Hope: Essays on the Reality of Science Studies*, trans. C. Porter, Cambridge, MA: Harvard University Press.

Latour, B. (2004), *Politics of Nature: How to Bring the Sciences into Democracy*, trans. C. Porter, Cambridge, MA: Harvard University Press.

Lau, C. K. (2014), "Bernhard Eillhelm: The Contemporary and Sartorial Remembrance," *Critical Studies in Fashion & Beauty*, 5 (2): 295–312.

Leach, W. (1993), *Land of Desire: Merchants, Power and the Rise of a New American Culture*, New York: Vintage.

Leary, M. R. and Tangney, J. P. (2012), "The Self as an Organizing Construct in the Behavioral and Social Sciences," in M. R. Leary and J. P. Tangney (eds.), *Handbook of Self and Identity*, 1–18, 2nd edn, New York: Guilford Press.

Lee, J. H. X. (ed.) (2015), *Chinese Americans: The History and Culture of a People: The History and Culture of a People*, Santa Barbara, CA: ABC-CLIO.

Lendvai, P. and Major, A. (2008), *One Day that Shook the Communist World: The 1956 Hungarian Uprising and Its Legacy*, Princeton, NJ: Princeton University Press.

Lennon, S. J., Johnson, K. K., Noh, M., Zheng, Z., Chae, Y., and Kim, Y. (2014), "In Search of a Common Thread Revisited: What Content does Fashion Communicate?," *International Journal of Fashion Design, Technology and Education*, 7 (3): 170–178.

Levey, S. M. (2010), "The Story of a Shirt: A Cautionary Tale with an Unexpected Ending," *Costume*, 44: 28–36.

Lévi-Strauss, C. ([1978] 2001), *Myth and Meaning*, London: Routledge.

Levy, S. (2002), *Ready, Steady, Go!*, London: Fourth Estate.

Lightfoot, K. G. (2005), *Indians, Missionaries, and Merchants: The Legacy of Colonial Encounters on the California Frontiers*, Berkeley, CA: University of California Press.

Linthicum, L. (2006), "Integrative Practice: Oral History, Dress and Disability Studies," *Journal of Design History*, 19 (4): 309–318.

Loder, A. R. and Çili, S. (forthcoming), *An Exploratory Investigation of Clothing as a Material Possession and Its Relationship with Autobiographical Memory, the Self, and Psychological Well-Being*. Manuscript submitted for publication.

Lofland, L. H. ([1978] 2019), *The Craft of Dying*, Cambridge, MA: MIT Press.

Lollar, K. (2010), "The Liminal Experience: Loss of Extended Self After the Fire," *Qualitative Inquiry*, 16 (4): 262–270.

Lomas, C. (2000), "'I Know Nothing About Fashion: There's No Point Interviewing Me': The Use and Value of Oral History to the Fashion Historian," in S. Bruzzi and P. Church Gibson (eds.), *Fashion Cultures: Theories, Explorations and Analysis*, 363–370, Abingdon: Routledge.

Loveday, C., Woy, A., and Conway, M. A. (2020), "The Self-Defining Period in Autobiographical Memory: Evidence from a Long-Running Radio Show," *Quarterly Journal of Experimental Psychology*, 73 (11): 1969–1976.

Loveday, V. (2014), "'Flat-capping it': Memory, Nostalgia and Value in Retroactive Male Working-Class Identification," *European Journal of Cultural Studies*, 17 (6): 721–735.

Loveless, N. (2019), *How to Make Art at the End of the World: A Manifesto for Research-Creation*, Durham, NC: Duke University Press.

Lowenthal, D. (2015), *The Past Is a Foreign Country, Revisited*, Cambridge, UK: Cambridge University Press.

Luck, R. (2002), *The Madchester Scene*, Harpenden, Herts: Pocket Essentials.

Lummis, T. (1987), *Listening to History: The Authenticity of Oral Evidence*, London: Hutchinson.

Lutz, D. (2017), *Relics of Death in Victorian Literature and Culture*, Cambridge, UK, New York and Melbourne: Cambridge University Press.

Macbeth, P. (2019), "A Matter of Life and Death," *Textile: The Journal of Cloth and Culture*, 17 (4): 340–346.

Maffesoli, M. (1996), *The Time of the Tribes: The Decline of Individualism in Mass Society* (Published in association with *Theory, Culture & Society*), London: Sage.

Mair, C. (2018), *The Psychology of Fashion*, London: Routledge.

Manchester Art Gallery (2019), "Platt Hall Redevelopment: Towards a Community Generated Museum." Available online: https://manchesterartgallery.org/news/platt -hall-redevelopment-a-community-generated-and-resident-focused-museum/ (accessed March 18, 2022).

Mara, C. (1998), "Divestments," in K. Dunseath (ed.), *A Second Skin: Women Write About Clothes*, 57–60, London: The Women's Press.

Maria, S. and Soep, E. (2005), "Introduction," in S. Maria and E. Soep (eds.), *Youthscapes: The Popular, the National and the Global*, xv–xxxv, Philadelphia, PA: University of Philadelphia.

Markus, H. and Nurius, P. (1986), "Possible Selves," *American Psychologist*, 41 (9): 954–969.

Mason, P. (2001), *The Lives of Images*, London: Reaktion.

Masuch, C. S. and Hefferon, K. (2014), "Understanding the Links between Positive Psychology and Fashion: A Grounded Theory Analysis," *International Journal of Fashion Studies*, 1 (2): 227–246.

Masuch, C. S. and Hefferon, K. (2018), "'It's Like a Souvenir of Something that was Important': The Role of Nostalgic Memorabilia in Psychological Well-being," *International Journal of Fashion Studies*, 5 (2): 342–361.

McAdams, D. P. (2015), "Three Lines of Personality Development: A Conceptual Itinerary," *European Psychologist*, 20 (4): 252–264.

McDowell, C. (1997), *Forties Fashion and the New Look*, London: Bloomsbury.

McLaughlin, N. (2000), "Rock, Fashion and Performativity," in S. Bruzzi and P. Church Gibson (eds.), *Fashion Cultures: Theories, Explorations and Analysis*, 264–285, London: Routledge.

McLean, K. C. and Syed, M. (2015), "Personal, Master, and Alternative Narratives: An Integrative Framework for Understanding Identity Development in Context," *Human Development*, 58 (6): 318–349.

McLean, K. C., Syed, M., Pasupathi, M., Adler, J. M., Dunlop, W. L., Drustrup, D., Fivush, R., Graci, M. E., Lilgendahl, J. P., Lodi-Smith, J., McAdams, D. P., and McCoy, T. P. (2020), "The Empirical Structure of Narrative Identity: The Initial Big Three," *Journal of Personality and Social Psychology*, 119 (4): 920–944.

McNeil, P. (1993), "'Put Your Best Face Forward': The Impact of the Second World War on British Dress," *Journal of Design History*, 6 (4): 283–299.

Medvedev, K. (2009), "Fashion And 'Crime' in the 1950s, 1960s and 1970s in Hungary," in I. Simonovics and T. Valuch, *Let's Dress up the Country! Fashion and Dress in Socialism*, 130–147, Budapest: Argumentum Kiado. [Trans. Z. Juhasz]

Mellers, W. and Hildyard, R. (1989), "The Edwardian Age and Inter-War Years," in B. Ford (ed.), *The Cambridge Guide to the Arts in Britain, Vol. 8: The Edwardian Age and the Inter-War Years*, 2–44, Cambridge, New York and Melbourne: Press Syndicate of the University of Cambridge.

Melly, G. (1972), *Revolt into Style*, London: Penguin.

MH Lace (no date), "[Hot Item] African French Swiss Lace Fabrics Nigerian Party Wedding Dress," *Made-in-China.com*. Available at: https://mh-chine.en.made-in -china.com/product/jdEJgFMYHxVr/China-African-French-Swiss-Lace-Fabrics -Nigerian-Party-Wedding-Dress.html (accessed March 6, 2022).

Mida, I. and Kim, A. (2015), *The Dress Detective: A Practical Guide to Object-based Research in Fashion*, London: Bloomsbury Academic.

Mikkelson, D. (2003), "Was the Weight of a Human Soul Determined to Be 21 Grams?." Available online: https://www.snopes.com/fact-check/weight-of-the-soul/ (accessed March 22, 2022).

Milcoy, K. (2017), *When the Girls Come Out to Play: Teenage Working-Class Girls' Leisure Between the Wars*, London: Bloomsbury.

Miles, S. (1995), "Towards an Understanding of the Relationship Between Youth Identities and Consumer Culture," *Youth and Policy*, 51: 35–45.

Millar, L. (2012), "Cloth and Memory, Salts Mill, Summer 2012," in L. Millar (ed.), *Cloth and Memory*, Tunbridge Wells: Direct Design Books.

Millbank, C. R. (1989), *New York Fashion: The Evolution of American Style*, New York: Harry N. Abrams.

Miller, D. (ed.) (2005), *Materiality*, Durham, NC and London: Duke University Press.

Miller, D. (2008), *The Comfort of Things*, Cambridge, UK: Polity Press.

Miller, D. (2010), *Stuff*, Cambridge, UK: Polity Press.

Miller, D. and Parrott, F. (2009), "Loss and Material Culture in South London," *Journal of the Royal Anthropological Institute*, 15: 502–519.

Miller, D. and Woodward, S. (2012), *Blue Jeans: The Art of the Ordinary*, Berkeley, CA: University of California Press.

Miller, J. (2008), "Hair Without a Head: Disembodiment and the Uncanny," in G. Biddle-Perry, and S. Cheang (eds.), *Hair: Styling, Culture and Fashion*, 183–192, Oxford: Berg.

Mills, H. (2016), "Using the Personal to Critique the Popular: Women's Memories of 1960s Youth," *Contemporary British History*, 30 (4): 463–483.

Mills, M. (1997), "Narrative Identity and Dementia: A Study of Emotion and Narrative in Older People with Dementia," *Ageing and Society*, 17 (6): 673–698.

Misztal, B. A. (2003), *Theories of Social Remembering*, Maidenhead: Open University Press.

Mitchell, C. (2012), *Doing Visual Research*, London: Sage.

Mitchell, E. S. (2018), "'Believe Me, I Remain . . .': The Mary Greg Collection at Manchester City Galleries," PhD thesis, Manchester Metropolitan University, UK.

Morrison, K. R. and Johnson, C. S. (2011), "When What You Have Is Who You Are: Self-Uncertainty Leads Individualists to See Themselves in Their Possessions," *Personality and Social Psychology Bulletin*, 37 (5): 639–651.

Munawar, K., Kuhn, S. K., and Haque, S. (2018), "Understanding the Reminiscence Bump: A Systematic Review," *PLOS ONE*, 13 (12), December 11. Available online: https://journals.plos.org/plosone/article?id=10.1371/journal.pone.0208595 (accessed January 28, 2020).

Nelson, K. and Fivush, R. (2004), "The Emergence of Autobiographical Memory: A Social Cultural Developmental Theory," *Psychological Review*, 111 (2): 486–511.

Neumann, M. (1996), "Collecting Ourselves at the End of the Century," in C. Ellis and A. Bochner (eds.), *Composing Ethnography: Alternative Forms of Qualitative Writing*, 172–198, London: Sage.

Nevinson, J. L. and Hope, T. (1973), *Designs of Modern Costume Engraved for Thomas Hope of Deepdene by Henry Moses, 1812*, London: The Costume Society.

Newman, D. B., Sachs, M. E., Stone, A. A., and Schwarz, N. (2020), "Nostalgia and Well-Being in Daily Life: An Ecological Validity Perspective," *Journal of Personality and Social Psychology*, 118 (2): 325–347.

Ng, S. (2018), "Clothes Make the Woman: Cheongsam and Identity in Hong Kong," in K. Pyun and A. Y. Wong (eds.), *Fashion, Identity, and Power in Modern Asia*, 357–378, New York: Palgrave Macmillan.

Niinimäki, K. and Armstrong, C. (2013), "From Pleasure in Use to Preservation of Meaningful Memories: A Closer Look at the Sustainability of Clothing via Longevity and Attachment," *International Journal of Fashion Design, Technology and Education*, 6 (3): 190–199.

Nora, P. (1989), "Between Memory and History: Les Lieux de Memoire," *Representations*, 26 (Spring): 7–24.

Norman, J. (2007), *Make Do and Mend: Keeping Family Afloat on War Rations*, London: Michael O'Mara.

Ogersby, W. (2014), *Subcultures, Popular Music and Social Change*, Newcastle Upon Tyne: Cambridge Scholars Publishing.

Olick, J. K. (2008), "'Collective Memory': A Memoir and Prospect," *Memory Studies*, 1 (1): 23–29.

Olick, J. K., Vinitzky-Seroussi, V., and Levy, D. (2011), "Introduction," in J. K. Olick, V. Vinitzky-Seroussi, and D. Levy (eds.), *The Collective Memory Reader*, 3–62, Oxford: Oxford University Press.

Otter, C. (2008), *The Victorian Eye: A Political History of Light and Vision in Britain, 1800–1910*, Chicago, IL: University of Chicago Press.

Oxford English Dictionary (2022). Available online: https://www.oed.com/ (accessed March 22, 2022).

Paller, K. A., Voss, J. L., and Westerberg, C. E. (2009), "Investigating the Awareness of Remembering," *Perspectives on Psychological Science*, 4 (2): 185–199.

Parker, R. (2019), *The Subversive Stitch: Embroidery and the Making of the Feminine*, rev. edn, London: Bloomsbury.

Parker, S. (2005), *Faith on the Home Front: Aspects of Church Life and Popular Religion in Birmingham 1939–1945*, Oxford and Bern: Peter Lang.

Parkes, C. M. (1997), "Conclusions II: Attachments and Losses in Cross-Cultural Perspective," in P. Laungani and W. Young (eds.), *Death and Bereavement Across Cultures*, 233–243, London: Taylor and Francis.

Passerini, L. (2005), "Introduction," in *Memory and Totalitarianism*, 1–20, 2nd edn, New Brunswick, NJ: Transaction.

Pasupathi, M., Mansour, E., and Brubaker, J. R. (2007), "Developing a Life Story: Constructing Relations between Self and Experience in Autobiographical Narratives," *Human Development*, 50 (2–3): 85–110.

Pechurina, A. (2020), "Researching Identities Through Material Possessions: The Case of Diasporic Objects," *Current Sociology*, 68 (5): 669–683.

Peffer, G. A. (1986), "Forbidden Families: Emigration Experiences of Chinese Women under the Page Law, 1875–1882," *Journal of American Ethnic History*, 6 (1): 28–46.

Peluchette, J. V., Karl, K., and Rust, K. (2006), "Dressing to Impress: Beliefs and Attitudes Regarding Workplace Attire," *Journal of Business and Psychology*, 21 (1): 45–63.

Phillips, A. (2016), "Against Biography," lecture, The Oxford Centre for Life Writing, Wolfson College, University of Oxford, February 16.

Physiopedia (2022). Available online: https://www.physio-pedia.com/Milwaukee_brace (accessed March 22, 2022).

Picardie, J. (2006), *My Mother's Wedding Dress: The Life and Afterlife of Clothes*, London: Picador.

Pickering, M. and Keightley, E. (2015), *Photography, Music, and Memory: Pieces of the Past in Everyday Life*, Basingstoke: Palgrave Macmillan.

Pillemer, D. B. (2001), "Momentous Events and The Life Story," *Review of General Psychology*, 5 (2): 123–134.

Pillemer, D. B. (2003), "Directive Functions of Autobiographical Memory: The Guiding Power of the Specific Episode," *Memory*, 11 (2): 193–202.

Pink, S. (2015), *Doing Sensory Ethnography*, 2nd edn, Los Angeles: Sage.

Plankensteiner, B. (2013), "African Lace: An Industrial Fabric Connecting Austria and Nigeria," *Anthrovision, Vaneasa Online Journal*, 1 (2). Available online: https://doi.org/10.4000/anthrovision.679 (accessed February 17, 2022).

Polhemus, T. (1994), *Streetstyle: From Sidewalk to Catwalk*, London: Thames and Hudson.

Poole, R. (2008), "Memory, History and the Claims of the Past," *Memories Studies*, 1 (2): 149–166.

Popular Memory Group (1982), "Popular Memory: Theory, Politics, Method," in R. Johnson, G. McLennan, B. Schwarz, and D. Sutton (eds.), *Making Histories: Studies in History-Writing and Politics*, 205–252, London: Hutchinson.

Prown, J. D. (1982), "Mind in Matter: An Introduction to Material Culture Theory and Method," *Winterthur Portfolio*, 17 (1): 1–19.

Prown, J. D. (2001), *Art as Evidence: Writings on Art and Material Culture*, New Haven, CT and London: Yale University Press.

Pryce, H. (2011), "Culture, Identity, and the Medieval Revival in Victorian Wales," *Proceedings of the Harvard Celtic Colloquium*, 31: 1–40.

Radstone, S. (ed.) (2000), *Memory and Methodology*, Oxford: Berg.

Rathbone, C. J., Moulin, C. J. A., and Conway, M. A. (2008), "Self-Centered Memories: The Reminiscence Bump and the Self," *Memory & Cognition*, 36 (8): 1403–1414.

Rauser, A. (2015), "Living Statues and Neoclassical Dress in Late Eighteenth-Century Naples," *Art History*, 38 (3): 462–487.

Redhead, S. (1991), *Football with Attitude*, Manchester, UK: Wordsmith.

Reed-Danahay, D. E. (ed.) (1997), *Auto/ethnography: Rewriting the Self and the Social*, New York: Berg.

Reynolds, H. (1999), "Your Clothes Are Materials of War: The British Government Promotion of Home Sewing during the Second World War," in B. Burman (ed.), *The Culture of Sewing: Gender, Consumption and Home Dressmaking*, 327–339, Oxford: Berg.

Ricoeur, P. (2006), *Memory, History, Forgetting*, trans. K. Blamey and D. Pellauer, Chicago, IL: Chicago University Press.

Riessman, C. K. (2008), *Narrative Methods for The Human Sciences*, London: Sage.

Roach-Higgins, M. E. and Eicher, J. B. (1992), "Dress and Identity," *Clothing and Textiles Research Journal*, 33 (4): 265–279.

Robb, J. (2009), *The North Will Rise Again: Manchester Music City 1976–1996*, London: Aurum Press.

Roberts, E. (1984), *A Woman's Place: An Oral History of Working-Class Women 1840–1940*, Basingstoke: Palgrave Macmillan.

Roberts, E. (1995), *Women and Families: An Oral History, 1940–1970*, Oxford: Blackwell.

Roberts, K. (2011), *Class in Contemporary Britain*, 2nd edn, Basingstoke: Palgrave Macmillan.

Rosaldo, R. (1989), *Culture and Truth: The Remaking of Social Analysis*, Boston, MA: Beacon Press.

Rose, D. (1995), "Official Social Classifications in the UK," Social Research Update, July 9. Available online: https://sru.soc.surrey.ac.uk/SRU9.html (accessed May 3, 2021).

Ross, E. (1985), "'Not the Sort that Would Sit on the Doorstep': Respectability in Pre-World War I London Neighborhoods," *International Labor and Working Class History*, 27 (Spring): 29–59.

Ross, M. and Wang, Q. (2010), "Why We Remember and What We Remember: Culture and Autobiographical Memory," *Perspectives on Psychological Science*, 5 (4): 401–409.

Rothblum, E. and Solovay, S. (2009), *The Fat Studies Reader*, New York: New York University Press.

Rouse, E. (1989), *Understanding Fashion*, London: John Wiley and Sons.

Rouse, W. (2009), *The Children of Chinatown: Growing Up Chinese American in San Francisco, 1850–1920*, new edn, Chapel Hill, NC: The University of North Carolina Press.

Rubin, D. C. (2005), "A Basic-Systems Approach to Autobiographical Memory," *Current Directions in Psychological Science*, 14 (12): 79–83.

Rubin, D. C., Rahhal, T., and Poon, L. W. (1998), "Things Learned in Early Adulthood Are Remembered Best," *Memory & Cognition*, 26 (1): 3–19.

Russell, D. (1999), "Associating with Football: Social Identity in England 1863–1998," in G. Armstrong and R. Giulianotti (eds.), *Football Cultures and Identities*, 15–28, London: Macmillan Press.

Sakka, L. S. and Saarikallio, S. (2020), "Spontaneous Music-Evoked Autobiographical Memories in Individuals Experiencing Depression," *Music & Science*, 3, October 4. Available online: https://journals.sagepub.com/doi/10.1177/2059204320960575 (accessed December 30, 2020).

Salk, S. (2007), *Celebrating WASP Style: A Privileged Life*, New York: Assouline Publishers.

Samuel, R. and Thompson, P. (eds.) (1990), *The Myths We Live By*, London: Routledge.

Sandino, L. (2007), "Speaking about Things: Oral History as Context," *Working Papers on Design* 2, University of Hertfordshire. Available online: https://www.herts.ac.uk/__data/assets/pdf_file/0017/12329/WPD_vol2_sandino.pdf (accessed March 22, 2022).

Sangster, J. (1994), "Telling Our Stories: Feminist Debates and the Use of Oral History," *Women's History Review*, 3 (1): 5–28.

Scholnick, R. J. (2005), "Extermination and Democracy: O'Sullivan, the Democratic Review, and Empire, 1837–1840," *American Periodicals*, 15 (2): 123–141.

Schulkind, J. (ed.) ([1976] 1989), *Virginia Woolf: Moments of Being*, London: Grafton Books.

Schulkind, M. D., Hennis, L. K., and Rubin, D. C. (1999), "Music, Emotion, and Autobiographical Memory: They're Playing Your Song," *Memory & Cognition*, 27 (6): 948–955.

Schuman, H. and Corning, A. (2014), "Collective Memory and Autobiographical Memory: Similar but Not the Same," *Memory Studies*, 7 (2): 146–160.

Schuman, H. and Scott, J. (1989), "Generations and Collective Memories," *American Sociological Review*, 54: 359–381.

Sebald, W. G. (2011), *Austerlitz*, trans. A. Bell, New York: Modern Library.

Sedikides, C. and Wildschut, T. (2018), "Finding Meaning in Nostalgia," *Review of General Psychology*, 22 (1): 48–61.

Sedikides, C., Wildschut, T., and Baden, D. (2004), "Nostalgia: Conceptual Issues and Existential Functions," in J. Greenberg, S. Koole, and T. Pyszczynski (eds.), *Handbook of Experimental Existential Psychology*, 200–214, New York: Guilford.

Sennett, R. (2008), *The Craftsman*, London: Allen Lane.

Sheller, M. (2015), "Vital Methodologies: Live Methods, Mobile Art, and Research-Creation," in P. Vannini (ed.), *Non-Representational Methodologies: Re-Envisioning Research*, 130–145, New York and London: Routledge.

Sherlock, A. (2014), "'It's Kind of Where the Shoe Gets You To I Suppose': Materializing Identity with Footwear," *Critical Studies in Fashion & Beauty*, 5 (1): 25–51.

Sherlock, A. (2016), "'This Is Not a Shoe' An Exploration of the Co-constitutive Relationship Between Representations and Embodied Experience of Shoes," PhD thesis, The University of Sheffield, UK.

Simonovics, I. (2015), "Fashion and Socialism. The History of Fashion in Hungary, 1945–1968," Doctoral diss., University of Pécs, Hungary. Available online: https://pea .lib.pte.hu/handle/pea/14970 (accessed July 14, 2021). [Trans. Z. Juhasz]

Simpson, J. M. (2014), "Materials for Mourning: Bereavement Literature and the Afterlife of Clothes," *Critical Studies in Fashion & Beauty*, 5 (2): 253–270.

Simpson, J. M. (2017), "The Haunted Wardrobe: Reflections on Clothing and Loss," conference paper, *Death, Dying and Disposal*, September 6–9, University of Central Lancashire. Available online: http://eprints.whiterose.ac.uk/121975/ (accessed March 14, 2022).

Simpson, J. M. (2019), "Remember Me This Way: The Role of Clothing in Contemporary British Death Practice," PhD thesis, University of Leeds, UK.

Singer, J. A. and Salovey, P. (1993), *The Remembered Self: Emotion and Memory in Personality*, New York: Free Press.

Sladen, C. (1995), *The Conscript of Fashion: Utility Cloth, Clothing and Footwear 1941–1952*, Aldershot: Scholar Press.

Slater, A. (2010), "Make-do-and-Mend: 'Leisure' or 'Work' in the Lives of Working-Class Women in Bolton and Oldham, Lancashire 1939–1945?," in R. Snape and H. Pussard (eds.), *Recording Leisure Lives: Sports, Games and Pastimes in 20th Century Britain*, 41–55, Eastbourne: Leisure Studies Association.

Slater, A. (2011), "The Dress of Working-Class Women in Bolton and Oldham, Lancashire 1939 to 1945," PhD thesis, Manchester Metropolitan University, UK.

Slater, A. (2014), "Wearing in Memory: Materiality and Oral Histories of Dress," *Critical Studies in Fashion & Beauty*, 5 (1): 125–139.

Slater, A. (2020), "Listening to Dress: Unfolding Oral History Methods," in H. Holmes and S. M. Hall (eds.), *Mundane Methods: Innovative Ways to Research the Everyday*, 32–48, Manchester: Manchester University Press.

Smith, L. and Campbell, G. (2017), "'Nostalgia for the Future': Memory, Nostalgia and the Politics of Class," *International Journal of Heritage Studies*, 23 (7): 612–627.

Smith, M. (2000), *Britain and 1940: History, Myth and Popular Memory*, Abingdon: Routledge.

Sohan, V. K. (2015), "'But a Quilt Is More': Recontextualizing the Discourse(s) of the Gee's Bend Quilts," *College English*, 77 (4): 294–316.

Sontag, S. (1977), *On Photography*, London and New York: Penguin.

Sorkin, J. ([2002] 2012), "Stain on Cloth, Stigma and Shame," in J. Hemmings (ed.), *The Textile Reader*, 59–63, London and New York: Berg.

Spence, C. (2007), "Making Sense of Touch: A Multisensory Approach to the Perception of Objects," in E. Pye (ed.), *The Power of Touch: Handling Objects in Museum and Heritage Contexts*, 45–61, Walnut Creek: Left Coast Press.

Spivak, E. (2014), *Worn Stories*, New York: Princeton Architectural Press.

Stallybrass, P. ([1993] 1999), "Worn Worlds: Clothes, Mourning and the Life of Things," in D. Ben-Amos and L. Weissberg (eds.), *Cultural Memory and the Construction of Identity*, 27–44, Detroit, MI: Wayne State University Press.

Stallybrass, P. ([1993] 2012), "Worn Worlds: Clothes, Mourning and the Life of Things," in J. Hemmings (ed.), *The Textile Reader*, 68–77, London and New York: Berg.

Stallybrass, P. and Jones, A. R. (2000), *Renaissance Clothing and the Materials of Memory*, Cambridge, UK: Cambridge University Press.

Stauss, R. (2020), "Passing as Fashionable, Feminine and Sane: 'Therapy of Fashion' and the Normalization of Psychiatric Patients in 1960s US," *Fashion Theory: The Journal of Dress, Body and Culture*, 24 (4): 601–637.

Steedman, C. (2001), *Dust*, Manchester, UK: Manchester University Press.

Steele, V. (2004), *Encyclopedia of Clothing and Fashion*, New York: Scribner Library.

Stevens, C. J. (2015), "Is Memory for Music Special?," *Memory Studies*, 8 (3): 263–266.

Stewart, S. (1993), *On Longing: Narratives of the Miniature, the Gigantic, the Souvenir, the Collection*, Durham, NC and London: Duke University Press.

Stewart, S. (1999), "Prologue: From the Museum of Touch," in M. Kwint, C. Breward, and J. Aynsley (eds.), *Material Memories*, 17–36, Oxford: Berg.

Stitziel, J. (2003), "On the Seam between Socialism and Capitalism: East German Fashion Shows," in D. F. Crew (ed.), *Consuming Germany in the Cold War*, 51–85, Oxford: Berg.

Stitziel, J. (2005), *Fashioning Socialism; Clothing, Politics and Consumer Culture in East Germany*, New York: Berg.

Straw, W. (1991), "Systems of Articulation, Logics of Change: Communities and Scenes in Popular Music," *Cultural Studies*, 5 (3): 368–388.

Strohm, P. (2014), "Was There Life-Writing in the Middle Ages?," lecture, The Oxford Centre for Life Writing, Wolfson College, University of Oxford, March 6.

Sturken, M. (1997), *Tangled Memories: The Vietnam War, The AIDS Epidemic, and the Politics of Remembering*, Berkeley, CA: University of California Press.

Sturken, M. (1999), "The Image as Memorial: Personal Photographs in Cultural Memory," in M. Hirsch (ed.), *The Familiar Gaze*, 178–195, Hanover, NH: University Press of New England.

Summers, J. (2015), *Fashion on the Ration*, London: Profile Books.

Suterwalla, S. (2013), "From Punk to the Hijab: British Women's Embodied Dress as Performative Resistance, 1970s to the Present," PhD thesis, Royal College of Art, London, UK.

Sutter, K. M., Schwarzenberg, A. B., and Sutherland, M. D. (2021), "China's 'One Belt, One Road' Initiative: Economic Issues," January 22. Available online: https://sgp.fas .org/crs/row/IF11735.pdf (accessed February 17, 2022).

Sutton, J. (1998), *Philosophy and Memory Traces*, Cambridge, UK: Cambridge University Press.

Sykas, P. A. (2013), "Investigative Methodologies: Understanding the Fabric of Fashion," in S. Black, A. de la Haye, J. Entwistle, A. Rocamora, R. A. Root, and H. Thomas (eds.), *The Handbook of Fashion Studies*, 235–257, London, New York, New Delhi and Sydney: Bloomsbury.

Talmey, A. (1946), "'No Progress, No Fun': Dorothy Shaver of Lord and Taylor – Unorthodox Store Strategist," *Vogue, US*, 107 (3): 158–159, 192, 194, 196, 198.

Tangney, J. P. and Dearing, R. L. (2002), *Shame and Guilt*, New York: Guilford Publications.

Tarrant, N. E. A. (1983), *The Rise and Fall of the Sleeve 1825–1840: A Catalogue of the Costume and Accessories in the Charles Stewart and Royal Scottish Museum Collections*, Edinburgh: Royal Scottish Museum.

Taylor, L. (1983), *Mourning Dress: A Costume and Social History*, Abingdon: Routledge.

Taylor, L. (2002), *The Study of Dress History*, Manchester, UK: Manchester University Press.

Taylor, L. (2013), "Beyond Words: An Embroidery in Memory of Anna Binderowska, Married 1864," *Textile: The Journal of Cloth and Culture*, 11 (3): 300–313.

Tebbutt, M. (1995), *Women's Talk? A Social History of 'Gossip' in Working-Class Neighbourhoods, 1880–1960*, Aldershot: Scholar Press.

Tebbutt, M. (2016), *Making Youth: A History of Modern Britain*, London: Palgrave.

Thomas, L. (2013), "Hermione Lee, The Art of Biography No. 4," *The Paris Review*, 205. Available online: https://www.theparisreview.org/interviews/6231/the-art-of -biography-no-4-hermione-lee (accessed February 9, 2021).

Thompson, P. (1975), *The Edwardians: The Remaking of British Society*, London: Weidenfeld and Nicolson.

Thornton, S. (1995), *Club Cultures: Music, Media and Subcultural Capital*, London: Polity Press.

Tiggemann, M. and Lacey, C. (2009), "Shopping for Clothes: Body Satisfaction, Appearance Investment and Clothing Selection in Female Shoppers," *Body Image*, 6: 285–291.

Tonkin, E. (1990), "History and the Myth of Realism," in R. Samuel and P. Thompson (eds.), *The Myths We Live By*, 25–35, London: Routledge.

Tosh, J. (1991), *The Pursuit of History: Aims, Methods and New Directions in the Study of Modern History*, London: Longman.

Toussaint, L. and Smelik, A. (2017), "Memory and Materiality in Hussein Chalayan's Techno-Fashion," in L. Plate and A. Smelik (eds.), *Performing Memory in Art and Popular Culture*, London: Routledge.

Trentmann, F. (2009), "Materiality in the Future of History: Things, Practices and Politics," *Journal of British Studies*, 48: 283–307.

Trilling, L. (1972), *Sincerity and Authenticity*, London: Oxford University Press.

Truman, S. E. (2021), *Feminist Speculations and the Practice of Research-Creation: Writing Pedagogies and Intertextual Affects*, New York and London: Routledge.

Tseëlon, E. (2012), "Outlining a Fashion Studies Project," *Critical Studies in Fashion & Beauty*, 1 (1): 3–53.

Tuite, R. C. (2014), *Seven Sisters Style: The All-American Preppy Look*, New York: Rizzoli.

Tulloch, C. (2002), "Strawberries and Cream: Dress, Migration and the Quintessence of Englishness," in C. Breward, B. Conekin, and C. Cox, *The Englishness of English Dress*, 61–76, Oxford: Berg.

Tulloch, C. (2010), "Style-Fashion-Dress: From Black to Post-Black," *Fashion Theory: The Journal of Dress, Body and Culture*, 14 (3): 273–303.

Tulloch, C. (2016), *The Birth of Cool: Style Narratives of the African Diaspora*, London: Bloomsbury.

Tulving, E. (1983), *Elements in Episodic Memory*, Oxford: Clarendon Press.

Tulving, E. (2002), "Episodic Memory: From Mind to Brain," *Annual Review of Psychology*, 53 (1): 1–25.

Turkle, S. (ed.) (2007), *Evocative Objects: Things We Think With*, Cambridge, MA: MIT Press.

Turner, F. J. (1893), "The Significance of the Frontier on American History." Available online: https://www.historians.org/about-aha-and-membership/aha-history -and-archives/historical-archives/the-significance-of-the-frontier-in-american -history-(1893) (accessed February 2, 2022).

Turner, L. (2017), "What Do We Do with the Clothing of Grief?." Available online: https://www.racked.com/2017/2/26/14677684/miscarriage-funeral-grief-clothing (accessed January 10, 2022).

Twigg, J. (2009), "Dress and the Narration of Life: Women's Reflections on Clothing and Age," in A. C. Sparkes (ed.), *Auto/Biography Yearbook 2009*, 1–18, Nottingham: BSA Auto/Biography Study Group, Russell Press.

Twigg, J. (2010), "Clothing and Dementia: A Neglected Dimension?," *Journal of Aging Studies*, 24 (4): 223–230.

Twigg, J. (2013), *Fashion and Age: Dress, the Body and Later Life*, London: Bloomsbury.

Tynan, K. (1988), *The Life of Kenneth Tynan*, London: Methuen.

Valuch, T. (2009), "The Changes in Urban Fashion in Hungary 1948–2000," in I. Simonovics and T. Valuch, *Let's Dress Up the Country! Fashion and Dress in Socialism*, 99–129, Budapest: Argumentum Kiado. [Trans. Z. Juhasz]

Van den Hoven, E., Orth, D., and Zijlema, A. (2021), "Possessions and Memories," *Current Opinion in Psychology*, 39: 94–99.

van der Kolk, B. (2014), *The Body Keeps the Score*, London: Penguin Books.

Vaughan, L. (2015), "A Wardrobe of Making," in R. Gibson (ed.), *The Memory of Clothes*, 23–24, Rotterdam: Sense Publishers.

Volonté, P. (2022), *Fat Fashion: The Thin Ideal and the Segregation of Plus-Size Bodies*, London: Bloomsbury.

Walford, J. (2008), *Forties Fashion: From Siren Suits to The New Look*, London: Thames and Hudson.

Walker, T. (2008), "Meet the Global Scenester: He's Hip. He's Cool. He's Everywhere," *The Independent*, August 14. Available online: http://www.independent.co.uk/life

-style/fashion/features/meet-the-global-scenester-hes-hip-hes-cool-hes-everywhere-894199.html (accessed April 8, 2011).

Walker Howe, D. (2007), *What Hath God Wrought: The Transformation of America, 1815–48*, Oxford: Oxford University Press.

Wang, Q. (2021), "The Cultural Foundation of Human Memory," *Annual Review of Psychology*, 72: 151–179.

Ward, R. and Campbell, S. (2014), "'Once I Had Money In My Pocket, I Was Every Colour Under The Sun': Using 'Appearance Biographies' To Explore The Meanings Of Appearance For People With Dementia," *Journal of Aging Studies*, 30: 64–72.

Ward, S. (2010), "Chemise Dress," in V. Steele (ed.), *The Berg Companion to Fashion*, 144–145, London and New York: Bloomsbury.

Watson, C. A. (2004), "The Sartorial Self: William James's Philosophy of Dress," *History of Psychology*, 7 (3): 211–224.

Webber-Hanchett, T. (2003), "Dorothy Shaver: Promoter of 'The American Look,'" *Dress*, 30: 80–90.

Weber, S. and Mitchell, C. (eds.) (2004), *Not Just Any Dress: Narratives of Memory, Body and Identity*, New York: Peter Lang.

Wenting, R., Atzema, O., and Frenken, K. (2011), "Urban Amenities and Agglomeration Economies?: The Locational Behavior and Economic Success of Dutch Fashion Design Entrepreneurs," *Urban Studies*, 48: 1333–1352.

Wertsch, J. V. (2002), *Voices of Collective Remembering*, Cambridge, UK: Cambridge University Press.

Wertsch, J. V. (2009), "Collective Memory," in P. Boyer and J. V. Wertsch (eds.), *Memory in Mind and Culture*, 117–137, Cambridge, UK: Cambridge University Press.

Whyman, B. (2019), "How can Material Culture Analysis of Fashionable Menswear Augment Biographical and Museological Interpretations? A Critical Analysis of Three Wardrobes of Menswear at the Victoria and Albert Museum and Fashion Museum, Bath," PhD thesis, University of the Arts London, UK. Available Online: https://ethos.bl.uk/OrderDetails.do?uin=uk.bl.ethos.794303 (accessed May 10, 2021).

Willander, J., Sikström, S., and Karlsson, K. (2015), "Multimodal Retrieval of Autobiographical Memories: Sensory Information Contributes Differently to the Recollection of Events," *Frontiers in Psychology*, 6 (1681): 1–7.

Williams, C. (ed.) (2012), *The Richard Burton Diaries*, New Haven, CT: Yale University Press.

Williams, G. (1996), "Manchester," *Cities*, 13 (3): 203–212.

Williamson, V. (2014), *You Are the Music: How Music Reveals What It Means to be Human*, London: Faber and Faber.

Wilson, E. ([1985] 2010), *Adorned in Dreams: Fashion and Modernity*, London: I. B. Tauris.

Wilson, E. (2009), "Fashion and Memory," in A. Aronowsky Cronberg and A. Lynge-Jorlén (eds.), *Vestoj: The Journal of Sartorial Matters*, 1: 61–71.

Wilson, E. (2013), *Cultural Passions: Fans, Aesthetes and Tarot Readers*, London: I.B. Taurus.

Wilson, E. and Taylor, L. (1989), *Through the Looking Glass: A History of Dress from 1860 to Present Day*, London: BBC Books.

Wong, B. (2020), "Here's Why It's a Big Deal to Capitalize the Word 'Black,'" *HuffPost*, September 3. Available online: https://www.huffpost.com/entry/why-capitalize-word -black_l_5f342ca1c5b6960c066faea5 (accessed February 17, 2022).

Wong, P. T. P. (2008), "Transformations of Grief through Meaning: Meaning-Centred Counselling for Bereavement," in A. Tomer, G. T. Eliason and P. T. P. Wong (eds.), *Existential and Spiritual Issues in Death Attitudes*, 375–396, New York: Lawrence Erlbaum Associates.

Wood, E. (2016), "Displaying Dress: New Methodologies for Historic Collections," PhD thesis, University of Manchester, UK.

Wood, S. (2020), "Treasured Garments: Exploring Value in the Wardrobe," PhD thesis, Manchester Metropolitan University, UK.

Woodward, S. (2005), "Looking Good, Feeling Right: Aesthetics of the Self," in S. Küchler and D. Miller (eds.), *Clothing as Material Culture*, 21–40, Oxford: Berg.

Woodward, S. (2007), *Why Women Wear What They Wear*, Oxford: Berg.

Woodward, S. (2008), "Standing Out as One of a Crowd," in L. Salazar (ed.), *Fashion V Sport*, 66–77, London: V&A Publishing.

Woodward, S. (2009), "The Myth of Street Style," *Fashion Theory: The Journal of Dress, Body and Culture*, 13 (1): 83–102.

Woodward, S. (2015), "The Hidden Lives of Things: Accumulations in Cupboards, Lofts and Shelves," in E. Casey and Y. Taylor (eds.), *Intimacies, Critical Consumption and Diverse Economies*, 216–231, Basingstoke: Palgrave Macmillan.

Woodward, S. (2016), "Object Interviews, Material Imaginings and 'Unsettling' Methods: Interdisciplinary Approaches to Understanding Materials and Material Culture," *Qualitative Research*, 16 (4): 359–374.

Woolf, V. ([1928] 2003), *Orlando: A Biography*, Ware: Wordsworth Classics.

Worth, R. (2020), *Fashion and Class*, London: Bloomsbury.

Wouters, C. (2002), "The Quest for New Rituals in Dying and Mourning: Changes in the We-I Balance," *Body and Society*, 8 (1): 1–27.

Yohannan, K. (2010), "Claire McCardell," in V. Steele (ed.), *The Berg Companion to Fashion*, 503–505, London and New York: Bloomsbury.

Yohannan, K. and Nolf, N. (1999), *Claire McCardell: Redefining Modernism*, New York: Harry N. Abrams.

Zborowska, A. (2014), "Uses and Abuses of History: A Case of a Comme des Garçons Fashion Show," *Critical Studies in Fashion & Beauty*, 5 (2): 233–252.

Zijlema, A., Van den Hoven, E., and Eggen B. (2019), "A Qualitative Exploration of Memory Cuing by Personal Items in the Home," *Memory Studies*, 12 (4): 377–397.

Zweiniger-Bargielowska, I. (2000), *Austerity in Britain: Rationing, Controls, and Consumption 1939–1955*, Oxford: Oxford University Press.

Index

www.ingramcontent.com/pod-product-compliance
Lightning Source LLC
Chambersburg PA
CBHW050418280326
41932CB00013BA/1913